LEXINGTON
AND
CONCORD

ALSO BY GEORGE C. DAUGHAN

Revolution on the Hudson

The Shining Sea

1812

If By Sea

Concord Bridge, a painting by Mark Fountain,
photographed by Ken Harvey.

GEORGE C. DAUGHAN

LEXINGTON AND CONCORD

THE BATTLE HEARD ROUND THE WORLD

W. W. Norton & Company

INDEPENDENT PUBLISHERS SINCE 1923

NEW YORK | LONDON

For information about permission to reproduce selections from this book,
write to Permissions, W. W. Norton & Company, Inc.,
500 Fifth Avenue, New York, NY 10110

For information about special discounts for bulk purchases, please contact
W. W. Norton Special Sales at specialsales@wwnorton.com or 800-233-4830

Manufacturing by Quad Graphics, Fairfield
Book design by Brooke Koven
Production manager: Julia Druskin

Library of Congress Cataloging-in-Publication Data

Names: Daughan, George C., author.
Title: Lexington and Concord : The Battle Heard Round the World /
George C. Daughan.
Description: First edition. | New York : W. W. Norton & Company, 2018. |
Includes bibliographical references and index.
Identifiers: LCCN 2017060269 | ISBN 9780393245745 (hardcover)
Subjects: LCSH: Lexington, Battle of, Lexington, Mass., 1775. | Concord, Battle of,
Concord, Mass., 1775. | United States—History—Revolution, 1775–1783—Causes. |
United States—History—Revolution, 1775–1783—Economic aspects.
Classification: LCC E241.L6 D38 2018 | DDC 973.3/311—dc23
LC record available at https://lccn.loc.gov/2017060269

W. W. Norton & Company, Inc., 500 Fifth Avenue, New York, N.Y. 10110
www.wwnorton.com

W. W. Norton & Company Ltd., 15 Carlisle Street, London W1D 3BS

1 2 3 4 5 6 7 8 9 0

For my father, William G. Daughan, an engineer and teacher with a lifelong interest in Irish and British history

and

My grandfather, George Harris, an Englishman with an abiding love of America

Let every single step taken in this most intricate affair be upon the defensive.

—Rev. William Emerson

The King's dignity, and the honor and safety of the Empire, require that, in such a situation, force should be repelled by force.

—Lord Dartmouth

The first stroke will decide a great deal.

—Lieutenant General Thomas Gage

Here English law and English thought
'Gainst the self-will of England fought.

—James Russell Lowell

Spirit, that made those spirits dare,
To die, and leave their children free.

—Ralph Waldo Emerson

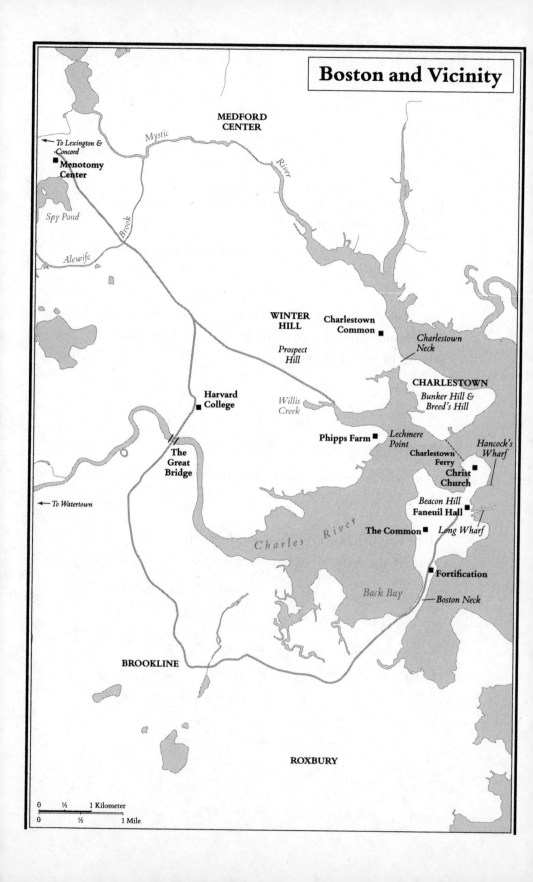

Boston and Vicinity

MEDFORD
CENTER

Mystic

River

To Lexington &
Concord

**Menotomy
Center**

Spy Pond

Brook

Alewife

WINTER
HILL

**Charlestown
Common**

*Charlestown
Neck*

*Prospect
Hill*

CHARLESTOWN

*Bunker Hill &
Breed's Hill*

**Harvard
College**

*Willis
Creek*

Phipps Farm

*Lechmere
Point*

*Hancock's
Wharf*

**The
Great
Bridge**

Charlestown
Ferry

**Christ
Church**

To Watertown

Beacon Hill
Faneuil Hall

Charles River

The Common

Long Wharf

Fortification

Back Bay

Boston Neck

BROOKLINE

ROXBURY

0   ½   1 Kilometer

0   ½   1 Mile

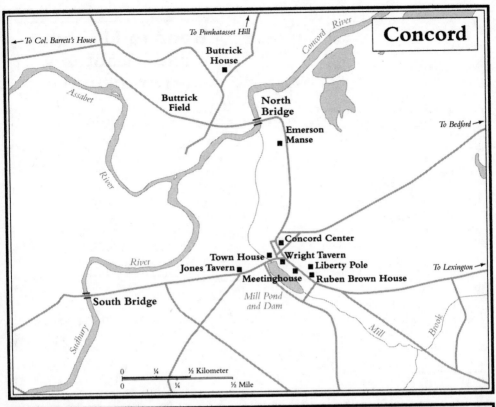

Concord

To Col. Barrett's House →

To Punkatasset Hill ↑

Buttrick House

Concord River

Assabet

Buttrick Field

North Bridge

Emerson Manse

To Bedford →

River

River

Concord Center

Town House

Wright Tavern

Jones Tavern

Liberty Pole

Meetinghouse

Ruben Brown House

To Lexington →

South Bridge

Sudbury

Mill Pond and Dam

Mill

Brook

| 0 | ¼ | ½ Kilometer |
| 0 | ¼ | ½ Mile |

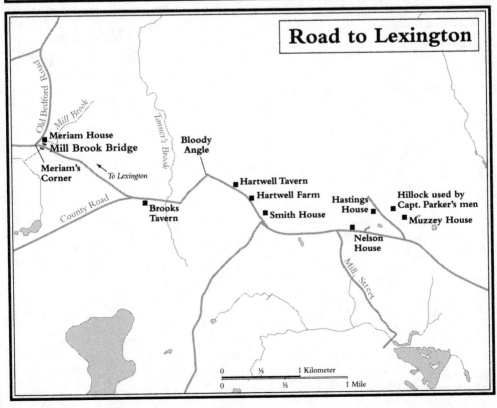

Road to Lexington

Old Bedford Road

Mill Brook

Tanner's Brook

Meriam House

Mill Brook Bridge

Bloody Angle

Meriam's Corner

← To Lexington

Hartwell Tavern

Hartwell Farm

Hastings House

Hillock used by Capt. Parker's men

Muzzey House

County Road

Brooks Tavern

Smith House

Nelson House

Mill Street

| 0 | ½ | 1 Kilometer |
| 0 | ½ | 1 Mile |

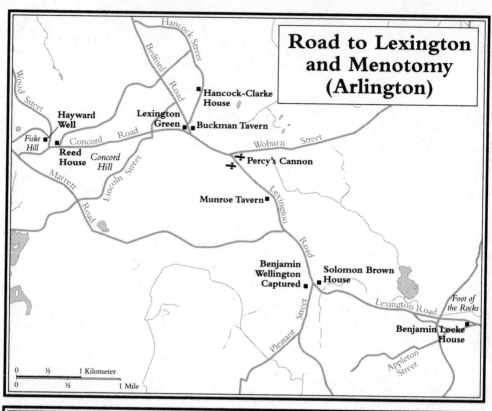

Road to Lexington and Menotomy (Arlington)

Hancock Street

Bedford Road

Wood Street

Hancock-Clarke House

Hayward Well

Lexington Green

Buckman Tavern

Woburn Street

Fiske Hill

Concord Road

Reed House

Concord Hill

Lincoln Street

Percy's Cannon

Lexington Road

Marrett Road

Munroe Tavern

Benjamin Wellington Captured

Solomon Brown House

Pleasant Street

Lexington Road

Foot of the Rocks

Benjamin Locke House

Appleton Street

0   ½   1 Kilometer
0   ½   1 Mile

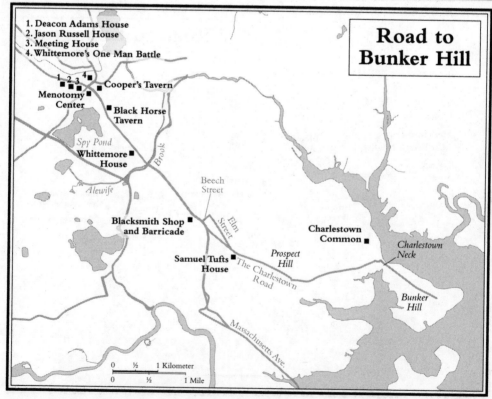

Road to Bunker Hill

1. Deacon Adams House
2. Jason Russell House
3. Meeting House
4. Whittemore's One Man Battle

1 2 3 4

Menotomy Center

Cooper's Tavern

Black Horse Tavern

Spy Pond

Whittemore House

Alewife

Brook

Beech Street

Elm Street

Charlestown Common

Charlestown Neck

Blacksmith Shop and Barricade

Samuel Tufts House

The Charlestown Road

Prospect Hill

Bunker Hill

Massachusetts Ave.

0   ½   1 Kilometer
0   ½   1 Mile

Contents

LEXINGTON
AND
CONCORD

Introduction

THE sheer number of Massachusetts militiamen who hurried from their homes on April 19, 1775, with muskets, powder, and ball to battle the column of redcoats marching to Concord via the Lexington Road amazed the British government. Before that day, no one in London knew if the men living comfortably in the Massachusetts countryside had the nerve to stand up to British regulars.

The most intriguing question that arose from the killing and maiming that ensued was why these well-off farmers were so aroused, and so confident, that they rose as one, and marched from small country towns to risk life and limb against one of the world's finest armies.

King George III and his supporters in Parliament were expecting just the opposite. During the preceding months, militiamen all over Massachusetts had been training in their towns, acquiring weapons and gunpowder from a variety of sources—including British smugglers—but there had been no actual fighting. His Majesty was confident that when the call to arms actually came, loudmouthed agitators in Boston like Samuel Adams would be deserted—embarrassed by the country people, who would be afraid to come out and die. Lord Percy, one of three brigade commanders in Boston, famously wrote, "I never believed, I confess, that they would have attacked the king's troops."

Even if a few militiamen found the courage to fire at the regulars, London was certain that the king's men would make quick work of them. Marine major John Pitcairn, who would play a leading role in subsequent events, reported to the first lord of the Admiralty, John Montagu, 4th Earl of Sandwich, "The deluded people are made to believe that they are invincible. A very impudent publication, lately came out, asserts that they are an over-match for all Europe in their own country. When this army is ordered to act against them, they will soon be convinced that they are very insignificant when opposed to regular troops."

Other British officers had even less regard for American fighters. One of the most strident was Captain W. Glanville Evelyn, who condemned all provincials as cowards. "The rebels, you know, have for a long time been making preparations as if to frighten us," he wrote to his father, "though we always imagined they were too great cowards ever to presume to do it."

The country people did not turn out to be either insignificant or spineless, however. To be sure, when they marched with their townsmen—many of them relatives—from village greens to the battle zone, they knew the risks they were taking: death or injury, a humiliating defeat, followed by merciless retaliation. The gruesome tales of British regulars, led by the Duke of Cumberland (the king's deceased uncle), hanging and beheading Jacobites after defeating them at the battle of Culloden (near Inverness) in 1746 were well known.

The militiamen on their way to fight knew the gamble they were taking. They could not even be sure how many of their comrades from other towns would be answering the call. Robert A. Gross, in *The Minutemen and Their World*, described the people of Concord as "reluctant revolutionaries." They were indeed, and so were their neighbors in the nearby towns of Lexington, Bedford, Acton, Sudbury, Carlisle, Billerica, Lincoln, Weston, Waltham, and Woburn. In fact, the same could be said of the militiamen in every Massachusetts town.

Reluctant or not, the farmers and artisans of the country towns were determined to fight it out. They were not going to allow London to rule them unchecked and turn them into the wretched peasants found in the British Isles. The standard of living in Massachusetts was higher than in any other part of the empire—higher, in fact, than anywhere else in the world. The country people were determined to protect it. The latest edicts of king and Parliament had convinced them that their not-so-benign rulers intended to take away their political power, appropriate their land, and impose the Anglican Church. They feared that Britain, if left unchecked, would reduce them to penury. It was no secret that Ireland's Catholics, who constituted perhaps 80 percent of the population—no census had ever been taken—were worse off than even the peasants of eastern Europe.

It was not hyperbole when the farmers and artisans of Massachusetts, who were ninety percent of the population, spoke of not wanting to become enslaved. It was a real danger. Benjamin Franklin, in letters home after a lengthy tour of Ireland and Scotland in the fall of 1771, explained why the people of Massachusetts would take up arms in defense of their rights. He described the misery inflicted on ordinary people living under British oppression in Ireland and Scotland. The comforts of New England stood in stark contrast, he wrote:

> I have lately made a tour through Ireland and Scotland. In these countries a small part of the society are landlords, great noblemen and gentlemen, extremely opulent, living in the highest affluence and magnificence. The bulk of the people tenants, extremely poor, living in the most sordid wretchedness in dirty hovels of mud and straw, and clothed only in rags. I thought often of the happiness of New England, where every man is a freeholder, has a vote in public affairs, lives in a tidy, warm house, has plenty of good food and fuel, with whole

clothes from head to foot, the manufactory perhaps of his own family. Long may they continue in this situation! But if they should ever envy the *trade* of these countries, I can put them in a way to obtain a share of it. Let them with three-fourths of the people of Ireland live the year round on potatoes and buttermilk, without shirts, then may their merchants export beef, butter, and linen. Let them with the generality of the common people of Scotland go barefoot, without shoes and stockings: and if they will be content to wear rags like the spinners and weavers of England, they may make cloths and stuff for all parts of the world.

Farther, if my countrymen should ever wish for the honor of having among them a gentry enormously wealthy, let them sell their farms and pay rack'd [impossibly high] rents; the scale of the landlords will rise as that of the tenants is depressed, who will soon become poor, tattered, dirty, and abject in spirit. Had I never been in the American colonies, but was to form my judgement of civil society by what I have lately seen, I should never advise a nation of savages to admit of civilization: for I assure you that in the possession and enjoyment of the various comforts of life, compared to these people every Indian is a gentleman: and the effects of this kind of civil society seems only to be, the depressing multitudes below the savage state that a few may be raised above it.

To Thomas Cushing, speaker of the Massachusetts General Court (House of Representatives), Franklin wrote:

Ireland itself is a fine country, and Dublin a magnificent city; but the appearances of general, extreme poverty among the lower people, are amazing: They live in wretched hovels of mud and straw, are clothed in rags, and subsist chiefly on potatoes. Our New England farmers of the poorest sort, in regard to the enjoyment of all the comforts of life, are princes when compared to them. Such is the effect of the discouragement of industry, the non-residence not only of pensioners but of many original landlords who lease their lands in gross to undertakers that rack the tenants, and fleece them skin and all, to make estates for themselves, while the first rents, as well as most of the pensions are spent out of the country.

Other observers, like the Frenchman St. John de Crèvecoeur, were also struck by the remarkable contrast in living conditions of ordinary people in America compared to those in Europe. Wealth in America was not concentrated in the hands of a few privileged noblemen, luxuriating in unimaginable affluence, while the rest of the people made do with next to nothing. Americans were overwhelmingly middle-class farmers who lived comfortably on land they owned. They were independent, economically and politically. They did not live at the mercy of a nobility that owned all the land and had all the political power.

The startling contrasts that Franklin and Crèvecoeur observed were well known to the people of Massachusetts. The living conditions inflicted on ordinary people in the British Isles, particularly in Ireland, were not a mystery.

———

As depraved as Great Britain sometimes looked to Americans, she was still the most advanced country in the world. People who gloried in her preeminence believed that her progressive institutions were responsible for it, and to a great degree they were. Compared to Europe's other monarchies, Britain was the epitome of ordered liberty, and a resounding economic success.

The commercial vitality of London and the country was stupendous, even though profits flowed to only a few. The Industrial Revolution began in England, and she remained at its forefront. Her manufacturers were ingenious in using newly invented technology to produce unheard-of amounts of merchandise for a trading empire that made her preeminent in world commerce.

A high percentage of Britain's trade flowed through London, where great merchant banks were essential partners of her manufacturers and traders, adding to the city's and the country's opulence. The Royal Navy protected this vast international commerce. No other country could hope to challenge Britain's preeminence at sea.

As the country's economy grew, so did its principal city. By the 1770s over five hundred thousand souls crowded into London's precincts. No one knew the exact number; the government had not taken a census. The actual population could well have been seven hundred thousand or more.

Continual tearing down and building up gave people the feeling of never-ending progress. Much of London's new construction was exceptionally beautiful, including residences for old families, as well as for the nouveaux riches, who were amassing fortunes from the new economy. The excitement of being in the British capital, particularly if one were young, was palpable. For gifted people like Samuel Johnson and his friend the actor David Garrick, prospects seemed endless.

For all of London's modernity, however, much of the old remained. Food still came into the city by wagon or boat, as it had for centuries. Open country began at Hyde Park. Farmers still drove their herds through the streets as they had since Roman times. Narrow roads lined with buildings, a legacy of the Middle Ages, continued to be the dominant feature of the urban landscape.

After the Great Fire of 1666, which destroyed nearly every half-timbered medieval building, the government had rejected Christopher Wren's grand scheme for an open city, retaining the meandering streets and alleys that made more sense as cow paths than grand boulevards for the most vibrant metropolis on earth.

London's vitality was on full display along her bustling streets. The alleys running off them were a scene of never-ending activity, with men, women, and children hawking everything from fruits and vegetables to scissors, almanacs, and coal. Apprentices stood outside their shops shouting for attention. Vehicles of every kind added to the din, their iron-rimmed wheels grinding into uneven stone pavement at either side of a center gutter. Urchins seeking food and money—appearing as if from nowhere—darted across the streets, braving traffic with amazing agility and courage.

If London's energy was on full display in her streets, so, too, was her shame. Gaunt beggars roamed side by side with pickpockets, footpads, and murderers. Stabbings and beatings were endemic. Prostitutes plied their trade (and diseases) to lord and commoner alike. With no effective policing, large, destructive mobs often roamed about unrestrained.

Franklin told a friend that "even this capital, the residence of the king, is now a daily scene of lawless riot and confusion." The only check on the mobs was the army, which the king called out periodically when things got out of hand. A brutal repression inevitably followed.

Not that London's beau monde was ever discouraged from flaunting itself on the streets. Alongside the human vermin roaming about on foot rode dazzling gilded carriages, their occupants pleasure seekers of extraordinary capacity, hurrying so as not to allow a single hour to pass unused in their relentless effort to amuse themselves with cards, dice, wine, whoring, and whatever whim their minds might invent. This was indeed the heroic age of dissipation.

Inexplicably, the same people, oblivious to society's ills, patronized a remarkable arts community that was as vital and extraordinary as the rest of London. Painters, sculptors, architects, musicians, composers, actors, playwrights, essayists, historians, novelists, and poets all thrived here. Johnson, Boswell, Reynolds, Garrick, Goldsmith, Burke, Gainsborough, Turner, the American John Singleton Copley, Hogarth, Pope, Richardson, Fielding, and Gibbon, to name a few, flourished in the city's free, tolerant, competitive atmosphere. The music of Bach, Haydn, Mozart, and Handel, whose *Messiah* was a favorite of the king, was performed to knowledgeable, enthusiastic audiences.

The fundamental rights enjoyed by all Englishmen formed the basis of this unique society that was the envy of the world. It was easy to see why Americans like Benjamin Franklin found Britain, in spite of its blemishes, so appealing.

London's sublime creative community was of little interest to most Americans, however. They rarely, if ever, came in contact with it. The flagrant inequities in English society were of greater interest.

America had developed a high level of prosperity that was accessible to anyone willing to work for it. Land was plentiful and affordable. There was no aristocracy that had inherited it, nor a desperately poor lower class of free white men who worked for next to nothing. Patriots wanted to keep it that way. Under no circumstances were they going to allow a self-serving aristocracy to transform their country into something resembling the British Isles.

At the same time, while they were shouting about not wanting to become slaves to Britain's upper class, Americans tended to forget about their own slaves, who now numbered a colossal five hundred thousand, or 17 percent of the population.

Most of the people in Massachusetts refused to defend slavery, but they were not going to fight to outlaw it either. They would have liked to do away with it in their own province, since the numbers enslaved were so few, but the Privy Council refused to let them, knowing that it would set a bad example and create difficulties for Britain's politically powerful West Indian planters, whose operations would be crippled if a movement to abolish slavery became widespread.

Native Americans, whose numbers were unknown but were substantial, particularly west of the Appalachian Mountains, were dismissed as savages, their land expropriated without any moral qualms. Since New England's Native American population had shrunk to insignificance after King Philip's War (1675–1678), they were not a factor in Massachusetts politics.

Although Americans refused to free their slaves, or treat Native Americans as anything but savages, they still championed freedom and a high standard of living for a larger swath of the population than existed in any other country. It was this prosperity that they were fighting to protect.

By February of 1775, Benjamin Franklin had become more disenchanted with the men who governed the empire than ever before. It was not just their condescending attitude toward Americans, it was how hopelessly mired in corruption they had become. "Here," he wrote from London, "numberless and needless places [jobs for the well connected], enormous salaries, pensions, perquisites, bribes, groundless quarrels, foolish expeditions, false accounts or no accounts, contracts and jobs devour all revenue, and produce continual necessity in the midst of natural plenty."

He added that, although disillusioned with British society, he would nevertheless "try any thing, and bear any thing that can be borne with safety to our just liberties rather than engage in a war with such near relations, unless compelled to it by dire necessity in our own defense."

The Massachusetts militiamen who answered the call on April 19 felt the same way. Only dire necessity made them take up arms in their defense. They understood what their fate would be if they did nothing. Paul Revere, looking back many years later, explained:

> The British covenanted with the first settlers of this country, that we should enjoy "all the liberties of free natural born subjects of Great Britain." [But that changed.] They were not contented to have all the benefit of our trade, in short to have all our earnings, but they wanted to make us hewers of wood and drawers of water. Their Parliament . . . declared "that they have the right to tax us and legislate for us, in all cases whatever— now certainly if they have a right . . . to take one shilling from us without our consent, they have a right to all we possess; for it is the birthright of an Englishman not to be taxed without the consent of himself, or representative.

It was not surprising that, given the awesome power of Great Britain, the patriots tried to settle their differences with king and Parliament around a conference table rather than on the battlefield. In the fall of 1774 the newly formed Continental Congress offered an easy way for London to enter into a dialogue. Since the Congress was a single body composed of fifty-six of the leading men from every colony except Georgia, it could speak for America, where people in overwhelming numbers wanted a peaceful resolution of their dispute with the mother country, not a civil war.

But the king and his supporters were having none of it. They saw no reason to negotiate when they had the upper hand. Their contempt for colonial fighters—so evident in the parliamentary debates that preceded the musket balls at Lexington and Concord—made them anxious for a showdown.

John Brooke, one of George III's more sympathetic biographers, wrote, "[T]he king could conceive of no middle ground for the colonies between independence and unconditional submission." And, of course, His Majesty would never countenance independence.

Reducing America's choices to these stark alternatives made reconciliation impossible. A negotiation with the Continental Congress might have produced other ways to view the issues facing the empire. But when the king ignored pleas for negotiations, and insisted on putting the patriots down by force, the country people resisted, coming out to fight on April 19 with uncommon courage and in numbers that London never anticipated.

The militiamen who fought the first battle of that war began a new epoch in human history. They are the heroes of this story, as are their families, who risked everything to defend their way of life and the freedom of future generations.

1

The Final Straw

O N January 19, 1774, John Hancock's merchant vessel *Hayley* reached Dover, England, with a cargo that included the latest newspapers from Boston. Their front pages were covered with the sensational story of an event that had taken place the night of December 16, 1773, in Boston Harbor. A huge crowd of Bostonians—numbering in the thousands—had gathered at Griffin's Wharf to watch in ceremonial silence as a hundred well-organized townsmen, thinly disguised as Mohawks, boarded the British cargo vessels *Dartmouth*, *Beaver*, and *Eleanor* and, working nonstop for almost four hours, dumped 342 smashed-open chests of the East India Company's tea—a whopping 92,000 pounds—into icy water to protest being taxed without their consent. It appeared that nearly the entire city of fifteen thousand was defying the British government and nothing was being done about it. Lawlessness reigned supreme.

While news of the dumping sped overland to London by word of mouth, the *Hayley* continued her voyage, under Hancock's most trusted skipper, James Scott. He shaped a course north around Margate to the Thames, and then upriver to Gravesend. From there, the incendiary newspapers were delivered to London's *St. James's Chronicle*, which published the story of Boston's Tea Party on Saturday, January 22. Two days later, the *Public Advertiser* had a full account as well. Soon the entire country knew what had happened.

The official report of the royal governor of Massachusetts, Thomas Hutchinson, arrived at Whitehall, the government's administrative offices, on January 27, confirming the newspapers' story. Deeply shaken, the British cabinet met the following evening at the grand London residence of one of its more belligerent anti-American members, Henry Howard, Earl of Suffolk. As was their custom, ministers, who included Lord North, the first (prime) minister, discussed the incipient crisis over a splendid dinner, including plenty of excellent French wine.j

They knew they had a major problem on their hands. The event in Boston was not a minor disturbance on the fringes of empire, but the latest in a series of direct challenges—dating back to the Stamp Act crisis in 1765—that Massachusetts radicals had directed at British authority. The angry ministers agreed that a powerful response was required. If left unchecked, Boston's malcontents could threaten the empire.

King George III was of the same mind. Even more upset than his ministers, he saw the Tea Party as confirmation of his long-held belief that Britain had mishandled the Americans for years. Time and again, London had foolishly tried to placate them, instead of demanding that they obey the laws passed by Parliament and threatening dire consequences if they did not. He was convinced that the Tea Party never would have happened had a resolute government stood firm and enforced the Stamp Act. He deeply regretted that he had ever allowed the law to be repealed.j

His Majesty was particularly incensed about the Tea Party because he had supported keeping a tax on tea back in 1770, when Lord North's government was repealing the Townshend duties (1767 to 1770), which had been conceived as a substitute for the Stamp Act. Colonists were so bitterly opposed to the Townshend taxes that they were doing more harm than good, and North wanted to get rid of them.

The ministry agreed with him in general, but split over whether to keep a single duty on tea. The king tipped the balance in favor of those who wanted to retain it. On March 5, 1770, he told North that even though "there is no inclination for the present to lay fresh taxes upon them. . . . I am clear that there must always be one tax to keep up the right, and as such I approve of the tea duty." North did as the king directed and kept the tax.

His Majesty felt that the challenge from Boston put the entire empire in jeopardy. If obedience to the mother country was not restored in Massachusetts, an unraveling could begin until Britain was reduced to an insignificant island off the coast of Europe. Restoration of London's authority became an obsession.

At this point in Britain's history the king had acquired enormous personal power. On a matter of this magnitude, he was easily able to obtain approval from the ministry and Parliament for drastic remedies to rid the colonies, particularly Massachusetts, of dissidents permanently.

Lord North was his willing, albeit at times uncertain, instrument. North was the son of the elderly Earl of Guilford, and was called "lord" as a courtesy. He was chancellor of the exchequer and first lord of the Treasury, as well as leader of the House of Commons, but he was not a prime minister in the modern sense. The British government was in transition at the time, moving, or more accurately muddling, its way toward a modern parliamentary system that would not emerge until after 1783, when William Pitt the Younger took the reins of power following George III's gross mishandling of the American crisis.

For Lord North to have been the actual, as well as titular, head of government, he would have needed strong convictions about how American discontent should be handled, and he would have needed to use his considerable parliamentary skill to have his policy adopted.

Earlier in the eighteenth century, strong parliamentary leaders such as Robert Walpole, Henry Pelham, and Thomas Pelham-Holles, 1st Duke of Newcastle, as well as William Pitt the Elder, had been able to lead the country, but they had had strong convictions that North lacked, and they'd had George I and George II to deal with, not George III. Pitt, of course, did have to contend with young George III, who ascended the throne in 1760, at the age of twenty-two. The young monarch turned out to be quite different from his predecessors. In spite of Pitt's great success during the Seven Years' War, His Majesty soon dismissed him, labeling him "mad Pitt" for wanting to expand the already long war to include Spain. The young monarch, under the influence of his mentor, Lord Bute, wanted to end it.

Lord North bore little resemblance to Pitt. He had scant knowledge of America and no firm convictions about how to deal with Massachusetts. The king, on the other hand, had a keen interest. He had studied the colonies and had acquired a surprising degree of information, albeit with little real understanding or sympathy. By 1774 he had developed strong convictions about what needed to be done to end colonial disturbances.

A confused, uncertain North rationalized his subservience to the monarch by insisting that the king's policies were what the House of Commons wanted, which was undoubtedly true. Nobody could read the temper of the House as well as North. In March of 1774, he tried to curry favor with both king and Commons by taking up the universal cry against the Tea Party. He stood in the House and solemnly declared, "Let it go forth to the world, that the Parliament of Great Britain will protect their subjects and their property." It was a pronouncement unworthy of a man with North's subtle mind. He must have had serious doubts about the king's approach to America, but he consistently refused to act on them.

North had always considered himself a man of the House, reflecting the opinion of a majority of its members. "I have been the creature of your opinion and your power," he told members toward the end of his long career, "and the history of my political life is one proof which will stand against and overturn a thousand wild assertions that there is a corrupt influence in the crown which destroys the independence of this House. Does my history show the undue influence of the crown? Or is it not, on the contrary, the strongest proof that can be given of the potent efficacy of the public voice?" By "public voice" North meant the opinions of the small number of landed aristocrats who held power in both houses of Parliament. In 1774 a firm majority of these landed gentlemen supported the king on most important measures, particularly those relating to America.

Even if North had schooled himself in the American problem and had developed his own approach to solving it, he would not have had an easy time implementing it, and probably would have been forced to step down as first minister. In slavishly following the king's dictates, he was simply bowing to political realities. Not only did he have an anti-American Parliament to deal with; his entire cabinet was solidly behind the king. The seven members who took an active part in developing and executing American policy were all hard-liners, except for North's brother-in-law, Lord Dartmouth, the secretary of state for America.

Unfortunately, Dartmouth had no firm convictions about what ought to be done with the colonies, except that, like North, he wanted to avoid a civil war—but not to the point where he was willing to stand up to the throne. He followed the king's lead, never exhibiting any independent judgment. It often appeared that he wanted to adopt a softer tone and seek accommodation, but he never felt strongly enough to fight for his views against a determined monarch with convincing support in Britain's upper class.

Benjamin Franklin, who knew Dartmouth well, had this to say about him: "It is a trait of that nobleman's character, who from his office is supposed to have so great a share in American affairs, but who has in reality no will or judgment of his own, being with dispositions for the best measures, easily prevailed with to join in the worst."

2

General Thomas Gage
and George III

ONE of the first things the king did after learning of the Tea Party was send for fifty-five-year-old General Thomas Gage, who knew more about America than any other British official, having served in the colonies continuously since 1755. By chance, Gage, the commander in chief of His Majesty's army in North America, happened to be in London enjoying his first visit home in eighteen years.

For a long time, he had been hoping to return to England for a visit, but he had been unable to arrange it until June 8, 1773, when he departed New York with his American wife, Margaret Kemble, and three of their five children for an extended vacation. The other two children were already in England attending school.

Gage had begun his American career under the ill-starred General Edward Braddock at the start of the French and Indian War. In the years of war and peace that followed, he had worked hard to distinguish himself in the eyes of Braddock and each of his successors: William Shirley; John Campbell, 4th Earl of Loudoun; James Abercrombie; and Jeffery Amherst, who eventually won the war with the indispensable help of General James Wolfe, the Royal Navy, and William Pitt.

Pitt's superb leadership in every phase of the war, including the handling of the American colonies, was responsible for Britain's stunning victory. He even became a favorite in Massachusetts, despite eliciting great sacrifices from the farmers and artisans of the countryside and the people of the seaport towns, including Boston.

General Gage had been an important figure throughout the war, even serving for a time with George Washington and forming a friendship with him. Gage was a brave fighter and a savvy political operator. By adroit maneuvering and a healthy dose of luck, he steadily advanced in rank. When the Seven Years' War was over in North America, he was appointed governor of Montreal, serving successfully from 1760 to 1763. Subsequently he became commander in chief of the army in North America, succeeding Amherst, whom Gage had made it his business to become close friends with—not an easy task with the aloof, ice-cold general. Gage was Amherst's most reliable administrator, and when Amherst went home, he and Gage remained close.

In 1765, two years after Amherst had returned to England, Gage was confronted with the Stamp Act crisis. He stood by with his troops ready to reestablish order, but he was never called upon. His headquarters were in New York, where strong protests took place. All his political skills were tested, as the unpopular, ultraconservative, seventy-two-year-old lieutenant governor, Cadwallader Colden (acting governor for nearly fourteen years), wanted Gage to crush the large-scale rioting. The army could not be used in any colony, however, unless both the governor and council requested them, and this was not going to happen in politically divided New York.

The explosive situation was resolved when the new governor, Sir Henry Moore, arrived to take over on November 13, 1765. He was determined to deal with the crisis peacefully. Calling out the troops was immediately ruled out.

To his credit, Gage did not overreact, in spite of moments that would have tried the patience of any British commander. He did not urge Moore to use military force. But he did feel that if military action had been threatened, the radicals, led by Isaac Sears and Alexander McDougall, could have been quieted more easily.

Parliament dealt with the crisis by rescinding the controversial Stamp Act, while simultaneously approving the Declaratory Act. The latter decreed that Parliament had the right to legislate "in all cases whatsoever." Although this boldfaced declaration was necessary to get angry lawmakers to repeal the controversial law, it was never accepted in the colonies. Even the conservative Stamp Act Congress, which met during the fall of 1765 in New York, rejected it. While paying due deference to the king and Parliament, the Congress declared in October 1765 that American colonists were entitled to the "inherent rights and privileges" of natural-born subjects in England, which meant, among other things, "that no taxes be imposed on them, but with their own consent, given personally, or by their representatives." Congress also underscored the importance of the right of trial by jury of one's peers.

A short time after the dispute over the Stamp Act, Gage was at the center of the storm over the Townshend duties. And he was prominently involved in every colonial crisis thereafter, exhibiting a capacity to keep a tight rein on his emotions when his every instinct urged taking strong action against protesters, including the use of force.

———

Not long after arriving in England in 1773, Gage had traveled to Montreal, General Amherst's estate in Kent County, for talks on American affairs. Nothing is known about what was said, but it's safe to assume that both of these experienced generals believed that if Britain meant to hold on to her colonies, a much larger military presence was necessary, coupled with the will to use it.

They were not unaware of how controversial this would be. Although Americans might tolerate a large British army in their midst for the purpose of protecting them from French, Spanish, and Native American threats, they strenuously objected to having troops there to police them, or worse, to enforce unpopular parliamentary laws. Despite knowing this, both generals advocated keeping a large military presence in the colonies, and coupling this with strengthening the powers of colonial governors, while weakening those of the lower house in the legislatures.

Talking with Amherst helped prepare Gage for his meeting with George III at King James's Palace on February 4, 1774. The conversation proceeded amicably. Their views appeared to be closely aligned. The general had long advocated taking tough action against the radicals in Massachusetts.

Since assuming command from Amherst, he had watched weak leaders in London give in to colonial protests over taxation. Compromising in this fashion, he believed, only invited more trouble. Enforcing the laws—using troops if necessary—was the only way to solve the American conundrum. When the present crisis was over, he was in favor of making far-reaching changes to the governmental structure of Massachusetts, which he had become convinced was the real source of the grief Britain was suffering.

Gage undoubtedly expressed these views to the king, just as he had in 1768 to Lord Hillsborough, the new, hard-line secretary of state for America during the crisis over the Townshend duties. "I know of nothing," he told Hillsborough, "that can so effectually quell the spirit of sedition, which has so long and so greatly prevailed here, and bring the people back to a sense of their duty, as speedy, vigorous, and unanimous measures taken in England to suppress it. Whereby the Americans shall plainly perceive that it is the general and determined sense of the British nation, resolutely to support and maintain their rights, and to reduce them to their constitutional dependence on the mother country."

Two years later, Gage expressed similar views to his close friend William Barrington, the secretary at war, during the brouhaha over the Boston Massacre. "I hope Boston will be called to strict account," he wrote. ". . . I think it must be plain to every man, that no peace will ever be established in that province, till the king nominates his council [the upper house of the legislature] and appoints the magistrates, and that all town meetings are absolutely abolished; whilst those meetings exist the people will be kept in a perpetual heat."

The Tea Party confirmed Gage's belief that stern punishment for Boston was the only effective way of reminding Massachusetts that the laws of the mother country must be obeyed. Anything less would only invite further, and worse, disturbances.

The king was delighted to hear Gage's views. Afterward he wrote to Lord North summarizing what had been said and urging him to speak with Gage himself. "Since you left me this day," he wrote,

> I have seen General Gage, who came to express his readiness, though so lately come from America, to return at a day's notice, if the conduct of the colonies should induce the directing of coercive measures. His language was very consonant to his character of an honest determined man; he says they will be lions whilst we are lambs, but if we take the resolute part they will undoubtedly prove very meek; he thinks the four regiments intended to relieve as many regiments in America, if sent to Boston, are sufficient to prevent any disturbance. I wish you would see him and hear his ideas as to the mode of compelling Boston to submit to whatever may be thought necessary; indeed, all men seem now to feel that the fatal compliance in 1766 [repeal of the Stamp Act] has encouraged the Americans annually to increase their pretensions to that thorough independency which one state has of another, but which is quite subversive of the obedience which a colony owes to its mother country.

His Majesty had a habit of sending similar letters after meeting with important people. The royal missives accurately portrayed the view from the throne but often distorted what the king's visitor had to say. On this occasion, His Majesty was probably assuming more agreement than there actually was. It's true that the general had long advocated strong measures, but there probably were significant differences on just what that might mean.

It's doubtful that Gage gave voice to whatever differences he may have had. If he wanted to keep his job in America, which he appeared to value above everything else, he had to agree with His Majesty or risk being replaced. There were plenty of officers, including fifty-seven-year-old General Amherst, who could take his place.

Nonetheless, it's hard to believe that Gage had no misgivings. He was discovering for the first time that despite their anger, the king and ministry were intent on subduing Massachusetts with words, not guns. They did not intend to employ additional troops, only strong legislation. It's unlikely that Gage believed only four regiments—fewer than two thousand men—could make Massachusetts submit to whatever punitive laws the king and ministry might fashion. He must have anticipated strong resistance when Bostonians saw the new legislation.

He had explained, time and again, to anyone who would listen, that a weak military presence only encouraged resistance. The king was apparently counting on the timidity of patriots like Samuel Adams, John Hancock, Thomas Cushing, Dr. Joseph Warren, Thomas Young, William Cooper, William Molineux, and their cohorts, when they had demonstrated through every crisis since the Stamp Act that they were fearless in defense of their rights. Yet George III and his supporters preferred to think that a large military presence wasn't necessary. They did not feel that having a weak garrison in Boston invited trouble. On the contrary, the king felt that the remedies he intended to apply were the best method for avoiding meaningful opposition.

He never believed that colonials would stand up to a professional army and navy. Throughout the crisis that led up to the Battle of Lexington and Concord, King George and his parliamentary allies consistently maintained that their American subjects were sure to shrink before the mighty British colossus. Lord North expressed the prevailing attitude when he bragged, "four or five frigates will do the business without any military force."

Years later, in answer to an inquiry from historian George Chalmers, Gage recalled that his conversation with the king was quite different than His Majesty remembered. Gage wrote: "The General [referring to himself] not long from his command by leave, and still holding it, made no objection to return to his duty, but was averse to taking the government of the Massachusetts Bay. He desired at length that a much larger force than four weak regiments might be sent out, and the town of Boston declared in rebellion, without which his hands would be tied up."

Gage's recollection, since it contradicted the king's in the critical matter of the proper size of the army to be kept in Boston, was at best inaccurate. In view of what happened later, he certainly would have liked to have had far more troops, but it's unlikely that he made an issue of it right then, for fear of being replaced.

3

Benjamin Franklin Excoriated

IMMEDIATELY after word of the Tea Party reached London, Benjamin Franklin became more deeply embroiled in a controversy with the government over a set of stolen letters he had acquired and then publicized. The ruckus over the letters had been going on for months, but the government was just now bringing the matter forward in order to link it in people's minds with the destruction of the tea, underscoring the depravity of Boston's protesters, and of Franklin himself. Since he was considered America's unofficial ambassador, who better to attack for both the tea and the letters?

Franklin reported to Cushing, "The transactions relating to the tea had increased and strengthened the torrent of clamor against us." He might have added that so, too, had agitation over the letters. In combination, they created a massive anti-American feeling throughout England, which the government wanted to encourage.

Franklin had been the agent for Massachusetts since 1770, and it was in that capacity that he was ordered to appear on January 29, 1774, before the Privy Council, which was considering a petition from the Massachusetts General Court to remove from office Governor Thomas Hutchinson and his brother-in-law Lieutenant Governor Andrew Oliver. The two had expressed controversial sentiments in a number of old private letters that Franklin had acquired from a person he refused to identify. The letters were addressed to Thomas Whately, a high official in the Grenville and North governments. Hutchinson could be certain that what he and Oliver wrote would come to the attention of the cabinet. Whately died in 1772. He was remembered as the man who wrote the Stamp Act.

There were thirteen surviving letters. Hutchinson wrote six in 1768–69, when he was chief justice and lieutenant governor of Massachusetts. Oliver, who was secretary of the Bay Colony at the time, wrote four, and men close to them wrote the others. The letters maintained that the people of Massachusetts were not entitled to the same rights and privileges as freeborn Englishmen. Hutchinson expressed the hope that London would gradually reduce colonial liberties in the interest of better governance. He wanted the democratic elements in Massachusetts slowly diminished until ordinary people had a negligible influence on the political decisions of their betters.

Knowing how explosive the letters would be if made public, Franklin, who had no use for Hutchinson, sent them to Speaker Thomas Cushing—a close ally of John Hancock and Samuel Adams—asking him to show them to a few important people but to otherwise keep them secret. The notion that they would remain confidential after Adams and Hancock got a look at them was unrealistic, and Franklin knew it. Nonetheless, he continued to hide the identity of the person who gave them to him. He admitted sending them to Cushing. Franklin was so tenacious about refusing to identify his source that we still do not know who the person was.

In the hands of Sam Adams, the letters were valuable propaganda. He used them to undermine Hutchinson and Oliver in Massachusetts, as Franklin knew he would. But Adams went much further and circulated them to like-minded political leaders in every colony, warning of the real plans that the British government had for America. The contents of some letters were even printed in the newspapers, and all of them were read to the Massachusetts House of Representatives.

On the appointed day, Franklin appeared before the Privy Council in the Cockpit, one of Parliament's large committee rooms in the rear of the old palace of Westminster. The unusual name dated back to the days of Henry VIII, who had used the space as a cockfighting arena.

A hostile audience had assembled. All thirty-five council members were present, and nearly the entire cabinet, including Lords North and Dartmouth. Edmund Burke, a leader of the opposition in Parliament, was also there, along with Generals Gage and Amherst. Anger at Boston over the Tea Party was palpable in the crowd, as was disquiet about the purloined letters. Burke observed that "[t]he [Privy] Council was the fullest I have ever known. It did not seem absolutely necessary from the nature of the case that there should be any public trial whatsoever. But it was obviously intended to give all possible weight and solemnity to the decision."

It was a foregone conclusion that the petition from the Massachusetts General Court to have Hutchinson and Oliver removed would be rejected. Gage later wrote to Hutchinson congratulating him on his victory.

With that bit of business out of the way, the government turned to the letters. Intercepting private mail was a common practice in England. Officials did it all the time. Lambasting Franklin for something he did not actually do—he was simply the recipient of the letters— was rank hypocrisy. Franklin's own letters were intercepted regularly, except for those he made special arrangements to keep secret. When writing, he always kept in mind that his letter could shortly wind up on a minister's desk.

The event in the Cockpit was memorable for the gratuitous personal attack that Alexander Wedderburn, the solicitor general, leveled at Franklin. The widespread outrage over the Tea Party heavily colored his remarks. This was what the audience had come to hear. They were not disappointed. Wedderburn's studied harangue against the living symbol of America more than lived up to expectations. At one point he shouted, "My Lords, Dr. Franklin's mind may have been so possessed with the idea of a Great American Republic, that he may easily slide into the language of the minister of a foreign independent state."

The reckless claim that Franklin was promoting independence was wide of the mark. In fact, he was doing just the opposite, searching for ways to reconcile the colonies with Britain, in the hope of avoiding a calamitous civil war. Announcing that American leaders were preparing the ground for a complete break was simply not true. There were a few, such as Sam Adams, who wanted independence, but they were a distinct minority. Insisting that they had wide support only added to their strength and increased the likelihood of the very separation that His Majesty was determined to prevent.

As if Wedderburn's scolding was not enough, the day after Franklin appeared before the Privy Council, he was dismissed as deputy postmaster general for North America, in spite of his unparalleled record of success. He had taken a practically defunct post office and resuscitated it, changing it from an enterprise that always lost money into one that produced £3,000 a year for the Crown—all the profit being dutifully shipped to London. It made no difference. The opportunity to publicly humiliate the symbol of America was irresistible.

A short time later, Franklin became aware of the government's extensive discussions about how best to punish Boston and Massachusetts for the Tea Party. He reported to Cushing that the ministry was contemplating major changes in colonial policy. In the current heated atmosphere, he did not expect anything good to come from their frenzied deliberations. On the contrary, he feared the worst. And although Wedderburn's lambasting had angered him deeply, he continued to do his best to warn the British of the misguided course they were on, in the hope of bringing about a reconciliation.

Needless to say, the ministry did not appreciate his efforts. There were even moments when he thought he was about to be arrested and thrown into Newgate prison. If he were, the charge could well have been treason. His suspicions were well founded. Lord Dartmouth thought seriously about arresting Franklin, but he never found the evidence he needed. He failed to find it because it didn't exist. Nonetheless, as long as Franklin remained in England, he was in danger of being seized on bogus charges that could bring the death penalty.

In spite of the danger, Franklin continued to issue statements to prominent newspapers criticizing the government's American policy. He was particularly incisive when asking what the end result of the legislation now being considered would be. He warned that trying to force Massachusetts to submit to the unholy bundle of laws being contemplated was bound to fail and could, in the end, seriously weaken Britain herself, not to mention the river of innocent blood that would flow.

As far as Franklin was concerned, an aroused king and ministry were rushing to produce legislation better suited to smite an enemy than a thriving colony. He tried to remind them that Americans were not implacable foes but loyal subjects. He also liked to point out that they knew how to fight. On April 15, 1774, the *Public Advertiser* published an open letter that Franklin addressed to Lord North, ridiculing the idea that America could be easily subdued by military means. He signed it sardonically, "A Friend to Military Government."

He reminded North that Americans were tough, experienced fighters who were "descended from British ancestors" and would defend themselves. They would not, as imagined now in London, "fly like sheep pursued by a wolf."

4

Britain Closes the Port of Boston

N o one in the government paid any attention to what Franklin had to say. He was thoroughly discredited. The king moved ahead, submitting to Parliament four pieces of far-reaching legislation designed to solve the colonial crisis once and for all. The new laws were approved in short order, one after the other, during the winter and spring of 1774. They were designed to deal with both the immediate problem of chastising Boston and the longer-term project of remaking the government and society of Massachusetts to ensure its permanent submission to the mother country.

Lord North had no trouble securing parliamentary approval. The king controlled enough votes to assure passage. His grip on Parliament was notorious. Through adroit use of the Civil List, he distributed special jobs requiring little or no work, but paid handsome salaries to favored members, their relatives, and hangers-on, guaranteeing votes on any important legislation. North's savvy undersecretary in the Treasury Department, John Robinson, kept careful track of who got what, and how they performed.

Even without the Treasury's careful oversight, widespread anger at Boston meant that opposition in Parliament would be weak. Edmund Burke, the agent for the colonial New York Assembly, explained to its members: "The popular current both within doors and without at present sets sharply against America. That you may not be deceived by any idle or flattering report, be assured that the determination to enforce obedience from the colonies to laws of revenue by the most powerful means seems as firm as possible, and that the Ministry appears stronger than I have ever known it."

Franklin reported to Cushing, "I suppose we never had since we were a people, so few friends in Britain. The violent destruction of the tea seems to have united all parties here against our province, so that the bill now brought into Parliament for shutting up Boston as a port till satisfaction is made, meets with no opposition."

The king's punitive laws were known as the Coercive Acts in Britain and in America. Much later, after the War of Independence was long over, they were labeled the Intolerable Acts, for intolerable they were to all the colonies, not just Massachusetts.

On March 14 Lord North brought the first of them, the Boston port bill, before the House of Commons. He rose from the Treasury bench and declared to a crowded chamber that Boston had been "the ringleader of all violence and opposition to the execution of the laws of this country. . . . Boston has not only, therefore, to answer for its own violence but for having incited other places to tumults."

North's remarks were well received by an audience that was irritated with the effrontery not only of a colony standing up to the mother country over a question of tax policy—which, in their minds, was a clear prerogative of Parliament—but of a city whose prosperity was an indicator of something far more ominous: the economic potential of, not just Boston, but of all the seaports, large and small, throughout the thirteen colonies. And beyond that, something even more disquieting: the vast economic potential of America, which, in time, could dwarf the economy of Britain herself. A single example illustrated the point.

The huge colonial trade of Great Britain was now done mostly in ships that were made in America and owned by Americans. Boston was the commercial and shipping center of New England, with a bright future. The rest of the colonies had similar prospects. It certainly must have crossed many minds in London that the time had come to regain control over the original thirteen colonies, to rein them in, before they became large enough to collectively constitute the most powerful country in the world. An aggressive policy to keep them divided and under firm supervision was long overdue. Little was said openly about this fear, but it was bound to be a factor in the thinking of Britain's rulers.

The Boston Port Act (March 25) would seal New England's most important seaport, closing it unceremoniously with little warning, as if it were the capital of a hostile power. Thousands would be thrown out of work, dealing a severe blow to the economy of Massachusetts and New England.

The bill's draconian measures directed that beginning on June 1, shipping in and out of Boston Harbor would be prohibited, except for coastal vessels carrying food and fuel, and these had strict controls placed on them. In addition, the colony's seat of government would be moved from Boston to Salem, and the customs house, which had always been in Boston, transferred to Salem, on the assumption that changing the seat of government would help calm things down.

The law would remain in effect until the East India Company was paid for the tea—a not inconsiderable £14,000—and the tax on it paid. Even then, strict controls would not be removed until the king was satisfied that conditions in Massachusetts warranted a restoration of the port and the reopening of trade. This meant that the people of the Bay Colony would be required to give proof of their willingness to submit to imperial authority. What exactly that meant was left unclear by design.

Burke explained to the New York Assembly that the legislation had broad implications. Much more was involved than recovering money, or even enforcing tax policy. An ambitious attempt was being made to reorient the entire relationship between colonies and mother country. He pointed out that Lord North was framing the vote in Parliament as a choice between submission to British law and independence. If members voted against the Boston Port Act, North warned, they were voting for independence. "Lord North's speech on the first opening of the matter," Burke explained, "turned on the absolute necessity of doing something immediate and effectual. For things were come to such a pass, by the evil disposition, the turbulent conduct, and the dark designs of many in the colonies, that the deliberation was no longer upon the degrees of freedom or restraint in which they were to be held, but whether they should be totally separated from their connection with, and dependence on the parent country of Great Britain. And that according to the part which gentlemen should take for or against the measure to be proposed, a judgment would be formed of their disposition to or against that connection and dependence."

North's gross misreading of the political temperament of Massachusetts, which reflected the king's, could only worsen the crisis he was trying to peacefully resolve. The fact was that people in the Bay Colony and in America generally, as Franklin was trying to point out, were not supporting independence, but wished overwhelmingly to remain part of the empire. Casting their political inclinations in an extreme light, as North was doing, only added to colonial alienation.

Both houses of Parliament approved the Boston port bill enthusiastically, and on March 31 a sanguine monarch signed it. At the same time, General Gage was appointed temporary governor of Massachusetts, replacing Thomas Hutchinson, who was sailing to England shortly to report on conditions in Massachusetts. He expected to return and resume his post after Boston had complied with the new law, which he and the king expected would be soon.

Having Gage as both political and military leader of the colony was highly unusual. The two offices had almost always been separated. Uniting them was more evidence of the king's determination to work his will on Massachusetts.

Although Gage's powers were thus enhanced, he still had only four regiments in Boston. Since he was also chief of the army in North America, he did have the option of bringing troops from Canada and New York to the city, but at the time, there were only around 3,500 regulars in all of North America.

While the fateful legislation sped through Parliament, Gage prepared to leave for Boston. He planned to travel alone. His family would follow two months later. He could not have been happy with the prospects before him. On April 7 he had a final meeting with the cabinet. Among other things, he wanted to determine under what conditions he could use the troops in Boston. The response was disappointing. Once again, as had been the case with the king earlier, he discovered that the ministers, who were publicly so anxious to clamp down on Massachusetts, expected it to be done without bloodshed and at minimal cost.

When Gage asked if he had the cabinet's approval to use force if necessary, he got an equivocal answer. Members assumed, as the king did, that Massachusetts would submit without a fight. They were gambling that when the people saw the severity of the law and viewed the four regiments prepared to act, they would be intimidated. When Gage pressed them on whether he could use troops if he had to, the ministers reluctantly approved.

The cabinet's attitude must have been small comfort for Gage, who knew, as the ministers should have known, that Boston's radicals would never meekly submit. Everything they had done in the past indicated that they would oppose the new law vigorously. And since the additional legislation being considered was directed at every town in Massachusetts, it could be assumed that the entire colony would be up in arms. It was also likely that, given past politically inspired disturbances, the radicals would attempt to unite all the American colonies in opposition.

The groundwork for doing so was already in place. Committees of correspondence had been operating in Massachusetts since 1772. Sam Adams had worked hard to establish them that year, when London quietly tried, once again, to remove the governor and judges from popular control by having the Crown, rather than the legislature, pay their salaries. His idea quickly caught on until all the towns in Massachusetts either had a committee of correspondence or had directed their selectmen to respond to communications from Boston's committee. The membership of the committees was usually around fifteen. In Boston it sometimes rose to twenty-one.

In March of 1773, Virginia's House of Burgesses, responding to

London's overreaction to the burning of a British revenue schooner, the *Gaspee*, in Rhode Island, picked up on Adams's idea and urged every province to establish committees of correspondence. The response was immediate and positive, as concern was growing over the Crown's increasing assertion of its authority. Once committees had been established in every colony, communication throughout America was markedly improved.

Although the willingness of Massachusetts, and particularly Boston, to stand up to London was clearly evident to Gage long before he left England, he nonetheless chose to go, passing up an opportunity to resign and avoid the confrontation he suspected lay ahead. Perhaps he was hoping that the king's strong commitment to enforcing the laws would at long last bring peace. Whatever his reasons, he put aside any qualms and sailed from Plymouth on April 16, 1774, aboard the 20-gun sloop of war HMS *Lively*, under Captain Thomas Bishop. On the same day, Franklin wrote to Cushing, "The torrent is still violent against America."

5

Declaring War on Massachusetts

THE day before Gage left for Boston, two more Coercive Acts were introduced in the House of Commons. The port bill was not enough for His Majesty; he wanted to use the anger swelling in Britain against Massachusetts to make more permanent reforms. The first and most wide-ranging was entitled A Bill for Better Regulating the Government of the Province of the Massachusetts Bay in New England, also known as the Massachusetts Government Act. It was referred to in Parliament as the Regulating Bill. A more accurate description would have been: "A bill to radically alter Massachusetts society for the purpose of dominating it." The far-reaching legislation swept through Parliament on a tide of anti-American feeling, and the king signed it on May 20. It was to go into effect in August.

The law's immediate objective was removing political power from the hands of the people, something Gage had been advocating for years. The new legislation nullified the Massachusetts Charter of 1691, and allowed the king and Parliament to rule the province directly. This had never been done before to any other colony. Not only was it meant as the beginning of a radical transformation of the province, but it was also a warning to every other colony. And it was taken that way. What it did not do was intimidate the colonists. Instead, it alerted them to a great menace that required united action to oppose.

The law dramatically expanded the authority of the royal governor, an appointee of the king, by giving him sole power to choose the Massachusetts Council, which served as both the upper house of the legislature and as an advisory board to the governor. The Charter of 1691 limited its membership to twenty-eight. Under the old charter the council was elected each year by the outgoing members and the House of Representatives meeting as a single body.

The House itself was composed entirely of representatives democratically elected in town meetings throughout the Commonwealth. Since the property qualifications for voting were so low, nearly every white male could participate, and as many as 90 percent or more did. Not all of the two hundred and fifty towns in Massachusetts sent representatives to Boston, although it was their right to do so. A surprising number did, however.

Under the new law, the power of the lower house, which Lord North liked to call the colony's democratic element, was curbed severely. The governor was placed beyond its control. He already had veto power over any legislation, and now his salary would no longer be subject to the approval of the General Court. The council would no longer be a check on him, either. Under the new law, the governor could appoint and remove all judicial and other officers without the consent of the council. For the first time, he was given exclusive power to select all sheriffs, justices of the peace, judges, and other court officials, and remove any of these officials at any time for any reason.

The election of juries, or any called by local constables, was also forbidden. Only sheriffs appointed by the governor could summon a jury, which meant that they would now be appointed by unelected sheriffs, removing the judicial system entirely from popular control. Heretofore, juries had been chosen by lists provided by the towns.

Determining who served on juries was now the sole prerogative of the representatives of the Crown, not the farmers and artisans, who made up the bulk of the population.

Even worse, beginning on August 1, town meetings, the heart and soul of popular government in Massachusetts, were banned, except for one to be held annually in the spring to choose town officers, and a representative to the General Court. No other meeting could take place without the governor's approval.

The third Coercive Act was the Administration of Justice Act. Gage and Amherst had both recommended that something like it be enacted. It allowed magistrates, customs officials, and their subordinates to use whatever means were necessary to suppress riots or enforce revenue laws. If any of them—including soldiers, naval personnel, and county sheriffs—were indicted for murder while carrying out their duties, the governor was permitted to transfer their trial to Great Britain or to another colony, effectively putting them beyond the law. The legislation, which patriots like George Washington termed the Murder Act, passed overwhelmingly, and on May 20 a triumphant king signed it.

The fourth Coercive Act was an amendment to the Quartering Act of 1765, by which colonists had been required to house British soldiers in barracks. By 1766, places of accommodation had been expanded to inns. The 1774 law again passed both houses of Parliament with convincing majorities, and it was signed by the king on June 2. It allowed military commanders to quarter troops outside barracks in abandoned buildings, "out-houses, barns, or other buildings."

The opposition in Parliament was appalled at the severity of the legislation. On April 19 Burke spoke at length in the House of Commons, deploring the path the administration was on. The old ways were much sounder, he told members.

> Again and again, revert to your old principles—seek peace and ensure it—leave America . . . to tax herself. I am not here going into the distinctions of rights, nor attempting to mark their boundaries. I do not enter into these metaphysical distinctions;

I hate the very sound of them. Leave the Americans as they anciently stood, and these distinctions, born of our unhappy contest, will die along with it. They and we . . . have been happy under that system. Let the memory of all actions, in contradiction to that good old mode, on both sides, be extinguished forever. Be content to bind America by laws of trade. . . . Do not burden them by taxes.

. . . Reflect how you are to govern a people, who think they ought to be free, and think they are not. Your scheme yields no revenue; it yields nothing but discontent, disorder, disobedience; and such is the state of America, that after wading up to your eyes in blood, you could only end just where you began; that is, to tax where no revenue is to be found.

Although in poor health, William Pitt, the Earl of Chatham, lent his powerful voice in opposition. He had consistently opposed taxing America, going back to the Stamp Act, and now found the Coercive Acts both repugnant and foolish. He was convinced that they would produce the exact opposite of what their authors intended. On May 26, 1774, he told the House of Lords that he condemned the riots in Boston, but found

the mode which has been pursued to bring them back to a sense of their duty to their parent state . . . so diametrically opposite to the fundamental principle of sound policy that individuals, possessed of common understanding, must be astonished at such proceedings. . . . the moment they perceived your intention was renewed to tax them, under the pretext of serving the East India Company, their resentment got the ascendant of their moderation, for I sincerely believe the destroying of the tea was the effect of their despair.

This . . . has always been my received and unalterable opinion, and I will carry it to my grave—that this country had no right under heaven to tax America. It is contrary to all the principles of justice and civil policy, which neither the exigencies of the state, nor even an acquiescence in the taxes, could justify upon any occasion whatever. . . . [I]nstead of adding to their miseries . . . adopt some lenient measures, which may lure them to their duty . . . instead of these harsh and severe proceedings, pass an amnesty on all their youthful errors. . . . [A]dopt a more gentle mode of governing America; for the day is not too far distant when America may vie with these kingdoms, not only in arms, but in the arts also.

Beyond the four Coercive Acts, Parliament further provoked the Bay Colony by passing the Quebec Act. The king signed the bill on June 22, but it was not to go into effect until May 1, 1775. The law applied to Canada, but patriots in Massachusetts thought that it had important implications for them as well.

The extensive legislation established a new governmental structure for Canada. After winning control of this vast territory as a result of the Seven Years' War, Britain was forced to create a new political system for a society that was almost entirely French, apart from an unknown number of Native Americans and an English enclave of a few hundred. The resulting bundle of compromises was intended to solidify British control and insulate the new province from the troubles to the south. The law even prepared Canada for possible use against the original thirteen colonies.

Since Quebec was overwhelmingly French and Catholic, an elected assembly was ruled out. Political power was placed exclusively in the hands of an English governor, assisted by an unelected council, whom he would appoint. Although the government was placed securely in British hands, French support was imperative. To guarantee this, a grand compromise was worked out, whereby the Roman Catholic Church, instead of being merely tolerated, was made part of the establishment. It would retain its privileged place in society, including its traditional ability to collect tithes and control parish schools for the indoctrination of the young. French civil law was also retained, which meant no trial by juries. And just as significant, if not more so, the feudal seigneurial landholding system was preserved.

In addition, Quebec's southern boundary was moved to the

Ohio River, massively increasing the colony's size. She would now reach from the Great Lakes to the Ohio River; and from the western boundary of Pennsylvania to the Mississippi. This huge territory would henceforth be closed to westward expansion of the original colonies.

Charles James Fox denounced the law: "to go at once, and establish a perfectly despotic government, contrary to the genius and spirit of the British constitution, carries with it the appearance of a love of despotism, and a settled design to enslave the people of America."

Patriots in Massachusetts and throughout the country thought the same thing. The Quebec Act appeared to contain some of the noxious policies that London intended to impose on the colonists. Dr. Joseph Warren wrote to John Adams, "the bill for regulating the government of Canada shows plainly that it would be very pleasing to the ministry to deprive the Americans totally of the right of representation."

The law did not sit well with Canada's French peasants, or *habitants*, as they were called, either. They made up the bulk of the population and worked the land. The church hierarchy, intent on maintaining its control, used parish priests to overcome resistance, but the peasants were never fully reconciled to the law. Since they had no political power and no means of resistance, they were forced to accept it.

No one in London gave any thought to the impact of the legislation on Massachusetts or the other colonies. The Roman Catholic Church was anathema to Protestant New Englanders, as was the feudal hierarchy of seigneurs the act was supporting. Patriots bitterly resented the establishment of a feudal society next door, all done to secure tight political control.

Taken together, the four Coercive Acts and the Quebec Act made General Gage's task of bringing about a reconciliation in Massachusetts impossible. Submission in the sense the king meant was never going to happen peacefully, and reconciliation on terms other than his own was never acceptable to the dull-witted monarch. Thus, from the beginning, dispatching Gage to Boston to enforce the new laws was simply lighting a train of gunpowder that would inevitably explode.

Nonetheless, the king and Parliament refused to consider that they were voting for war when they enacted the new legislation. They continued to insist that they were voting for an end to the troubles in Massachusetts, that the people of the Bay Colony would meekly submit without the need to use the small garrison in Boston. And their political blindness extended far beyond Massachusetts. They never anticipated that twelve other provinces would stand solidly behind the Bay Colony.

6

Support for Boston Broadens

O N May 24 Virginia's House of Burgesses showed just how wrongheaded the king and Parliament were. When news arrived at the regular sitting in Williamsburg that the Boston port bill was going into effect in seven days, the burgesses were outraged. They immediately proposed that June 1 be "a day of fasting, humiliation, and prayer, devoutly to implore the divine imposition for averting the heavy calamity, which threatens destruction to our civil rights, and the evils of civil war, and to give us one heart and one mind to firmly oppose, by all just and proper means, every injury to American rights."

With George Washington, Patrick Henry, and other famous Virginians in attendance, the burgesses approved the message wholeheartedly. The governor, John Murray, Earl of Dunmore, was so upset he dissolved the House the following morning.

Virginia's solid support for Massachusetts was a great boost to patriot morale, as was support from every other colony, with the exception of Georgia, which, at the moment, was in a struggle with the powerful Creek Nation and needed British arms and ammunition from St. Augustine. This allowed Governor James Wright to block a strong move by Georgia patriots to support Massachusetts.

And what of France? Could the patriots expect significant help from Britain's traditional enemy, still smarting from her humiliating defeat in the Seven Years' War? On both sides of the Atlantic, people were wondering what the French were going to do with the opportunity Britain was presenting to them.

Massachusetts patriots took it for granted that French support would be forthcoming immediately. They were counting on it. But on May 10, 1774, great uncertainty arose when Louis XV died of smallpox, in the fifty-ninth year of his reign. His grandson, a sheltered youth of nineteen and a complete unknown, all of a sudden became Louis XVI, king of France. With no governmental experience, he was elevated overnight to the throne of, not only a great European power, but England's most formidable rival.

The young man's immaturity and modest intellect meant that the men he appointed as his ministers would be far more important than they had been under his grandfather. The youthful monarch's unpredictability was soon made evident by his choice of Charles Gravier, Comte de Vergennes, as secretary of state for foreign affairs. Although practically unknown in Paris, Vergennes was a diplomat with long experience and conventional views. Like most Frenchmen, he considered Britain the country's natural enemy, and saw as his chief mission humiliating her for what she had done to France in the Seven Years' War.

From the beginning of his tenure, developments in Massachusetts were of great interest. Vergennes watched for ways to help the patriots without embroiling France in a war with Britain that she was not ready for. Like Europe's monarchs, Vergennes had no regard for the ability of George III. The French minister was expecting him to make mistakes that would offer France her opportunity. By the same token, he had to be careful. He did not want to stumble into a war before France was ready. Her fleet, which was rebuilding, was far from adequate, even when combined with Spain's.

The dons had their own score to settle with the hated English, but allying with France would still not be easy, nor would it guarantee success. The other European monarchs, including Frederick the Great of Prussia and Catherine II of Russia, watched events with great interest as well, but they had no desire to get involved in a struggle between Britain and France. They were decidedly neutral, at least for the moment.

Although Paris found events in America promising, the Americans were still British colonies. If they suddenly reconciled with London, France could find herself, once again, at odds with both. Vergennes understood the need to be careful.

British spies reported what the French were doing. Very little escaped their notice, but London was not anxious to get into a brawl with Paris. Even though Vergennes might be helping the American rebels, as long as French aid was kept at a low level, Britain complained, but otherwise did nothing.

Vergennes' views were not shared by all of Louis XVI's advisors. The powerful finance minister, Anne Robert Jacques Turgot, was utterly opposed to any involvement in America, on the grounds that a serious conflict with England would be disastrous for the French treasury. Turgot argued that the English would probably lose their American colonies, even if France remained neutral. On the other hand, if Britain managed to crush colonial resistance, the cost of keeping the Americans down would be so massive that England's ability to act elsewhere in the world, particularly in Europe, would be circumscribed. There was, thus, no reason for France to intervene, and every reason to remain aloof.

The young monarch listened to both Vergennes and Turgot. He took the warnings of his finance minister seriously but in the end found the views of his foreign minister more attractive. Vergennes had a distinct advantage. He was offering the prospect of achieving what every Frenchman wanted—revenge.

French hostility was not of great concern to the king and Parliament. They were confident that the business with America would be over quickly. There wouldn't be time for serious French intervention. And France was still unprepared at sea. She was embarked on a serious naval buildup, but her fleet was far from ready. Her army, of course, was vastly superior to Britain's. She was a great land power. But without a stronger sea force, her options with regard to America were limited.

———

On April 9, just before Gage left for Boston, Lord Dartmouth presented him with his final orders. Based on more wishful thinking, they lacked any understanding of the situation he would face. At least as an afterthought, Dartmouth admitted that Gage might find less than smooth sailing. If that turned out to be the case, he allowed that perhaps the general might have to use his troops. There was no indication that the number of regiments allotted to him was inadequate, however. He was to make do with what he had.

The orders must have brought a smirk to Gage's face. Dartmouth wrote:

> His Majesty trusts that no opposition will, or can, with any effect be made to the carrying the law into execution, nor any violence, or insult offered to those to whom the execution of it is entrusted: should it happen otherwise, your authority as the first magistrate, combined with your command over the King's troops, will, it is hoped, enable you to meet every opposition, and fully to preserve the public peace, by employing those troops with effect, should the madness of the people on the one hand, or the timidity or want of strength of the peace officers on the other hand, make it necessary to have recourse to their assistance. The King trusts, however, that such necessity will not occur, and commands me to say that it will be your duty to use every endeavor to avoid it, to quiet the minds of the people, to remove their prejudices, and by mild and gentle persuasion, to induce such a submission on their part to this law and such a proper compliance with the just requisitions it contains, as it may give full scope to His Majesty's clemency and enable His Majesty to exercise the discretionary power given him by the act, of again restoring to the town of Boston those commercial

privileges and advantages, which it has long enjoyed, and which have raised it to its present state of opulence and importance.

At the same time the sovereignty of the King-in-Parliament over the colonies requires a full and absolute submission. . . .

Dartmouth then did an about-face, contradicting everything he had just said. "The last advices from Boston," he warned, "are of a nature to leave little room to hope that order and obedience are likely to take the place of anarchy and usurpation; His Majesty, however, confides in your fortitude and discretion."

Gage would need all the fortitude and discretion he could muster to remain on course in the troubled waters he was sailing into. Long before he arrived in Boston, rumors had circulated about drastic measures Parliament was considering above and beyond the port bill. While Boston's patriots were contemplating this disturbing news, on May 10 the full text of the port bill arrived aboard the merchant vessel *Harmony*. The law turned out to be every bit as noxious as reported.

Two days later the committees of correspondence from eight towns surrounding Boston met with the city's twenty-one-member committee. Sam Adams chaired the meeting. They quickly decided to send urgent messages to the other colonies declaring Boston's distress to be everyone's and urging an immediate and total suspension of trade with Great Britain. The following day, the Boston town meeting endorsed the idea and dispatched Paul Revere to carry a message south to New York and Philadelphia, urging all the colonies to join in an embargo against Britain. The king's belief that the city would quietly submit to the port bill had been from the start a dangerous illusion.

The committees of correspondence were functioning well inside and outside Massachusetts. Although unifying provinces as diverse and competitive as the American colonies would not be easy, the unrestrained attack on Massachusetts left the other provinces feeling as if they had no other choice. Just the way Parliament's aristocrats spoke about "their colonies" was sobering. If ever Americans believed they were full British citizens, the debates in both Lords and

Commons over the Coercive Acts showed them that their hereditary rulers certainly did not think so.

"For what purpose," Lord Carmarthen asked during the debate over the Massachusetts Government Act, "were they [the colonists] suffered to go to that country, unless the profit of their labor should return to their masters here?"

7

Defiance Escalates

O N May 13 General Gage sailed into Boston Harbor, having made the passage from England in near record time—less than four weeks. Voyages to America often took two or three months. Instead of resting for a day and then going directly to town, he retreated to Castle William, a fortress located in the harbor a short distance off shore, for talks with sixty-three-year-old Governor Hutchinson, who had taken refuge in the fort. Gage assumed that rumors about the severity of the port bill had already reached Boston, and he naturally wanted to know what to expect when he got there.

The report he received wasn't encouraging. Hutchinson saw nothing to be hopeful about. "It is hardly time yet to form a judgment how the new acts of Parliament will operate," he said, "but I hear nothing of giving way, nor is there any proposal from any quarter of making compensation to the East India Company. Everybody seems apprehensive of the great calamity that is to come upon the town of Boston; but nobody appears to propose measures to extricate it."

The political climate had actually grown much worse than even

Hutchinson imagined. Resistance was building. Both he and Gage had assumed that Britain's military prowess would give even trouble-makers like Sam Adams, John Hancock, Dr. Joseph Warren, and their associates some pause. But it had not. The resolution of Boston's patriots, their determination and courage, had grown, as had their support from the rest of Massachusetts and the other colonies. The king had failed to instill the fear he had been counting on to cow the provincials.

Unable to delay any longer, on May 17 Gage left the peace of Castle William and entered the maelstrom in Boston. The gover-nor's handsome barge brought him to Long Wharf, the harbor's most prominent landmark. Built sixty-five years earlier, the famous pier extended King Street, the city's central thoroughfare, two thousand feet into deep water.

A fine welcoming ceremony awaited the general, almost as if the city was celebrating his arrival. Soldiers from regular British regi-ments lined the pier, along with John Hancock's well-trained, splen-didly attired Corps of Cadets. Dignitaries from state and town were also there, including the Governor's Council, the Massachusetts General Court, and the city's seven selectmen, led by John Scollay.

Two hours later, Gage was treated to a formal dinner at Faneuil Hall. He responded by toasting the city graciously and expressing his intention to carry out the port bill with as much consideration for the welfare of the people of Boston as possible. All of this was received without a murmur, but when he proposed a toast to departing Gov-ernor Hutchinson, his words were greeted with loud hissing.

The defiant tone was only a taste of what was to come. Relations deteriorated rapidly. The first serious confrontation occurred on May 25, when Gage summoned the Massachusetts General Court for its annual meeting. As their first order of business, representatives met with the outgoing Governor's Council and nominated twenty-eight men for the new council.

Everything was proceeding normally until Gage, unhappy with the political sympathies of many nominees, rejected thirteen of them—an unheard-of number. Among them were John Adams, James Bowdoin, and John Winthrop, Hollisian professor of mathematics and natural philosophy at Harvard and a direct lineal descendant of the first governor of the Bay Colony, John Winthrop.

The rejection looked as if it was meant as a shot across the bow of the town's malcontents. Gage seemed to have forgotten his pledge to carry out his mission with restraint.

Dismissing the councilors was just the beginning. The next day Gage followed with something far more unsettling. He announced that the government of the Commonwealth, including the customs house, was moving to Salem, and would remain there until Boston complied with all the terms of the Port Act. The legislature was to reconvene in Salem on June 7. The announcement came as a complete surprise. Transferring the seat of government would create even more economic hardship in Boston, which it was meant to do.

Before the move to Salem could begin, more startling news reached the city. On June 2, only one day after the port bill went into effect, word arrived that the king and Parliament had enacted two additional Coercive Acts. Four days later the *Boston Gazette* printed the full text of both. The provisions stunned the patriots.

Anger and alarm surged through Massachusetts and the whole country. The extent to which the new laws altered the government of the Commonwealth was deeply disturbing. People became convinced that the challenge from London had to be forcefully resisted or their entire way of life would be transformed into something resembling Ireland's.

The distrust and suspicion, indeed the hatred, exhibited in the new laws played powerfully into the hands of Sam Adams and his associates. Even before news of the additional Coercive Acts had spread, they had been moving fast to counter the port bill. Adams's immensely talented protégé, Harvard-educated, thirty-three-year-old Dr. Joseph Warren, acting as spokesman for the Boston committee of correspondence, sought support for Boston everywhere.

On June 5 he urged all the colonies to join in a Solemn League and Covenant to boycott all British goods. Eight nearby towns, through their committees of correspondence, immediately lent their support: Roxbury, Dorchester, Brookline, Newton, Charlestown, Cambridge, and even Lexington. Under the covenant, no imports would be allowed after August 31, 1774, and after October 1, non-consumption of anything manufactured in Britain would start.

Gage reacted immediately, issuing a proclamation threatening to arrest anyone who signed the covenant. In response, nearly every adult male in Boston signed. The opposition of many merchants to the proposed boycott was overcome when news of the new Coercive Acts arrived.

Sam Adams was careful to draw a distinction between boycott and violence. He wanted to avoid what he called "premature conflict." He told Stephen Hopkins, the patriot leader in Rhode Island, "I hope by refraining from every act of violence, we shall avoid the snare that is laid for us by the posting of regiments so near us."

On June 17 the Boston town meeting, with Sam Adams as moderator, approved the Solemn League and Covenant overwhelmingly. Adams was anxious to get economic warfare going. He did not want to wait until a general congress of all the colonies, which many in America were calling for, convened and discussed what to do. He feared that months would pass before any action was taken, lessening the shock value of a boycott on Britain's manufacturers and merchants.

Adams was surprised that his rush to counter the Coercive Acts did not meet with universal approval. Many people in the other colonies, and even in Massachusetts, felt that he was moving too fast. In their view, finding an effective remedy for London's aggressive legislation required more thought. They were concerned that Adams's insistence on an immediate boycott might not have the effect he intended. He was counting on British merchants and manufacturers pressuring Parliament, but he knew nothing of their present mood. In fact, they were divided, not the solid block of opinion he imagined. Many of them agreed with the king that Massachusetts had to be reined in before other colonies followed her example.

Miscalculating the immediate effect of economic warfare was not the only thing Adams got wrong. The other colonies, although deeply concerned about the Coercive Acts, wanted to hold a Continental Congress in order to have a dialogue with each other, and ideally with the British, on where the relationship between the two countries was going after the present crisis had passed, before deciding what to do about the Coercive Acts. No colony, and this included Massachusetts, wanted to proclaim independence. They hoped for a reconciliation, not a separation.

If Adams wanted to maintain his political clout, even in Massachusetts, he had to put aside the Solemn League and Covenant and push instead for a Continental Congress to meet in early September. He had no trouble making the adjustment. His long-term goal of independence remained, but he was willing to make whatever tactical changes were necessary to get there. Virginia had already called for a Continental Congress, an idea that eleven other colonies were enthusiastic about.

Many influential people, including John Hancock and Benjamin Franklin, had been calling for a Congress. On March 5, 1774, when Hancock gave the annual oration commemorating the Boston Massacre at South Meeting House, he had urged the calling of a continent-wide Congress. By then, rumors of tough legislation being put through Parliament had already reached the city. Hancock appealed for continued support for the committees of correspondence, as well as for convening a general Congress.

Franklin was also lending his support. On February 18, 1774, while still upset about the attack on him in the Cockpit, he wrote to his old friend Joseph Galloway in Philadelphia, "I wish most sincerely with you that a constitution was formed and settled for America, that we might know what we are and what we have, what our rights and what our duties, in the judgement of this country as well as in our own. Till such a constitution is settled, different sentiments will ever occasion misunderstandings. But if 'tis to be settled, it must settle itself, nobody here caring for the trouble of thinking on it."

Meanwhile, with opposition to the Coercive Acts mounting, General Gage had to think about how he was going to use his regiments, if it came to that. What was clear—as it likely had been since his meeting with the king back in January—the force he had was woefully inadequate. He would soon be required to transfer units from New York, Halifax, and Quebec to Boston. The Twenty-Third Regiment (the Royal Welch Fusiliers) was in New York and the

Fifty-Ninth at Halifax. He also had a detachment of artillery with twenty guns in New York.

Gage was searching for alternative strategies as well, and none appeared more promising than bribing Boston's radicals. The tradition of bribing political opponents was an old one in Britain. It was a painless way to avoid a bloody confrontation. He focused on Sam Adams, who stood out as both powerful and poor, the kind of political figure never found in Britain. There was no doubt that if Gage succeeded with Adams, the patriot cause in Boston, and the colonies in general, would suffer a grievous blow.

Hutchinson had famously described Adams as the "Great Incendiary." Few would have disagreed. His power came from an ability to dominate three key institutions: Boston's three political caucuses, the Boston town meeting, and the Massachusetts House of Representatives.

With immense energy and dedication, the caucuses (North, Middle, and South) directed Boston's politics. The North Caucus was particularly potent. It had something of an executive committee, known as the Long Room Club, whose seventeen members included the most prominent patriots in the city. Sam Adams was their leader. All were Harvard graduates. They planned strategy in a room above the print shop of Benjamin Edes and John Gill, publishers of the *Boston Gazette*, the town's most powerful patriot newspaper. The city's Tories had no comparable organization or newspaper, and suffered badly from the lack of them.

No other political figure could match Samuel Adams's political strength, and this included John Hancock, who brought significant talent, experience, and wealth to the patriot cause but found he had to work with Adams to get anything done.

Educated at Harvard, Sam Adams was a gifted polemicist, who devoted every waking moment to politics, exhibiting a degree of energy and commitment beyond the capacity or interest of any of his contemporaries. He also had a wealth of political experience that dated back to the 1740s and the bitter fight with Parliament and wealthy Boston merchants like the Hutchinsons over creation of a land bank. The controversy was part of the recurring problem of insufficient currency that all colonies faced. It was a dispute that Adams's side lost, and that he would never forget.

Adams was also a popular politician, admired by the people of Boston for his courage in standing up to the British, especially since Gage had arrived. Although threatened with being arrested and packed off to England and oblivion, he stood fast and would not be silenced. He had a mighty ambition to lead America to what he called "independency," and he knew that he had no hope of doing it without the aid of Britain's misguided leaders. On May 14, 1774, he wrote to his friend William Checkley, "By her multiplied oppressions [Britain] is now accelerating that independency of the colonies which she so much dreads, and which in process of time must take place."

Other committed patriots, including John Hancock and Thomas Cushing, were more than willing to remain in the empire if the king would compromise and allow Massachusetts to resume the self-government she had enjoyed prior to the present troubles. Adams, on the other hand, was single-mindedly devoted to achieving independence. Whatever compromising he did was for the purpose of advancing that goal. Britain's furious reaction to the Tea Party added immeasurably to his power.

Although Adams was careful not to be found actually breaking the law, he was unquestionably the prime mover behind the destruction of the tea. It's hard to imagine that he anticipated the Tea Party's producing near hysteria in Britain's body politic, but he must have been delighted when it did. Always looking to the future and the ultimate need for colonial unity, he was a tireless correspondent, maintaining contact with leading patriots in the other provinces. Among them were Charles Thomson, Thomas Mifflin, Joseph Reed, and Christopher Marshall of Philadelphia; Silas Deane in Connecticut; Christopher Gadsden and Thomas Lynch in South Carolina; Richard Henry Lee and Patrick Henry in Virginia; Samuel Chase, William Paca, and Thomas Johnson in Maryland; John Sullivan in New Hampshire; Samuel Ward and Stephen Hopkins in Rhode Island; William Hooper and Cornelius Harnett in North Carolina; and Isaac Sears, Alexander McDougall, and John Lamb in New York. As powerful as

Sam Adams was, however, he did not command an army. The potential for creating a patriot military force lay in the countryside. Only the thousands of farmers and artisans outside Boston could provide the manpower.

Gage and Hutchinson were only dimly aware of the fighting potential of the country people. They had no idea of the immense anger building in the Massachusetts towns. The power of the farmers was not yet understood. Out of their ranks would come men who marched to their own drummer and did not need Sam Adams for leadership. Some of them were even more radical than he was. Nevertheless, Adams was a potent leader, and if Gage could bribe him, opposition to the Coercive Acts would receive a serious setback without having to sacrifice any troops. Gage went after Adams as early as late June, when it had already become apparent that the Coercive Acts were not going to be accepted in Boston. He did not know what percentage of the population outside the city were radicals, but his experience so far indicated that the number was high. The huge amount of supplies being delivered to Boston after her port was closed was evidence enough.

Gage sent a Colonel Fenton to offer Adams a handsome sum to switch sides. The amount would have tempted almost anyone— £1,000 annually for life and a similar amount for his son. To Gage's great surprise, the puritanical Adams spurned the offer. For years Adams had railed against corruption in Britain. He was not about to dive into that cesspool himself, especially when a permanent break with the mother country was more likely than it had ever been. Money was not what he was after; it was fame—history's accolades for leading America to independence.

Adams had been thinking about independence for a long time, even as far back as his master's thesis defense at Harvard in 1743, when, drawing on John Locke, as he often did, he answered the following question in the affirmative: "[w]hether it be lawful to resist the Supreme Magistrate, if the Commonwealth cannot be otherwise preserved?"

As an alternative to bribing the Great Incendiary, Gage might have done what many had expected him to do already—arrest him, and one or two others, like John Hancock, and send them to England, where they would be jailed, tried, and then put to death for treason, or given long prison sentences in the Tower of London.

Gage was reluctant to arrest any patriot leader, however, for fear that a sudden move like that could trigger a widespread uprising, which he was not prepared for. Bribery seemed a safer course. Although Adams rejected the bribe, he was undoubtedly pleased to have received the offer, since it indicated how weak Gage was and how desperate he had already become. Actually, what Gage was doing was trying to accomplish his mission quickly and painlessly with what was, after all, an insignificant amount of money to the British.

Although he failed to bribe Sam Adams, he succeeded with several others, the most notable of whom was Dr. Benjamin Church, a trusted member of the patriots' inner circle. But Church was not Sam Adams. He could not do for Gage what Adams could, even though he was of more help than any of the other informants.

8

A Deepening Crisis

THE Royal Navy was working closely with Gage to enforce the port closure. Rear Admiral John Montagu, the cousin of the First Lord of the Admiralty, the 4th Earl of Sandwich, with whom he shared a first name, was in command of the North American squadron. His headquarters were in Boston. Montagu had been in charge of the squadron since 1771. He was set to return to England as soon as his replacement, Vice Admiral Samuel Graves, arrived.

To enforce the Port Act, Montagu had his flagship, the 64-gun *Captain*, as well as two fast escorts, the 16-gun sloop of war *Active* and the 16-gun sloop of war *Kingfisher*, under Captain James Montagu, his nephew. The 20-gun *Lively* would arrive three days later to supplement them. In addition, he had three small warships, making a total of seven to police the extensive harbor.

Ever since Admiral Montagu had taken command of the North American station, political trends in Boston and the colonies had upset him. In this he reflected the general view of the navy's leadership. On March 3, 1773, Montagu had written to Lord Sandwich, "without some measures are taken to check these people, it must in a little time be attended with fatal consequences.

"The town [Boston] is managed by what is called a town meeting, who have set the whole province in a flame by their resolves, and every town is addressing Boston and agreeing with them in their resolutions. In short, they are almost ripe for independence, and nothing but the ships prevents their going greater lengths."

On June 1, 1773, Admiral Montagu sent another dire warning to Sandwich. "Boston is taking great pains to influence the whole continent. . . . I am greatly afraid [if] the situation of this province is not attended to with the seriousness that it requires: be assured, my Lord, if they are not checked in time, it will end in fatal consequences."

Montagu's distaste for colonials and their society was well known, particularly in Massachusetts, and it was cordially reciprocated. John Adams wrote of him: "An American freeholder, living in a log house twenty feet square without a chimney in it, is a well-bred man, a polite, accomplished person, a fine gentleman, in comparison with this beast of prey. This is not the language of prejudice, for I have none against him, but of truth. His brutish, hoggish manners are a disgrace to the Royal Navy and to the king's service."

Montagu's reports to Lord Sandwich were exactly what the earl wanted to hear. For a long time the first lord, who was always a potent force in the cabinet, had wanted to crack down on Boston's radicals. He thought that they would present no problem once His Majesty took a firm stand against them. He had scant knowledge of the colonists and felt no sympathy for them. He was a naval administrator devoted to strengthening the king's fleet against what they were all nervous about—France's naval buildup. By all accounts he was doing an excellent job, more than keeping pace with the French.

Sandwich, who had been first lord since 1771, led a remarkable double life. In private he was a voluptuary. His wife was genuinely mad, and his son a useless wastrel. The earl kept a wild-living mistress, Martha Ray, but she was never enough for his insatiable appetite. He had an unequaled knowledge of all that was base in human nature, and used it to satisfy his bizarre needs.

If this was all there was to him, he could be written off as yet another self-indulgent nobleman, but there was far more. In his official capacity he was a very different person. Horace Walpole said of him, "The Admiralty, in which he had formerly presided with credit, was the favorite object of Lord Sandwich's ambition; and his passion for maritime affairs, his activity, industry, and flowing complaisance, endeared him to the profession, reestablished the marine, and effaced a great part of his unpopularity. No man in the Administration was so much the master of business, so quick, or so shrewd, and no man had so many public enemies who had so few private; for though void of principles, he was void of rancor and bore with equal good humor the freedom with which his friends attacked him, and the satire of his opponents."

Sandwich had been in government at the highest levels and in various capacities since 1744. He had even served as first lord of the Admiralty (1748–51). No member of the cabinet had more experience. He was always taken seriously, in spite of his private life, which he did nothing to hide.

Lord North had a high regard for Sandwich's expertise in naval matters, and when he brought him back to the Admiralty in 1771, he was not disappointed. During the next few years, in spite of North's determination to shrink the national debt, Sandwich, with a limited budget, managed to strengthen the fleet, always with a close eye on what the French and Spanish were doing.

His views on the American colonies were straightforward. Unlike North or Dartmouth, Sandwich simply advocated clamping down on them, which he mistakenly believed would be easy. The men he appointed to serve in America, like Admirals Montagu and Graves and marine major John Pitcairn, agreed with him.

Since the American station was not important in Sandwich's view, he had no qualms about appointing favorites to command there, as long as they shared his political views. Competency was never an issue. Samuel Graves was one of his worst appointments. It didn't matter that Admiral Graves was old and inept; the Graves clan were important in the navy, and this was an easy way to throw them a bone. Having command of the North American station was an opportunity for the sixty-one-year-old Graves to line his pockets before retirement.

Graves had had long experience as a sea officer but had never been entrusted with an important command. As a lieutenant, he fought at Cartagena in 1741. Later, he served credibly as a captain during the Seven Years' War under Admirals George Anson and Edward Hawke. In 1759 he took part in the all-important battle of Quiberon Bay, which knocked the French fleet out of the war and helped Jeffery Amherst and James Wolfe win a great victory in Canada.

Graves had no knowledge of America. His opinion on how to handle Boston and Massachusetts was simply to threaten naval destruction of their seacoast towns. And his threats were real. He had no reservations about bombarding defenseless cities like Boston or Charlestown or Falmouth (now Portland), in the Maine District of Massachusetts. On more than one occasion Gage had to restrain him from carrying out destructive attacks on places like Cambridge because of the political damage it would do. Graves had no feel for politics.

Since his first priority was accumulating as much money as he could in the shortest amount of time, he made no effort to work closely with Gage. An example of his outsized greed was his fishing policy in Boston Harbor. Although British troops were desperately in need of food during the long winter of 1774–75, Graves would not allow anyone to fish in the huge harbor without obtaining an expensive license from his secretary, George Gefferina.

Graves did not arrive in Boston until the end of June. On the thirtieth he sailed into the harbor aboard his 50-gun flagship, HMS *Preston*. He had a total of nineteen warships in the North American squadron. Seven were in Boston Harbor. Five more would soon be sent from England, and he was authorized to buy two additional schooners in Marblehead.

———

Hard as they might try, the British could never actually seal the port of Boston. Clever patriots found ingenious ways to circumvent the blockade. The Royal Navy could never stop small boats from sneaking in during the night or in bad weather.

All the surrounding towns, as well as the other colonies, sent food and fuel to help sustain the beleaguered city. The generosity of colonists up and down the coast was heartwarming. The response was overwhelming. Israel Putnam even brought 130 sheep from his Connecticut farm. Numerous Massachusetts seaports were doing even more. Instead of using Boston's difficulties to gain a step on the city's merchants, they offered their facilities to Boston's traders so that they could keep their businesses going.

Within the confines of Boston Harbor, Graves did not have to worry about his ships being attacked. The patriots had no sea militias comparable to their land militia. The colonists had always relied on the Royal Navy. Nonetheless, Graves was concerned about the safety of his warships. When he looked at the extensive coastline around Boston Harbor, he saw innumerable small craft that troubled him. On any given night, a host of them filled with armed men could surprise any of his warships, including the largest men-of-war, and overwhelm them with numbers. More than one warship could be seized at the same time, run out of the harbor, and hidden. The coastline was so extensive, it would be hard to find them.

Graves feared that the rebels would see the opportunity and make an attempt, which is one of the reasons he ran guard boats around his warships every night. The other was to prevent desertion, something that plagued him the entire time he was in Boston. Anyone caught was in for an ugly reprimand. Despite the draconian punishments, attempts were made constantly—most of them successful. Dozens of seamen fled. Graves admitted to 160. But the number was growing, and was probably much higher after his report.

While patriots in all the colonies were trying to sustain Boston, Admiral Graves was doing his best to hinder their efforts and to pocket whatever money he could from the city's plight. He was making it exceptionally difficult for larger vessels to get food and fuel to Boston under the Port Act. Each vessel had to be cleared by customs at Salem and unloaded at Marblehead, all of which created opportunities for the voracious admiral. The goods would then be brought overland in wagons to Boston, a round-trip of twenty-eight miles.

James Bowdoin complained bitterly to Franklin, "The Port-Act in all conscience cruel enough, is made much worse than it is in itself by the executors of it, who have laid restraints not warranted by the act, and in many instances of their conduct have appeared destitute of every sentiment of humanity."

———

While General Gage was busy enforcing the Coercive Acts, Sam Adams and his colleagues were working hard organizing resistance. On June 17 Adams, through some deft maneuvering, got the Massachusetts General Court, now meeting in Salem, to agree to send five delegates to a Continental Congress scheduled to meet in Philadelphia the first week of September. Adams arranged a novel way of raising £500 to cover their expenses, circumventing the governor, who, of course, would never have approved the expenditure, since according to the British government, a Continental Congress was illegal.

Gage responded by dissolving the General Court. Without the governor intending it, the old colonial government was now a thing of the past. The General Court as a colonial body never met again. In its place would come a Provincial Congress composed of representatives of the towns dedicated to defying the Coercive Acts and, if necessary, defending Massachusetts against any attempt by Gage at enforcement. Remarkably, only one town, Marshfield, did not support the Provincial Congress. The near unanimity of the towns was a powerful political statement with strong military implications.

———

As the summer progressed, patriots were busy in Boston counteracting the ill effects of the Port Act. The town meeting launched public works projects to give people jobs. Thousands needed them. The entire waterfront, which had been accustomed to handling over twelve hundred merchant vessels every year, was completely shut down. The thousands of workmen and specialists who processed goods moving in and out and repaired and serviced the ships were suddenly unemployed. Taverns and shops were either closed or barely surviving.

While trying to help the unemployed, patriots were doing their best to make life difficult for the redcoats, sabotaging them in every way they could, including burning hay, and sinking barges piled high with bricks or other materials. Carpenters refused to build barracks or anything else; in fact, there was a general refusal to help the king's men at all. And to taunt them, public signings of pledges not to purchase British goods were conducted.

While Gage was in Salem, attempting to conduct the government, Lord Percy was in charge in Boston. He did not arrive until July 5. The eldest son of the Duke of Northumberland, one of the most powerful men in the kingdom, Percy had scant knowledge of Boston. Like his fellow officers, he thought colonials were cowards. Long before he got there, he wrote to a friend, "Surely the people of Boston are not mad enough to think of opposing us."

On July 5, 1774, the day he sailed into Boston Harbor, he wrote to his father, "You will perceive by the date of this (for we only came about an hour ago) that we have had a very bad passage. I have the misfortune, for I must think it so, of commanding the camp here. The people by all accounts, are extremely violent and wrongheaded, so much so that I fear that we shall be obliged to come to extremities." He had no doubts about who would prevail.

After being in Boston for a few weeks Percy wrote again to his father, "General Gage has done his duty with great coolness and firmness. If Administration does not support him they never again deserve to be well served."

He did not have similar compliments for the people whose city he was occupying. In the same letter, he wrote, "The people in this part of the country are in general made up of rashness and timidity. Quick and violent in their determinations, they are fearful in their execution of them (unless, indeed, they are quite certain of meeting little or no opposition, and then, like all other cowards, they are cruel and tyrannical). To hear them talk, you would imagine that they would attack us and demolish us every night; and yet, whenever we appear, they are frightened out of their wits."

Regardless of the contempt British officers had for the citizens of Boston, no explosion occurred, in good part because Gage was ruthless in keeping his men in check, even while the patriots were rubbing shoulders with them every day and getting under their skin in small and large ways, including enticing soldiers to desert. Gage retaliated by publicly executing any unfortunate who got caught.

Incidents between citizens and soldiers continued to disturb the peace. The problem never went away. And Gage kept disciplining his men. Naturally, they resented it, feeling as if they were being punished more than the townspeople. Traditional problems like drunkenness and prostitution were rampant. Boston was a seaport town, after all, known by sailors around the world for something other than its Calvinist rectitude.

Even as cool a head as Lord Percy came to hate the citizenry. After being in town a month he wrote, "The people here are a set of sly, artful, hypocritical rascals, cruel and cowards. I must own I cannot but despise them completely." Percy's annoyance did not extend to Gage, however, unlike his fellow officers, who bitterly resented the restraints put on them. Lieutenant John Barker was one of them. He wrote: "Yesterday, in compliance with the request of the selectmen, General Gage ordered that no soldier in future appear in the streets with his side arms. . . . Is this not encouraging the inhabitants in their licentious and riotous disposition? Also orders are issued for the guards to seize all military men found engaged in any disturbance, whether aggressors or not. . . . *Tommy* feels no affection for his army."

Percy understood that Gage was in a tight spot, fearing that a small incident might blow up into a major one. Gage did not have the troops to contain it, especially if it brought massive help from the countryside. He intended to maintain the peace at all costs, while waiting for new instructions and, he hoped, more troops from London.

"Tommy" received no plaudits from the patriots for maintaining the peace in Boston, either. The most criticism Gage received, however, was from London. The king did not understand why his general, who had talked so boldly back in January, was not taking the initiative and forcing the colonials to knuckle under. His Majesty wanted a more spirited commander to frighten the provincials into submitting. He thought Gage had plenty of troops, as well as an adequate fleet, to do the job. Gage, on the other hand, believed he was performing something of a miracle by keeping everyone from one another's throats. Unfortunately, that's not what the king expected.

All the while, Bostonians who had relatives outside the city were leaving to get out of harm's way, and Tories from the countryside were moving in. They were undergoing harassment in many towns, and wanted to get to a safe place before the persecution turned to something worse, and they were killed or had their homes and possessions destroyed.

9

The Counties Strike Back

THE Massachusetts Government Act was not scheduled to go into effect until August 6, but its contents had been known since the first week of June, and they had already had a profound impact on the country towns.

According to the law, the people in the towns could no longer govern their communities as they had in the past. The threat of losing control of local and provincial government produced a fierce reaction in each of the fourteen Massachusetts counties, and in all of their 240 towns, with the sole exception of Marshfield. Circumventing the prohibition against town meetings became a major preoccupation. Attention was drawn early to the omission in the hated law of any ban on county meetings.

This was an oversight by a Parliament whose anti-American members had been in such a rush to pass the legislation that they overlooked the Massachusetts counties, while focusing their attention exclusively on town meetings, which had been irritating them for a long time. The leveling tendencies of these gatherings were particularly odious. The notion that government should be in the hands of ordinary people was an alien concept.

In Britain around four hundred families dominated the political landscape. This did not mean that they were unified. They had serious differences, but on the American question a strong majority sided with His Majesty. He was their king. They felt he was one of them. The last two monarchs were Germans who did not even speak English. George III was an Englishman through and through. He spoke the language as a native because he was one, and the great families loved him for it.

———

Berkshire County, at the far western edge of Massachusetts, was the first county to take action against the Government Act. On July 6, three weeks before the law was to go into effect, 60 delegates from 19 towns and districts met at a county convention in Stockbridge, 130 miles from Boston. A few courageous Tories attended the meeting, but they were a small minority and could do nothing except protest. This was the case in all the county conventions held during the summer. Tories were politically crushed, causing many to flee to Boston for protection.

General Gage did nothing to stop the Berkshire gathering. The county was beyond his reach. The only thing he could do was protest. He wasn't willing to gamble that the militiamen would back down if he challenged them. Sending Lord Percy with a body of troops all the way to the western part of a hostile colony could result in a bloody defeat. Just getting there with hundreds of men would be a major undertaking. A lone rider would need four days to make the trip. Even the landscape would be a problem. Much of it was still wilderness, complete with mountain lions, bears, and wolf packs. Percy's men could be attacked going and coming, and while he was away from Boston there could be an uprising. Admiral Graves might then come into play, and there was no telling what he might do. Gage really had no choice but to keep his troops in Boston.

He also had to contend with the fact that the county's towns were now in constant communication with Boston's committee of correspondence. Since the Boston committee had initiated the committee system, the towns looked to it for leadership, demonstrating how united the patriots were. Whenever the western counties did not agree with Boston, it was always to urge more strident action. The overriding need for unity, however, kept them from going their own way.

The one lever that Gage might have had to bring pressure on the western part of Massachusetts was the Mohawk Nation in eastern New York, but due to some unique circumstances, the Mohawks were not available to him at the moment.

William Johnson, the legendary British superintendent of Indian affairs for the northern colonies, had been so successful in becoming a major influence on the Iroquois Nation, and in particular the mighty Mohawks, that Gage had hoped to use him to bring about an alliance of the Iroquois and the British against the Massachusetts rebels. Unfortunately, Johnson unexpectedly died of a stroke on July 11, 1774, and left a political vacuum that no one else could fill, right at the moment when Gage most needed help. Johnson's Mohawk brother-in-law, Joseph Brant (Thayendanegea), who would later play a major part in the Revolutionary War against the colonists, and who might have given Gage some help, was just a simple Mohawk farmer at the time, and not politically aware.

The most the patriots could expect from the Native Americans was neutrality. The Iroquois, who despised the colonists, nonetheless leaned in the direction of neutrality. They had a realistic view, from long experience, of the unreliability of British friendship.

———

The limits on Gage's power were demonstrated again on August 9, when members of the committees of correspondence from twenty-two Worcester County towns assembled in the town of Worcester to discuss how to oppose the Government Act. They sent a letter to the Massachusetts delegates going to the Continental Congress in Philadelphia, and a second letter to the towns that could not send representatives to the meeting. The letter was a solemn declaration of opposition to the Government Act. "All that is valuable in life is at stake," it declared. The language was not an exaggeration, but a sober recognition of what would happen to them if they did nothing. The great majority of country people felt the same.

The Worcester County meeting passed a resolution reminding King George that the Massachusetts Charter of 1691 pledged His Majesty "to protect and defend us, his American subjects, in the free will and full enjoyment of each and every right and liberty enjoyed by his subjects in Great Britain."

Gage was furious. He thought seriously about taking action. Worcester was much closer to Boston than Berkshire County. Making an example of Worcester could save him from trouble with the other counties later on. In the end, though, he decided, once again, to just protest. Dispatching Percy and a brigade to Worcester might spark an uprising in Boston. Gage did not have enough troops to deal with Worcester and Boston at the same time. Percy might also be subject to harassment on his way to Worcester, which could bring on a fight Gage was not prepared for.

———

Gage had never anticipated the predicament he was now in. Although he had been expecting a far stronger reaction from the colonists over the Coercive Acts than had the king and his naïve supporters, he was still surprised. The way the towns were uniting all over the Commonwealth was something he never would have predicted. He was also expecting that Massachusetts Loyalists would be far more numerous, and much braver than they turned out to be. It was embarrassing having them consistently defeated in every county meeting.

And, of course, he was astonished to find the entire continent supporting Massachusetts. He never anticipated that either. He later told Dartmouth, "Nobody here or at home could have conceived that the Acts made for the Massachusetts Bay could have created such a ferment throughout the continent and united the whole in one common cause; or that the country people could have been raised to such a pitch of frenzy as to be ready for any mad attempt they are put upon."

Perhaps the greatest surprise for Gage, and his biggest disappointment, was London's lack of understanding. The hard-liners, particularly the king, were unhappy that he wasn't taking action. They had expected him to challenge the patriots, under the assumption that the king's troops, no matter their number, would frighten the colonials into submission. This infuriating blindness left Gage without a strategy. He was being blamed for a situation he had no control over. And things were getting worse. Other counties soon held conventions. The most important was Suffolk County, which contained Boston and was larger than present-day Suffolk County, encompassing a greater area of eastern Massachusetts.

Representatives of some of the Suffolk County towns met in Stoughton on August 16, but there weren't enough of them, so the meeting was postponed until September 6. Gage wasn't encouraged by this. He knew that they would meet on the sixth and that he wouldn't like what they did.

———

Another illustration of the ominous drift of events occurred in Salem on August 20, when the committee of correspondence called a town meeting without the governor's approval, as required under the Government Act. Selectmen normally called town meetings, but this time it was different. It didn't matter to Gage which body had called the meeting; he had not given his approval, as stipulated in the new law. And since his headquarters were in Salem, he took it as a particularly egregious challenge to his authority.

He denounced the proposed meeting as illegal, ordered that it not take place, and threatened action if the town went ahead, which it did. The meeting was held on August 24.

Infuriated, Gage attempted to punish those involved, particularly the ringleaders. He ordered two companies of the Fifty-Ninth Regiment, which were now stationed in Salem, to unceremoniously bust up the meeting, but the troops arrived too late. It was over before they got there.

Gage then tried to arrest the men who had called the meeting, but he was stopped. To his utter amazement, hundreds of militiamen from surrounding towns assembled with their arms to prevent any arrests. No one knew the exact number of armed men who showed up; it could have been well over a thousand.

They were not a mob. Many of them, including all their leaders, were experienced ex-soldiers who had fought against the French in the last war and knew their business. With no other viable option, Gage wisely backed off, not wanting to start a war over this issue, or begin one with an embarrassing rout. He wisely ordered his troops back to their barracks.

Gage was defied again on August 30–31, this time when the Worcester County Meeting refused to allow the Court of General Sessions to sit in the town of Worcester because the governor had appointed the judges under the Government Act. To underscore the seriousness of the move, on August 26 hundreds of patriot militiamen marched into Worcester and paraded on the common. Gage was again forced to back off, and the court could not meet.

Even more ominous, two days earlier, patriot leaders from four counties, Suffolk, Worcester, Middlesex, and Essex, met at Faneuil Hall in Boston to organize an alternative government for Massachusetts. They hoped to establish a Provincial Congress that could speak for the colony as a whole. Agreement to establish one was easily obtained, since the need was obvious. Gage knew what was going on, but he did not feel strong enough to stop them.

Dr. Joseph Warren was chosen chairman of the convention. Elbridge Gerry, an Essex County delegate, ably assisted him. They wanted the proposed Congress to develop "an effectual plan for countering the systems of despotism" embodied in the Coercive Acts. Dr. Warren expressed the sense of outrage building all over Massachusetts when he denounced the acts as "a complete system of tyranny. . . . persons are appointed to fill certain offices of government in ways and under influences wholly unknown before in this province. . . . no power on earth has a right, without the consent of this province, to alter the minutest tittle of its charter."

Delegates urged the towns to arm themselves and drill their militiamen in case Gage used his troops to enforce the offensive laws. The towns needed no encouragement. Military preparations were already under way in every one of them except Marshfield.

The counties not in attendance at Faneuil Hall accepted the recommendations, agreeing to hold the first meeting of the Provincial Congress on October 11 at Concord.

———

By the end of August and early September it was clear to Gage, if it hadn't been before, that the Coercive Acts had severed whatever trust existed between colony and mother country. Without a high level of trust, he had no power to enforce the Government Act or any of the other Coercive Acts, with the exception of the Boston port bill, which depended on the navy, and even that was limited. The great majority of ordinary people were now so deeply suspicious of Britain's motives that only a dramatic reversal of the king's policies could prevent a war.

In view of this, Gage decided to leave Salem and retreat back to Boston for protection. Remaining in Salem was obviously impractical, given the nature of the opposition there, and indeed throughout the Commonwealth. By the end of August he had moved the entire government. His strategy became purely defensive. He had given up any hope of Massachusetts accepting the Coercive Acts. The king's strategy had failed. No law, no matter under what government, could be effective, if people refused to obey it under any circumstances.

Gage faithfully communicated this unpleasant reality to London, and waited impatiently for a reply. He planned to keep the lid on in Boston, while awaiting new instructions. They would be a long time in coming. Just getting messages back and forth would consume weeks; and a major change in policy, of the kind Gage was seeking, would take the home government even more time—that is, if Britain's leaders were inclined to change policies. They might think that they needed a new general, not new policies.

———

During the first week of August, Gage's problems had been compounded by the arrival in Boston of forty-two-year-old former British Lieutenant Colonel Charles Lee, a self-appointed champion of American rights. His career in the British army had reached a point where he had no further hope of promotion. He was working hard to ingratiate himself with the Americans, hoping to become their military leader. With a sharp tongue, a facile pen, and a puffed-up résumé, he had already acquired a following among patriot leaders.

Not only did Lee profess devotion to the patriot cause, but he told those who admired him that the British army in Boston was vastly overrated. He assured the patriots that the Massachusetts militias were potentially much stronger. The British regulars in Boston were not hardened veterans from victorious battles, he said, but rather "the refuse of an exhausted nation, few of whom have seen any action." They would be opposed by Americans "animated in defense of everything they hold most dear and sacred." The men of Massachusetts, he observed, were "vigorous yeomanry, fired with the noble ardor we see prevalent throughout the continent, all armed, all expert in the use of arms almost from their cradles."

Lee emphasized that Massachusetts had nothing to fear from the regulars. "I mean," he wrote,

> that it is very possible for men to be clothed in red, to be expert in all the tricks of the parade, to call themselves regular troops, and yet, by attaching themselves principally or solely to the tinsel and shew of war, be totally unfit for real service. This, I am told, is a good deal the case of the present British infantry: If they can acquit themselves tolerably in the puerile reviews exhibited for the amusement of royal Masters and Misses in Hyde Park or Wimbledon Common, it is sufficient.
>
> In the beginning of the late war [the French and Indian

War], some of the most esteemed regular regiments were sent over to this country [America]; they were well dressed; they were well powdered; they were perfect masters of their manual exercise; they fired together in platoons; but fatal experience taught us that they knew not how to fight.

Dr. Warren reported the many incidents of defiance in Massachusetts to members of the First Continental Congress in Philadelphia, just as they were about to convene on September 5. The news would influence their deliberations significantly.

10

His Majesty Refuses to Bend

WHILE Dr. Warren, Samuel Adams, and their colleagues in the counties of Massachusetts were organizing opposition to the Coercive Acts, Governor Hutchinson boarded the *Minerva* in Boston on June 1 and sailed for London. His passage was unusually fast, and on the twenty-ninth he landed at Dover, sixty-seven miles southeast of London. He had no time to rest; the king wanted to see him right away.

The following day a post chaise brought him directly to the capital. It was not an easy ride, especially after a month at sea in a comparatively small vessel, but he had no choice—His Majesty was waiting. Early the next morning, July 1, Hutchinson went to the American Office in Whitehall to meet Lord Dartmouth, who greeted him warmly. After a brief conversation, Dartmouth brought him directly to the king, who was understandably eager to hear the latest news from Boston.

The attention being given Hutchinson was just what he wanted. He saw himself as uniquely qualified to fashion a reconciliation between Britain and America. He intended to use whatever influence he had to broker a compromise and avoid an armed conflict. Sadly, the middle ground he sought did not exist. Even Hutchinson's own views would be a problem. The great majority of people in Massachusetts were not willing to turn their affairs over to the management of their "betters," as Hutchinson conceived them. The time for that had long since passed. The democratic elements in the colony had deep roots. The citizens demanded control of their own affairs.

After meeting with Hutchinson, His Majesty, as he often did, wrote to Lord North. "I have seen Mr. Hutchinson late Governor of Massachusetts," he said, "and am now well convinced that they will soon submit." He explained that Hutchinson believed, as he himself did, that "the Boston Port Bill was the only wise, effectual method that could have been suggested for bringing [Boston's radicals] to a speedy submission, and that the change in the legislature [Council] will be a means of establishing some government in that province, which till now has been a scene of anarchy."

It's hard to believe that Hutchinson reported that Boston's malcontents would soon submit. It's quite possible, of course, that he suddenly grew timid in the presence of his august monarch and glossed over the truth, but it's more likely that the king heard only what he wanted to. In any event, the note to North was a clear way of telling him that His Majesty intended to stay the course.

Hutchinson, who had departed Boston before the Port Act went into effect, did not know precisely what the reaction in Boston would be. Naturally, he hoped for the best, but he certainly didn't believe that Boston would submit, pay for the tea, and accept Parliament's supremacy in all matters whatsoever, which is what the king was predicting would happen.

On July 7 Hutchinson met with Lord North for a long conversation. It wasn't encouraging. North told him that there was no going back now. His high tone reflected the prevailing belief in London that the colonists, consumed with fear, would submit in the near future. He told Hutchinson there were two things Massachusetts had to do to regain the king's favor—pay for the tea and acknowledge Parliament's authority in all matters.

Hutchinson must have realized that this attitude, which reflected the thinking of the great majority of England's ruling class, was a sure path to civil war. Nothing like what North and the king were predicting was ever going to happen. On August 2 Hutchinson received word that a Continental Congress was going to meet in Philadelphia, which was firm evidence of how far defiance had already progressed.

By this time Hutchinson also knew of the other Coercive Acts, particularly the Government Act, which he thought misguided and ill-timed. Nonetheless, he kept this opinion to himself and continued a seemingly endless round of conversations with London policy-makers, hoping to fashion some sort of compromise. While he did, the situation in America grew worse by the day. As early as July 18, Gage explained to his friend Lord Barrington, "The seditious here have raised a flame in every colony." If Gage had had more political acumen, he might have seen that "the seditious" were not looking to raise flames but to negotiate. The flame was being lit in London.

Three days before Gage wrote this, he had strengthened his army by ordering the Twenty-Third Regiment of Royal Welch Fusiliers from New York to Fort Hill in Boston, and the Fifty-Ninth Regiment from Halifax to Salem. In addition, he moved a detachment of artillery with twenty guns from New York and stationed them on Boston Common. They arrived the first week of August.

Although this strengthened his army, it was far from what he needed, as the incidents of defiance in August showed. Having two companies of the Fifty-Ninth Regiment in Salem did nothing to intimidate the rebels. It emboldened them. When the militiamen turned out to defy Gage, they outnumbered his men by a large margin.

The king and his supporters found it impossible to adjust to the fact that instead of submitting, the colonies were preparing for a mighty confrontation. The Continental Congress had already been successfully organized, and it had the potential to lead them. Since this was the exact opposite of what the king had been predicting and his sycophants had been echoing, everything now depended on how His Majesty would react to the new challenge.

While the Continental Congress was a threat, it was also an opportunity. Since nearly every province was represented by its foremost leaders, it was a perfect body with which to negotiate a grand compromise and keep the empire together. Lords North and Dartmouth could have been sent to lead a distinguished delegation to Philadelphia for a high-level conference. That would have stopped people like Sam Adams in their tracks. They would have been forced to go along. Adams would have been marginalized, overshadowed by other leaders who better represented the thinking of most people, who wanted compromise.

The king continued to reject any talks, however. He would not give an inch. When he had discovered in July that a Continental Congress would be meeting in September, he considered it a threat, not an opportunity. He wanted the colonies divided. Uniting in this fashion was a signal defeat. Instead of viewing the Congress as an ideal vehicle for negotiations, he went on the offensive, suddenly informing Lord North that he wanted the cabinet to dissolve the present parliament, which had been prorogued, or adjourned, on June 22, 1774, after passage of the Coercive Acts and the Quebec Act. He thought a new parliament would strengthen his hand for even tougher measures, if they were needed.

On August 24, 1774, he wrote to North, asking him to make arrangements for the new election. Ordinarily, one would not have taken place until the spring of 1775. He cautioned North not to make an announcement until a week before the campaigns for office were to begin. He wanted to keep the opposition, weak as it was, off balance. The notice that a new parliamentary election would begin on September 30 remained a tightly held secret until September 22.

The aristocrats who dominated the House of Lords and the House of Commons, as well as the upper levels of administration, were on lengthy vacations at the time—dispersed to their country estates, enjoying the unsurpassed English countryside in summer. Massachusetts was far from their thoughts. When word came of the new elections, it caught them by surprise. Their attention was suddenly on politics for six weeks, but after that, they returned to their pleasurable lives.

Lord North presented the results of the election to the king on

November 14, and His Majesty was quite pleased. He had achieved his objective of strengthening his already strong majority.

The new Parliament would not convene until November 29, and by then the Christmas season would be in full swing—further distracting the country gentlemen. When the new parliament finally did meet, the king gave a belligerent opening address to receptive ears. He made it clear that rather than seeking peace through compromise, he wanted to strengthen his hand against a united America. He was preparing for a showdown. He expected Parliament to support whatever measures he might take against his American subjects, including war.

While the king was preparing to force the colonies, by one means or another, to accept parliamentary supremacy, Americans were bracing to assert their rights as freeborn Englishmen, even if it meant armed conflict, which, as the weeks went by, it looked more and more as if it would.

11

The Powder Alarm

DURING the first week of September, an even more powerful display of disaffection occurred near Boston. The incident became known as the Powder Alarm. It began on August 27, when Colonel William Brattle, Loyalist commander of the First Regiment of Middlesex militia and major general of the Massachusetts militia, sent a letter to Gage warning him that the selectmen in the town of Medford, adjacent to Charlestown, had removed all the town's gunpowder that had been stored in a locked storehouse on Quarry Hill in Charlestown known as the powder house (now Powder House Square in Somerville). The other towns in Middlesex County had already quietly removed their powder—including Charlestown, which had begun withdrawals as early as July. The only powder left in the storehouse was the king's, which Brattle feared would soon be taken as well.

Gage responded quickly. On the morning of September 1, well before sunrise, thirteen ship's boats were assembled at Long Wharf in Boston, and 260 British regulars climbed in. With seamen from the fleet manning the oars, they sped up the Mystic River unnoticed, landed at Temple's farm, and made their way to Quarry Hill to remove the king's gunpowder.

No one was around; the regulars had achieved complete surprise. They quickly loaded the powder and two old cannon they had also seized on wagons that Gage had quietly moved to the hill. Before anyone knew what was happening, the troops returned to their boats and were soon back in their barracks, while the heavily loaded wagons made their way unnoticed to the waterfront. Boats were waiting at the dock to transport the munitions to Castle William. From beginning to end, the operation was flawless.

But that was not the end of it. A firestorm soon erupted. The atmosphere was so politically charged that a slight movement of troops in the middle of the night sparked hysterical rumors that Gage was attempting to disarm the inhabitants of Boston and seizing all the ammunition throughout Massachusetts, while the fleet in Boston was threatening to bombard the city, and the troops at Castle William were organizing for a thrust into the countryside.

Wild rumors and stories of atrocities led patriots from surrounding towns, and even as far away as Worcester and Connecticut, to grab weapons and rush to Cambridge. Tales began circulating that the Royal Navy was actually firing on Boston. Hundreds and then thousands of militiamen were soon marching toward Cambridge. A battle with Gage's troops appeared imminent.

——

On September 2 at six o'clock in the morning, Dr. Warren was awakened at his home in Boston and told that armed patriots, in unprecedented numbers, were marching along the roads toward Cambridge, coming from as far away as Sudbury. He was alarmed, worried that a fight could break out between Gage's regulars and patriot militiamen. Fearing the worst, he moved swiftly to alert as many members of Boston's committee of correspondence as he could find, before heading to the scene of action, hoping that he would not be too late to prevent a disaster. Several committee members went with him. They took the ferry to Charlestown, where Warren discussed the dangerous situation with members of the town's committee of correspondence before continuing on to Cambridge.

Along the way, Warren ran into Lieutenant Governor Thomas Oliver, who lived in Cambridge and was hurrying to Boston. Oliver told him that he was going "to the general, to desire him not to march his troops out of Boston." Warren was relieved to hear that. While Oliver went on to Boston, Warren and his entourage soon reached Cambridge, where they found an agitated multitude assembling. It was eight o'clock. Warren's presence, along with the other members of the Boston committee of correspondence, had a calming effect. The mob scene they feared had not yet developed.

But the crisis was far from over. Warren soon learned that more militia were coming to Cambridge from as far west as Hampshire County. The size of the force, which continued to grow, was already impressive. Warren reported later to Sam Adams in Philadelphia, "Had the troops [regulars] marched only five miles out of Boston, I doubt whether a man would have been saved of their whole number."

Since Gage had already recovered the gunpowder from Quarry Hill, the mission was complete, and he did not have to back down again, but he would have if it had come to that. He was not capable of taking on a force as large as the one that turned out. The thousands of militiamen who appeared were a grim eye-opener. The response gave him a good indication of what he was up against. Perhaps most impressive, their numbers were not the result of intense preparation. What would his position be like when the patriots really got organized? He did not know, but it was clear that he needed a force at least five times larger than the one he had.

The Powder Alarm had come close to a tragic bloodletting that neither side wanted or was prepared for. In the end no blood was shed, but it was close. Three days later Gage ordered General Frederick Haldimand in New York to bring all his troops to Boston and sent transports to pick them up. He sent transports to Quebec for troops as well.

On September 8 Gage received more bad news. The rebels had

taken an important battery, complete with guns and supplies, from Charlestown. When he sent men in longboats to investigate, they found the entire battery and all ammunition and equipment gone. To prevent the captured cannon from being used, Gage asked Graves to move the powerful *Lively* to a position between North Boston and Charlestown in the ferry way as a warning that any use of the captured cannon would bring merciless retaliation against Charlestown and Cambridge.

Meanwhile, Gage was turning Boston into an impregnable fortress. He put four big field guns at Boston Neck, which he intended to bolster with four new brass cannon, but he soon discovered that the rebels had already taken the brass cannon from their place near Boston Common. He was livid. They were his best weapons.

On September 25, three weeks after the Powder Alarm, Gage sent his report to Dartmouth. "Upon a rumor propagated with uncommon dispatch through the country, that the soldiers had killed six people, and that ships and troops were firing upon Boston, the whole country was in arms, and in motion, and numerous bodies of the Connecticut people had made some marches before the report was contradicted. From present appearances there is no prospect of putting the [Coercive] acts in force but by first making a conquest of the New England provinces."

On September 2, the day after the Powder Alarm began, but before the countryside erupted in anger and turned it into a full-blown crisis, an exasperated Gage had given Dartmouth his assessment of the general situation. "Civil government is at an end," he had declared. To restore it would require a substantial reinforcement. He did not intend to make a move until he had one. In the meantime, he planned "to avoid any bloody crisis as long as possible, unless forced into it by themselves, which may happen. . . . Nothing that is said at present can palliate; conciliating, moderation, reasoning is over. Nothing can be done but by forcible means."

On September 12 Gage had written again to Dartmouth. By then he had passed through the powder crisis and had been deeply affected by it. "As far as it can be seen," he told the secretary, "nothing less than the conquest of almost all the New England provinces will procure obedience to the late acts of Parliament for regulating the government of the Massachusetts Bay; and it is somewhat surprising that so many in the other provinces interest themselves so much in the behalf of this. I find they have some warm friends in New York and Philadelphia, and I learn by an officer who left Carolina the . . . end of August, that the people of Charles Town are as mad as they are here."

The very same day, September 12, in a private letter to Hutchinson, Gage outlined what he thought were the real alternatives London had to choose from in order to avoid a civil war. He assumed that Hutchinson would discuss them with Dartmouth.

The first option, Gage wrote, was for the government to suspend the Coercive Acts and ask Massachusetts to send representatives to London for negotiations. The second option, and the one he said he preferred, was for the government to enforce the Coercive Acts by dispatching a powerful army to Massachusetts, including foreign mercenaries from Germany, to force the colonists to submit.

Lack of an adequate army had circumscribed all of Gage's actions. It was obvious now to everyone that his writ did not extend beyond Boston. He felt besieged. The fortifications begun around Boston Neck proceeded apace. He told Barrington that "the fury of the people is so much increased since the receipt of the new acts" that he had to protect himself in Boston against a possible attack by the country people, supported by an uprising in the city. Bostonians were over fifteen thousand strong and well armed.

The patriots were quick to protest Gage's new fortifications on the neck. They did not want the only land route into Boston being blocked. The Suffolk County Convention, which had begun its meetings on September 6, appointed a committee, headed by Dr. Warren, to meet with Gage and ask him to remove the new fortifications. After an exchange of views, the committee concluded by telling Gage, in the words of Dr. Warren, "that no wish of independency, no adverse sentiments or designs towards His Majesty, or his troops now here, actuate his good subjects in this colony; but that their sole intention is to preserve pure and inviolate those rights to which, as men and English-Americans, they are justly entitled, and which have been guaranteed to them by His Majesty's royal predecessors."

As might have been expected, Gage was unmoved. The fortifications would remain. At the same time, he needed new instructions from London, but these would be a long time in coming.

12

The Colonies Unite

O N August 10 the Massachusetts delegates to the First Continental Congress, Thomas Cushing, Robert Treat Paine, and
the Adamses, left Boston for the long journey to Philadelphia.
The fifth delegate, James Bowdoin, was sick and could not go with
them. They rode in Cushing's well-appointed carriage. Two mounted
armed guards were in front, and four slaves in livery were behind, two
on horseback and two on the coach. They traveled at a leisurely pace,
stopping from time to time to confer with political leaders in Connecticut, New York, and New Jersey about the great issues of the day.
John Adams wrote to Abigail, "We have had opportunities . . . to form
acquaintances with the most eminent and famous men, in the colonies
we have passed through. We have been treated with unbounded civility, compliance, and respect." Strange as it might seem, this was the
first time Sam Adams had traveled outside Massachusetts.

When they reached the outskirts of Philadelphia, on August 29,
political leaders from the city were there to greet them, including
Joseph Reed, Dr. Benjamin Rush, and Thomas Mifflin, a sometime

correspondent of Sam Adams. Although Reed was not an actual delegate, he was closely associated with those who were. The Philadelphians lost no time warning the men from Massachusetts to tone down whatever radical sentiments they might have, lest they alienate moderates and conservatives in Congress and doom their efforts from the start. They did not need to be told this. They understood, perhaps more clearly than anyone else, that unity was paramount: It was their colony, after all, that was under assault.

Sam Adams, who was keeping abreast of events in Massachusetts, had been sounding the same theme there—unity was fundamental to success. He had been particularly anxious that this all-important message be conveyed to the Suffolk County Convention, meeting in Dedham. With Adams away, Dr. Joseph Warren was leading the convention, and stressing the need for unity. He did not want the Suffolk County delegates doing anything that might alienate the more conservative members of the new Congress. Warren and Adams were particularly worried about the western counties supporting aggressive action against the British prematurely. Adams wanted the emphasis to be on defense, not offense. He and Warren were especially anxious to head off any mob violence.

In a letter to a friend, John Adams explained the delicate situation they were dealing with:

> Their [the Philadelphia delegates'] opinions . . . are fixed against hostilities and ruptures. . . . [A]n action . . . would make a wound [they believe] which . . . would fix and establish a rancor, which would. . . . render all hopes of a reconciliation with Great Britain desperate. It would light up the flames of war, perhaps through the whole continent, which might rage for twenty years, and end, in the subduction of America, as likely as in her liberation.

Since the Massachusetts delegation had arrived in Philadelphia seven days before the first session of Congress began, they had plenty of time to socialize with the other delegates. Hours of talk in taverns and rooming houses and while riding around town and the countryside allowed everyone to get acquainted in a short time and, more importantly, relieve the anxiety some members of Congress felt about their political views. It also gave the Massachusetts delegates an opportunity to make a case for countering the Coercive Acts with strong measures.

John Adams remembered, "When we first came together, I found a strong jealousy of [the members] . . . from New England, and . . . Massachusetts. . . . Suspicions were entertained of designs of independency—an American Republic—Presbyterian principles— and twenty other things. Our sentiments were heard in Congress, with great caution—and seemed to make but little impression: but the longer we sat, the more clearly they saw the necessity of pursuing vigorous measures."

———

While the Massachusetts delegation had been on the road to Philadelphia, relations between Britain and America had deteriorated further. The traumatic events of August and early September in Massachusetts made the first meeting of the Congress appear even more urgent than it already was. People across the country realized that what was decided in Philadelphia could have an enormous impact on events.

His Majesty had already reacted to the mere calling of the Congress by having Lord North make arrangements for dissolving Parliament and holding new elections. The successful calling of a Congress was a significant defeat for the king. On the other hand, it was not beyond the realm of possibility that the Congress would fail, leaving Massachusetts isolated and the king triumphant. The differences between the northern, southern, and middle provinces could make it impossible for them to agree on anything.

Even if the men in Philadelphia did manage to work together, the king had no intention of softening his position. He condemned their gathering as an illegal body whose members were guilty of treason. Nothing they did would satisfy him except abject submission to the Coercive Acts. Absent that, he intended to ignore whatever petition the Congress presented to him. The idea that he might recognize it as a legitimate body and possibly negotiate an end to the present crisis was never a possibility.

Franklin wrote to Cushing that the meeting "is an unexpected blow to the ministry, who relied on our being neglected by every other colony. . . . They are now a little disconcerted, but I hear yet from that quarter no talk of retreating or changing of measures."

The king was confident that the Congress would be marked by endless wrangling. General Gage thought that the entire enterprise would fail and hostilities would break out but be confined to Massachusetts. If the fighting could be isolated to one colony, Britain would be victorious in a year or so, he thought. The other colonies had slaves and Indians to worry about. That would minimize any help they could extend to Massachusetts.

At the moment, however, after the Powder Alarm and the defiance of the Massachusetts counties during the summer, Gage's thoughts were mainly on managing his immediate problems in the Bay Colony.

———

When Congress finally began formal deliberations in Carpenter's Hall on September 5, the first order of business was deciding how to vote—would it be by colony, each one having a single vote, or would the larger, more populated provinces have more votes than the smaller ones? The decision wasn't easy. The small colonies fought tenaciously for each province to have a single vote regardless of size. If they lost, their influence would be negligible. They might even go home. The larger colonies were forced to give way in the interests of unity. The first great problem was thus solved by a difficult, not entirely satisfactory, compromise. It would not be the last one.

As members were debating this critical issue, on September 6 news of the Powder Alarm reached Philadelphia. Rumors of gun battles, and of warships firing on Boston, created confusion. The hostilities that delegates had been sent to avert might have already started. Events appeared to be spinning out of control. The Congress might be forced to direct a war instead of develop a plan to avoid one.

John Adams wrote to Abigail:

We have received a confused account from Boston of a dreadful catastrophe. The particulars we have not heard. We are waiting with the utmost anxiety and impatience, for further intelligence.

The effect of the news we have both upon the Congress and the inhabitants of this city, was very great—great indeed! Every gentleman seems to consider the bombardment of Boston, as the bombardment of the capital of his own providence. Our deliberations are grave and serious indeed.

A short time later, word came that perhaps these early accounts were exaggerated. On September 10, reliable news arrived of what had actually happened, and things calmed down. But that did not end the matter. The unsettling events could not help but influence the deliberations. If nothing else, the Powder Alarm underscored the need for Congress to act quickly. A sense of urgency began to permeate Carpenter's Hall that had not been there before. If delegates wanted to achieve a peace instead of preside over a war, they needed to reach decisions as rapidly as possible. But that was not easy, given the newness of the body and the magnitude of the problems it was wrestling with.

Two great tasks were before them. The first was to agree on a list of rights and grievances, along with countermeasures if the complaints were not addressed. The second was to fashion a new constitutional arrangement between America and Britain that would allow them to work together amicably without the continuous bickering that had strained relations for the past ten years.

Although there was a need for speed, members were careful about their work, knowing that their decisions would have far-reaching consequences. Congress was in the unique position of having to act as an alternate government that could speak for the colonies as a whole, while at the same time being tasked with producing a formula for making America a contented part of the empire again. At no time did any member advocate independence.

13

The Suffolk Resolves

THE fact that Congress was committed to negotiations was read in London as weakness and fear. It made the king and his supporters more anxious than ever for a military show-down. Impatience with Gage was mounting. He appeared to be doing everything he could to avoid using military force.

Although Congress wanted a reconciliation, not a shooting war, there were grievances that delegates intended to voice and insist on being corrected. It was with this firmly in mind that they held their meetings, which were conducted in secret to allow frank discussions. Fifty-six leaders from twelve of the colonies were in attendance. The assembly was probably the finest collection of political leaders America has ever produced.

Among the distinguished delegates were George Washington, Patrick Henry, Richard Henry Lee, and Peyton Randolph from Virginia. Randolph would have the tough job of moderating the Congress. The other colonies sent equally talented men. Among them were John Jay and Philip Livingston from New York; William

Livingston of New Jersey; the two Rutledges, John and Edward, as well as Christopher Gadsden from South Carolina; Roger Sherman and Silas Deane from Connecticut; Caesar Rodney of Delaware; and Charles Carroll of Maryland.

Charles Thomson, whom many considered the Sam Adams of Philadelphia, was kept off the conservative Pennsylvania delegation by its leader, Joseph Galloway. Unhappy with this bit of maneuvering, Sam Adams, Richard Henry Lee, and other like-minded delegates countered by seeing to it that Thomson was chosen secretary of the Congress, to the chagrin of Galloway and other conservatives. Thomson was a presence throughout the deliberations.

Although John Adams generally had a high regard for his colleagues, at times they drove him to distraction. "I am wearied to death with the life I lead," he wrote to Abigail one day.

> The business of the Congress is tedious, beyond expression. This assembly is like no other that ever existed. Every man in it is a great man—an orator, a critic, a statesman, and therefore every man upon every question must show his oratory, his criticism, and his political abilities.
>
> The consequence of this is that business is drawn and spun out to an immeasurable length. . . .
>
> The perpetual round of feasting too, which we are obliged to submit to, make[s] the pilgrimage more tedious to me.

———

Although in the end Congress was able to rise to the challenge and reach agreement on the fundamental issues before them, the "great men" got off to a poor start. After deciding that each colony would have one vote, the delegates placed their entire operation in jeopardy by forming an unwieldy, twenty-three-member committee—nearly half the members of Congress—to draft a statement of rights and grievances.

A long delay followed, as the committee debated on and on, unable to find common ground. Frustration and anxiety mounted; ten long, contentious days went by. Delegates began feeling an urgent need to decide something. The atmosphere in and out of Carpenter's Hall grew tense. If the Congress deadlocked over perhaps its easiest task, His Majesty would have won an easy victory by default.

A destructive pessimism began to take hold, when Paul Revere galloped into Philadelphia from Dedham on September 16 with the answer to Congress's problem—the Suffolk Resolves. This poignant declaration provided a way out of the hole delegates were digging for themselves.

The resolves were the work of Dr. Joseph Warren. They were an elegant statement of the grievances felt by Massachusetts, coupled with a clear plan of action. They also contained a strong statement on independence, insisting that colonists were not interested in separating from Great Britain; they were simply exercising their rights as good Englishmen to protest and seek redress. They expressed a strong desire to solve their differences with the mother country peacefully, in the hope of resuming the agreeable relationship they had had in the past. The language of the resolves satisfied the needs of radicals and moderates and even, to a degree, conservatives.

In the very first resolve, Warren emphasized the "allegiance and submission" to His Majesty, George the Third, of all the people protesting the Coercive Acts. This was plainly a call, not for separation, but for a redress of legitimate grievances from loyal subjects. These sinister acts, Warren wrote, show "the power, but not the justice, the vengeance, but not the wisdom of Great Britain." He argued that "our venerable progenitors, who bequeathed to us [a] dear-bought inheritance, who consigned it to our care and protection—the most sacred obligations are upon us to transmit the glorious purchase, unfettered by power, unclogged with shackles, to our innocent and beloved offspring."

He then pledged to resist, and never accept the "voluntary slavery" that Parliament was attempting to impose. He described the Coercive Acts as "the attempts of a wicked administration to enslave America," and said that therefore no obedience was due them. He supported the formation of a Provincial Congress in Massachusetts and advised that all taxes be paid to it rather than to General Gage's government in Boston until the hateful acts were repealed and the army of occupation removed.

Warren urged every Massachusetts town to elect their militia officers and to make sure that townsmen "acquaint themselves with the art of war as soon as possible, and . . . for that purpose appear under arms at least once a week." Readiness was imperative. At the same time, he emphasized that "from our affection to His Majesty, which we have at all times evidenced, we are determined to act merely upon the defensive, so long as such conduct may be vindicated by reason and the principles of self-preservation, but no longer."

The pledge to act only on the defensive was of signal importance. Warren and Sam Adams wanted to make certain that people in the colonies and in England understood that the only way independence could come about was if London forced the issue and refused any compromise.

Actually, Sam Adams and Dr. Warren, but especially Adams, believed that in the long run independence was inevitable. There was no need to hurry it along; the British would do that for them. At the moment, they stressed defensive preparations to keep the conservatives and moderates in Philadelphia happy.

In the fourteenth resolve Warren warned of retaliation should Gage seize any patriot leader. He then urged an end to all "commercial intercourse" with Great Britain, Ireland, and the West Indies, and abstention from consumption of all British "merchandise and manufactures," until Parliament saw the light and reversed its policies.

Warren included in the resolves a recognition that the Continental Congress was beginning to assume the role of an alternate government for America. He promised "that this county, confiding in the wisdom and integrity of the Continental Congress now sitting at Philadelphia, [would] pay all due respect and submission to such measures as may be recommended by them to the colonies, for the restoration and establishment of our just rights, civil and religious, and for renewing that harmony and union between Great Britain and the colonies, so earnestly wished for by all good men." He went on to warn his own supporters against engaging "in any routs, riots, or licentious attacks upon the properties of any person whatsoever."

This was not a call for independence but a plea for negotiations to restore harmony and remove the danger of war. At the same time, Warren was warning London that the patriots would not be frightened into submission.

The Suffolk Resolves received an unusually warm reception. They were desperately needed by a Congress that had reached a dangerous impasse. If the resolves were adopted, Congress would be making a strong statement that outlined a peaceful path forward. Lacking an alternative, delegates eagerly grasped the lifeline Warren was throwing them, and on September 18 they adopted the resolves unanimously.

This bold move saved the Congress while offering Britain a chance to avoid a ruinous war. Unfortunately, the chance was missed. Although surprised by the unanimity in Philadelphia, London rejected any compromise. The parliamentarians and the king, who were pushing the Coercive Acts so hard, never expected a uniform rejection from "their" colonies. From the beginning of the troubles, they had been convinced that they could easily work their will because America would be divided. Unanimous support for the Suffolk Resolves demonstrated that this comfortable assumption wasn't true.

The Massachusetts delegation was overjoyed by the vote. John Adams wrote, "The esteem, the affection, the admiration for the people of Boston and . . . Massachusetts which were expressed, and the fixed determination that they should be supported, were enough to melt a heart of stone. I saw the tears gush into the eyes of the old, grave, pacific Quakers of Pennsylvania."

The conservative delegates, after considerable soul-searching, had voted for the resolves, even though they did not approve of them. They were hoping that when they proposed something at least as important, the "republican faction," as they liked to call Sam Adams and his associates, would reciprocate and vote for their proposals in the interests of unity, just as they were doing.

Joseph Galloway, the Speaker of the Pennsylvania Assembly and the leading Loyalist in Congress, later claimed that there were other, more sinister reasons why conservatives voted in favor of the resolves.

He alleged that threats were made, that the republicans had a mob outside in case the vote did not go their way. His accusation was a boldface lie, designed, no doubt, to explain to London why he had voted in the affirmative. In fact, mob action was precisely the kind of thing that Warren and Sam Adams were doing their best to prevent in Massachusetts. Adams was surely not going to encourage similar capers in Philadelphia when he was doing so much to prevent them at home.

14

Congress Completes Its Work

T HE next item to occupy Congress was the thorny issue of trade sanctions. A spirited debate lasted for two days before members agreed on December 1, 1774, as the date when nonimportation of all goods from Great Britain would start. The West Indies was conspicuously left out. Rather than continuing to haggle over this item, it was set aside for later consideration.

News of the decision on nonimportation was quickly reported to Lord North by one of the conservative members, probably Joseph Galloway. North had confided to Hutchinson that he had reliable reports of the deliberations in Congress. Even the London newspapers regularly reported on the "secret" meetings in Philadelphia.

Agreement on nonimportation was the easiest part of the trade issue to resolve. Nonexportation was far more divisive, and had the potential to rip Congress apart, setting region against region. The interests of the cod fishermen, shipbuilders, traders, lumbermen, and small farmers of Massachusetts, New Hampshire, Connecticut, and Rhode Island, for instance, had little in common with those of the rice, tobacco, and indigo planters of South Carolina; the pitch, tar, and turpentine producers of North Carolina; the tobacco barons of Maryland and Virginia; or the grain and livestock producers of New York, Pennsylvania, Delaware, and New Jersey.

Since the question of when to start nonexportation was so difficult, Congress postponed discussion of it and on September 28 took up a proposal that conservatives calling themselves the "loyal party," such as Joseph Galloway and James Duane of New York, were advocating. It was nothing less than a grand constitution to govern relations between America and Britain. Galloway called it "A Plan of Union."

He proposed creating a Grand Council or legislature for America, to be elected by the colonial legislatures. The council would be chosen every three years and would meet once a year. It would regulate all general policies and affairs in matters involving Britain and the thirteen colonies, or more than one colony. The colonies would retain their governments and powers over internal affairs as before. The king would appoint a chief executive or president general, who would have veto power and be subject to removal only by the monarch. The council would be an inferior and distinct branch of the British parliament, and legislation could be initiated in either body. General statutes would require approval of both.

Galloway's proposal attracted little support. It was discussed for only a day and then, by a vote of six to five, set aside. Five colonies wanted to reject it outright, while six wanted to postpone consideration. One colony refused to vote. The plan never had any chance of passing; Congress did not take it up again. There wasn't enough interest. And since no other member presented a viable alternative, the whole matter of attempting to create a constitution that would govern relations between Britain and America was deemed a waste of time.

Even if the delegates had taken Galloway's plan seriously, London certainly would not have. The king intended to ignore it, as he planned to do with all of Congress's pronouncements.

Franklin thought as little of Galloway's plan as Congress and the king, albeit for different reasons. On February 25, 1775, he wrote to Galloway, who remained a friend in spite of their political differences. Franklin began by telling Galloway that he knew his friend had sent his proposal to Lord Dartmouth, seeking support from that quarter. This struck Franklin as hopelessly naïve, an unfortunate trait he found in most American Tories. Dartmouth was never going to show this to the ministry, and certainly not to the king.

Franklin then told Galloway that he would make only one comment on the proposal:

> When I consider the extreme corruption prevalent among all orders of men in this old rotten state, and the glorious public virtue so predominant in our rising country, I cannot but apprehend more mischief than benefit from a closer union. I fear they will drag us after them in all the plundering wars which their desperate circumstances, injustice, and rapacity may prompt them to undertake; and their wide-wasting prodigality and profusion is a gulf that will swallow up every aid we may distress ourselves to afford them. . . .
>
> To unite us intimately, will only be to corrupt and poison us also.

The next order of business for Congress was the difficult question of nonexportation. Early in the debate members were reminded that the West Indies had been omitted from the prohibition on importation approved earlier. As everyone knew, this was not an oversight but a deliberate attempt to allow goods to come in that certain economic interests, like distillers and distributors of rum, wanted. After a lengthy debate, the West Indies were added to the prohibition.

Congress then turned to the even more difficult question of when to begin nonexportation. Virginia wanted to wait until the current tobacco crop had been sold, which meant putting off prohibition until September of 1775. Members were understandably opposed to granting this year of grace, but Virginia held firm, and she was too powerful to turn down. After more spirited debate, members voted on September 30 to begin halting exports a year hence, on September 10, 1775.

The declaration of rights and grievances was next on the agenda.

Discussion of this was finished on September 22, but the declaration was not voted on until October 14. Congress denied that Parliament had jurisdiction over all colonial matters, including internal ones, or the right to set aside any colonial charter at will. The Declaratory Act of 1766, which proclaimed Parliament's right to legislate on any subject, was thus declared invalid. The Coercive Acts and the Quebec Act were pointed out as egregious examples of Parliament's lack of restraint. Congress demanded that they be repealed, calling them not only "unjust and cruel" but a direct threat to "religion, laws, and liberties." Congress then—after much additional debate—accepted Parliament's right to regulate the external trade of the colonies for the benefit of the empire as a whole.

In addition to these matters, Congress was anxious to end the prohibition against expansion west into Native American territory. There was little controversy about this. That these vast lands belonged to a variety of Native American nations, and that seizing their territory was a species of imperialism as reprehensible as what the king was planning, did not matter. No hesitation was in evidence. The delegates were eager to agree to it, even though it would inevitably bring on warfare and the deaths of thousands.

While insisting on the right of westward expansion into land controlled by Native Americans, members were forgetting that should their efforts at reconciliation with London fail and a civil war ensue, Native Americans would inevitably be involved, in which case the colonists would be in the position of wanting them as allies, or at a minimum neutral, while the British, who had far better relations with the tribes, would be aggressively seeking their support. The hard fact was that so many colonists thought of Native Americans as savages that treating them as potential allies, as the British from time to time were able to do, was impossible.

In addition to claiming the right to Native American territory, Congress insisted that every colonist enjoyed the same basic rights as freeborn Englishmen, describing them as a treasured inheritance that would never be given up. The right to life, liberty, and property were their foundation. These could never be abridged without the consent of the governed, certainly not by a Parliament in which the colonists were not represented. The right of trial by a jury of one's peers in a nearby location was underscored as also of great importance.

Congress went on to maintain that "in all cases of taxation and internal polity," provincial legislatures had jurisdiction. Furthermore, keeping a standing army in the colonies in peacetime was illegal without explicit consent from colonial legislatures. The appointment of Legislative Councils exclusively by the crown was also denounced. Thus, Congress repudiated almost every important piece of legislation passed by Parliament for the colonies since the end of the Seven Years' War in 1763.

The final item that Congress took up was creating a method of enforcing its edicts against nonimportation, nonconsumption (scheduled to begin on March 1, 1775), and nonexportation—the basic tools that members hoped would move Britain to withdraw the Coercive Acts and the Quebec Act.

Most members assumed that colonial merchants would attempt to circumvent the extensive trade restrictions, which meant that a policing mechanism was essential. Delegates settled on a method that became known as the Continental Association, or simply the Association. It extended Congress's control into every community in America, further moving it toward becoming a separate government. The Association involved organizing what amounted to revolutionary committees in every county, town, and city throughout the colonies. They would be chosen by voters in their communities. It was assumed that only individuals who supported every measure Congress had approved would control them, which turned out to be the case. Forming the Association meant that the American patriots, while offering to negotiate with London and remain in the empire under certain specified conditions, were, at the same time, forming a revolutionary government.

The great majority of delegates were counting on the nonimportation, nonconsumption, and nonexportation agreements, coupled with the Association, to move the British government toward negotiations. Simply pleading with the king appeared useless. Nonetheless, before adjourning, Congress approved a petition to His Majesty, reiterating where the colonies stood, along with their hope for reconciliation.

Most members, including George Washington and the entire Massachusetts delegation, doubted the petition would have any effect. They considered it a public relations ploy more than anything else.

In the end, despite an uncertain start that might have proven fatal, Congress had moved with lightning speed for a deliberative body, especially one that was untried and controversial, and reached agreement on the big issues before them. It was nothing short of a political miracle. As its last bit of business, members voted to reconvene on May 10, 1775, if the problems being addressed had not been solved by then.

———

The demands that Congress enunciated, as well as the promise of economic warfare if they were not met, reached London two weeks before Christmas. They were greeted with derision. Anger at the presumption of the colonists was widespread. Opinion among the upper class was so negative that it acted as strong support for the throne.

General Gage expressed contempt as well. He saw no basis for considering talks. He told Barrington on February 10, 1775, "Never was a greater piece of insolence offered a country, yet the factions rely upon it as their sheet anchor, and even those termed friends of government have their doubts. Your next advices will clear up that and all other matters respecting this country, and leave no doubt upon our minds. I hardly think it possible that any of the opposition can support the resolves of the Congress, for surely you would be better without colonies than to accept the terms they have sent you."

On October 20, 1774, the very day that Congress sent its list of rights and grievances to London, the king prohibited the sale of arms and ammunition to America in preparation for a possible conflict.

Notice of the king's Privy Council order prohibiting the export of gunpowder or any other warlike stores to America reached Philadelphia on December 1, 1774, the same day that the Continental Association went into effect. The two countries remained on a collision course.

15

Slaves

ONSPICUOUSLY absent from the deliberations in Philadelphia was the issue of human bondage. Accusations that Britain was attempting to enslave the colonists were common among the patriots, but the question of their own enslavement of over five hundred thousand African men, women, and children appeared to be overlooked—that is, until October 6, when an item appeared on a list, indicating that Congress intended to include in its boycott items from countries and places other than the British Empire. One of the items was the slave trade. Congress was prohibiting it, apparently without a serious debate. The matter was handled quietly. The prohibition looked as if it had been inserted almost as an afterthought.

It was an odd way to treat a problem of such magnitude. As everyone in Philadelphia knew, no other issue had greater potential to rip apart colonial unity than this one. The differences between the colonies were profound. The most obvious one was between those where slave labor was the basis of the whole economy (for example, South Carolina, North Carolina, and Virginia) and those where it was not, such as Massachusetts. Yet all the colonies, including Massachusetts, had slaves.

A less obvious difference was between those colonies in which most people believed that black Africans were human beings and those in which most insisted that they were lesser creatures, destined to permanent servitude, including sexually. People who knew that slaves were human beings, deserving the same rights as everyone else, existed in all the colonies, but in significantly larger numbers in those where slavery was not the basis of the economy. In colonies like South Carolina, the belief was widespread that black Africans were not human beings in the same sense as white people, and that therefore one could, without committing a sin against God, employ them as a better form of cattle and still attend church with a clear conscience.

At the same time, slave owners in places like the Carolinas found it necessary to soothe their conscience through endless criticism of slaves, just as the British did in Ireland when demeaning Irish Catholics. A deep, unacknowledged sense of guilt elicited a steady stream of accusations against those whom they knew, at some level, they had profoundly wronged.

The enslavement of hundreds of thousands for nothing more noble than profit or personal convenience was so morally repugnant that a serious movement to eradicate it had already begun in Massachusetts, as well as in Connecticut and Rhode Island. The Massachusetts legislature had made three attempts to pass a law that would eliminate the slave trade, the first in 1771 and the others in 1774, but when Governor Hutchinson submitted them to the Privy Council for approval, they were immediately turned down. The West Indian planters in Parliament wouldn't approve; they believed that all their operations required slave labor to produce a maximum profit from plantations that provided more money for the British treasury than any other overseas operation.

How serious the Massachusetts General Court was about the issue wasn't certain. Sam Adams was using the proposal to embarrass and discredit his enemy, the governor. But there's no doubt that many people in the Bay Colony found slavery reprehensible and wanted to get rid of it.

Any formal discussion of slavery by the Continental Congress was sacrificed to the need for unity. The Massachusetts delegation understood this from the start. Among the first persons to greet John Adams and the others when they first arrived in Philadelphia was John Rutledge of South Carolina. Although there is no record of his bringing up the slave issue, it is hard to imagine that he did not. It's also hard to believe that he did not make clear that tackling this at the same time as the other issues that had to be dealt with would end whatever hope there was for unity.

He must have been pleased to discover that the Massachusetts men understood the concerns of the colonies that relied on slavery. In many of them, slaves constituted at least half the population. South Carolina had a hundred thousand slaves in a total population of around one hundred and eighty thousand. Virginia had over two hundred thousand slaves. Massachusetts had less than five thousand.

The four Massachusetts delegates had no intention of destroying the unity of the colonies by initiating a debate on slavery. Thus one of the great issues that Congress might have faced was settled quietly without a vote—in fact, without even being discussed. That did not mean the issue had gone away. Abigail Adams wrote to her husband wondering if "the passion for liberty [can be as] strong in the breasts of those who have been accustomed to deprive their fellow creature of theirs." Her husband had to assume that it did.

Even though Abigail's own father had slaves, she abhorred the practice. She wrote again to John in Philadelphia, "I wish most sincerely there was not a slave in the province. It always appeared a most iniquitous scheme to me—fight ourselves for what we are daily robbing and plundering from those who have as good a right to freedom as we have."

Her husband was in no doubt about where she stood, but there was nothing he could do about slavery at the moment, and even if he could, he did not agree with her. He thought that only gradual abolition over a long period of time would work, but he was not going to champion the cause. He could live with the issue unresolved for the time being.

Abigail saw what John could not see, and that was how differ-ently women viewed slavery than men. Female slaves, particularly attractive ones, were used by their owners as whores, and they pro-duced legions of children. Nobody knows how many, but given the widely accepted practice of owners having sex with slaves anytime they pleased, the figure must have been a very large one. The life of women under the system was thus inevitably more horrifying than for men, which is what Abigail understood and John could not, or at least not in the same way.

As far as the new Congress was concerned, liberty did not include freedom for enslaved Africans. If delegates insisted on including the subject in their deliberations, members from colonies where slavery was an integral part of the economy would go home, and the colo-nies would remain divided and impotent. And nothing would have been done about eliminating slavery, either.

Rutledge and his southern colleagues must have been relieved that slavery was not the contentious issue they feared it might be. Before arriving in Philadelphia, they must have been apprehensive about the first stirrings of a serious antislavery movement in Massachusetts and in New England generally. They must also have been concerned about a similar movement in Britain, where certain religious groups were repelled by the idea of human bondage and were gathering an impressive amount of political support, although opposition from West Indian planters was still too strong to overcome.

Slavery was simply too big a question for Congress. Members did not have the time or the inclination to get into it. Doing something about human bondage in America would require redoing the whole of society, particularly in the South. And it would mean the end of a unified Congress. Massachusetts would be left to its fate. Members were determined not to let that happen and quietly gave big slave owners a significant victory.

If unity was to be preserved, the most that could be hoped for by members who felt that slavery was an abomination was a commit-ment to end the slave trade. Some support for this could come even from slave owners like Christopher Gadsden, who had no interest in liberating slaves but did favor prohibiting further importation, because a massive influx of Africans could dramatically lower the market value of his own.

For the most part, to say that one wanted to end the slave trade, as everyone knew, was empty rhetoric. The slave trade would go on as before. The pledge was meaningless. Despite many such resolves over the years, more than a quarter of the African slaves imported into the United States came after the Declaration of Independence.

To show to what degree Congress considered the issue untouchable, the largest slave trader in America, Henry Laurens of South Carolina, was elected president of Congress immediately after John Hancock resigned.

Men like George Washington and Patrick Henry never stooped to defending slavery. It was simply the system they had inherited, and they could see no easy way to get rid of it. They knew it was profoundly wrong when they thought about it, yet they saw themselves trapped in a system they had no way of jettisoning.

On January 18, 1773, Henry wrote the following in a letter to a Virginia Quaker who believed slavery was morally wrong.

> Is it not amazing, that at a time when the rights of humanity are defined and understood with precision, in a country above all others fond of liberty, . . . we find men . . . adopting a principle as repugnant to humanity as it is inconsistent with the Bible and destructive to liberty.
>
> Every thinking honest man rejects it in speculation, how few in practice from conscientious motives? . . .
>
> Would anyone believe that I am master of slaves of my own purchase! I am drawn along by the general inconvenience of living without them; I will not, I cannot justify it. However culpable my conduct, I will so far pay my devoir to virtue as to own the excellence and rectitude of her precepts and to lament my want of conforming to them. . . .
>
> I know not where to stop; I could say many things on this subject, a serious review of which gives a gloomy perspective to future times.

Since the Virginia economy was based on slavery, the great slave owners who dominated society were certain that changing it would tear the economy and their world apart. They had no desire to do it. Living with the system, which was personally so kind to them, was much easier. They never considered that a free society would be vastly more productive and enrich them far more than the morally bankrupt one they presided over. The greatest economist of the time, Adam Smith, argued that free labor was infinitely better, and indeed less expensive than slave labor. Benjamin Franklin thought the same thing. It was also the case, as later economists, as well as experience, would confirm, that a free society was far more productive than any other. It wasn't by chance that the poorest states in America were those handicapped by slavery.

Virginians never understood how costly a slave society was to maintain. They had to do much more than simply live with a noxious system. They had to be jailers, and incarcerating people who yearned to be free was expensive.

Large slave owners never liked to dwell on the fact—or in most cases even acknowledge—that the humans they held in bondage yearned to be free, just as they did. Phillis Wheatley, a young, precocious, enslaved African American poet who lived in Boston, reminded all the colonists that the desire for freedom dwelled in the breast of every human being, including African slaves. Slave owners had to think, whether they admitted it or not, that black Africans were a lesser species, and that being enslaved was better for them than being free. To believe as Wheatley did would make incarceration an evil so large they couldn't bear it.

As a practical matter, keeping Africans in bondage required what in modern terms would be called a police state. Slaves had to be controlled, and every heartless precaution to ensure this was used, from armed militias, to the strict prohibition against teaching any slave to read or write, to vicious beatings.

Not only did the slave system require men like Washington and Henry to be vigilant jailers, ever alert for revolts, but it also made their cries for freedom sound absurdly hollow. Every human in bondage in America in 1775 was a living rebuke to Henry, who shouted,

". . . give me liberty, or give me death!" He had no such commitment. His cry was obviously not for universal freedom. He rationalized his hypocrisy by claiming that he alone could do nothing about the vast, cruel, unholy system that defaced so much of the country. Even in New York, 20 percent of the population were slaves; most worked the land, as slaves did in the South.

The British understandably found it hard to take seriously the cries of people to be free when America enslaved so many. Of course, the British were monumental hypocrites themselves, as their West Indian plantations attested to.

In any kind of civil war, Britain was sure to use slaves against the patriots. They would certainly offer them incentives to run away and encourage revolts. They could then put them to use in their armies doing labor that was as hard as, or harder than, the labor that the slaves were doing in the colonies.

16

The Perverse Effects of
the Powder Alarm

Lᴛʜᴏᴜɢʜ General Gage scoffed at the pretentions of Congress and was confident that London would reject any of its proposals, his situation in Massachusetts was continuing to deteriorate. He had even reached the point of thinking that without a much larger army, casting off the colonies might be necessary. Otherwise, leaving the situation as it was and pretending that his small number of troops could force Massachusetts to accept the Coercive Acts could only lead to bloodshed and defeat. He never mentioned this to Dartmouth, and perhaps never even admitted it to himself, but that's where the logic of his position led.

To make matters even worse for Gage, on October 17, 1774, just as the Continental Congress was approaching the end of its work, the long-planned Massachusetts Provincial Congress held its first meeting, presided over by John Hancock. The Congress had the support of every Massachusetts town except Marshfield. Representatives from 239 towns were eligible to attend, and the great majority did. A few smaller towns could not afford to send a representative, but they still supported the cause.

The Provincial Congress was, in effect, a separate government, funded with tax receipts from the towns. Money was collected as before, but it was now sent to a receiver general, Henry Gardner of Stow, instead of to the royal provincial treasurer in Boston.

The first order of business was building a military force as rapidly as possible. As early as October 26, 1774, the Provincial Congress established an executive arm, the Committee of Safety, and appropriated £20,000 for munitions. John Hancock presided over this all-important committee.

There had already been a scramble for weapons and gunpowder in Massachusetts, as all the towns—and the rest of New England— rushed to arm themselves. Gunsmiths were overwhelmed with work. Entrepreneurs of every stripe, recognizing the need for the patriots to acquire munitions, particularly gunpowder, worked hard to fill the need. Dutch, French, and British merchants, as well as Americans, were involved in the arms trafficking. There was plenty of money to be made.

The people of Boston were also involved, sending what arms they could to the Congress. At times they were slipping out of the city a hundred muskets a day—not an insignificant number. Women in the countryside were melting pewter plates to make bullets, as well as doing multiple tasks to prepare the men, and themselves, for combat.

The king and the ministry had been so unimpressed with the fighting qualities of the provincials that they had not gotten around to prohibiting the export of gunpowder and other weapons of war until October 19, 1774. Dartmouth's order did not arrive in Boston until December 15. Admiral Graves received a similar order on the same day from Philip Stephens, the secretary to the British Admiralty.

While the patriots were preparing for a possible military confrontation with Gage, and he was nervously pleading for more troops, London was feeling more confident than ever that the king's will could be worked in Massachusetts with the forces Gage already had. The Powder Alarm had not caused the hard-liners in the cabinet, or the king, to question their American policy. They had expected an easy time of it when they hurriedly approved the Coercive Acts, and the Powder Alarm proved to them that they had been right. The thousands of farmers who came to fight Gage's regulars that day appeared to London as a leaderless mob that a disciplined army could easily handle.

Gage would have been flabbergasted to learn that this interpretation of the Powder Alarm was so prevalent at home. As impossible as it would be for him to understand, his report of the incident, which arrived in London the first week of October, confirmed the general belief that the rebels were never going to be a military threat. The fast frigate HMS *Scarborough* brought the comforting report while the king and North were in the midst of the snap parliamentary election His Majesty had called.

Thus the Powder Alarm, which Gage was counting on to show how much he needed reinforcements, instead reassured Britain's leaders that they had been right all along; the Coercive Acts could be enforced by the army already in Boston. Gage's complaints that he did not have enough troops could be brushed aside as the desire all theater commanders had for larger armies.

No matter what Gage wrote, he could not secure any change in policy. His dismal reports in September and October did not produce the reaction he expected. To be sure, the king wasn't happy with the state of affairs his field commander was describing, but he blamed the whole business on Gage. As far as His Majesty was concerned, the Powder Alarm, instead of proving how badly Britain needed to rethink her relationship with America, revealed the shortcomings of a local commander who did not have the brass to use his troops against poorly trained amateurs. So far as George III was concerned, Gage's weak response was the root cause of the continuing disturbances in Massachusetts, not the Coercive Acts. The additional troops Gage was calling for weren't needed, nor were they immediately available. Producing reinforcements on the scale Gage was asking for would be difficult. The entire British army amounted to fewer than fifty thousand men. Given their many duties in places like Ireland, Scotland, and England against foes foreign and domestic, they could not be spared in large numbers for America.

As frustration mounted in London, so did anger at Gage. A movement to replace him had already started and was growing. The notion that all would be well if Gage would only use the force that he had did not change in the weeks ahead; it led directly to the fateful orders that Lord Dartmouth would send to Gage in the spring of 1775 that precipitated the Battle of Lexington and Concord.

———

Back on September 11, His Majesty had reminded Lord North that his basic policy was the same. It had not changed, nor would it. The note to North was sent weeks before the king knew of the Powder Alarm or of Gage's bleak assessment of the situation in New England. "The die is now cast," His Majesty had famously declared. "The colonies must either submit or triumph." By triumph he meant declare independence. He went on to observe: "I do not wish to come to severer measures, but we must not retreat; by coolness and an unremitting pursuit of the measures that have been adopted, I trust they will come to submit."

When Gage reported that the colonists were not submitting, and that he needed far more troops, the king's reaction was to assure him that his basic policy remained in place. On October 10, 1774, His Majesty wrote to Dartmouth, telling him to inform Gage that "though the conflict is unpleasant, Great Britain cannot retract." The king thought this might reassure Gage that if he stood up to the radicals, London would support him.

On October 17 Lord Dartmouth sent the king's response to Gage's most recent description of the situation in Massachusetts. The dispatch arrived at Province House in Boston on December 3. It must have been deeply disturbing. The king's position indeed had not changed. No more troops would be forthcoming. Dartmouth insisted that they just were not available. He did not add that they weren't needed. Dartmouth told Gage that instead of the huge army he was requesting, three more sail of the line, the *Asia*, the *Somerset*, and the *Boyne*, would be sent, along with a contingent of five hundred marines.

The tiny reinforcements seemed, at first, a curious evasion. It was hard to imagine what good they could do, unless they were meant to give Admiral Graves additional firepower to mercilessly incinerate a few unsuspecting towns—Charlestown or Cambridge or Falmouth (now Portland) in the Maine District of Massachusetts—as a warning to the malcontents in all the colonies and to the Continental Congress. One wonders if the king and the enthusiasts who supported this strategy, like Lord Sandwich, wanted Graves to warn his victims before he destroyed their homes and their cities, or if they expected him to take the colonists by surprise and kill as many as possible. In any event, it appeared that His Majesty wanted to use terror to bring his subjects to heel, if that's what it took. Firebombing coastal towns would allow him to cow the provincials at minimal cost, which had been his intent all along. The type of reinforcements he was sending spoke clearly enough about what strategy he preferred.

Admiral Graves was an advocate of using terror, and had been since he arrived in Boston, but Gage wouldn't permit it. The general never commented on what he must have seen as a policy he could not support, not just from a humanitarian point of view but because of the adverse political effects it was bound to produce. It would anger and unite the Americans as nothing else could. The task of subduing them, already difficult, would inevitably get worse.

17

The March to War

THE Provincial Congress was well aware that a disciplined army was needed, and fast. It began creating one by first reorganizing the town militias. If this had not already been done, each town was to replace the Crown appointees, who ran the old, royalist militias of the past, and elect new officers. They were also to choose leaders for the larger regiments to come.

In addition, the Congress established a fast response force that became known as minute men. These special units were required "to equip and hold themselves in readiness, at the shortest notice from the Committee of Safety, to march to the place of rendezvous." The minute man companies would consist of at least fifty men, or a quarter of the number of the original companies in each village.

While focusing most of its attention on military preparations, the Congress was soon confronted with an issue they wished to ignore—slavery. A group of literate Massachusetts slaves had sent the Provincial Congress a request to end human bondage in the colony. They wanted to know why liberty did not apply to everyone, regardless of skin color. Most members of the Congress found slavery indefensible and were in favor of getting rid of it. For them, this discussion was long overdue. But for Hancock and the other leaders, this was not the time. They refused to consider it, even though the number of slaves in Massachusetts was so small that freeing them would not have been a major undertaking, as it would have been in places like the Carolinas and Virginia. Doing it immediately, however, would have interfered with the struggle against Britain. The unity of the Continental Congress could have been undermined. Hancock did not want to risk it. He had word from Philadelphia that doing something like this might cause problems. Estimates were that one in five Massachusetts households had slaves, although no one really knew, and this number was doubtless exaggerated.

———

London misinterpreted the defensive preparations advocated by the Continental Congress and put into effect by the Massachusetts Provincial Congress as preparations for an aggressive war. It made the king even more anxious for Gage to take immediate action. For the patriots, the preparations were entirely defensive, and they were not going to desist, no matter how much London protested and threatened. While Gage watched and His Majesty fumed, the countryside grew stronger. The town militias trained in earnest under their newly elected officers, most of whom were combat veterans from the French and Indian War.

In the town of Lexington, John Parker, the militia leader, had been a veteran of the war, as had Concord's Colonel James Barrett and Major John Buttrick. So too, were all the men at the rank of sergeant or above. Barrett was also colonel of the combined militias of Middlesex County. Drilling began right away and continued through a winter that everyone remembered as unusually mild. The Provincial Congress supported the town militias, keeping up a flow of supplies, particularly gunpowder. Gage paid close attention to their activities. He had spies among the delegates. They had been much easier to bribe than Sam Adams. The traitors reported what was going on in detail. The most valuable of them was still Dr. Benjamin Church.

Patriot leaders like Hancock and Adams had known for a long time that Church had a mistress, but they never expected him to sell out his country in order to keep her. Without their suspecting it, she had increased his need for money dramatically. Gage's handsome bribe—probably the same one he offered Sam Adams—had forced Church to choose between his pleasure and his country. He chose pleasure, spying on his erstwhile comrades for over a year before he was discovered and arrested in Cambridge on September 27, 1775. He was subsequently tried and convicted by a board of officers with Washington presiding. The Continental Congress then jailed him in Connecticut under close scrutiny. On May 14, 1776, he was released on bail because of ill-health but remained closely guarded.

There was some thought given to exchanging him for a high-level prisoner in British hands, but when Congress considered how much Church knew about the American army, it set aside that idea. He was eventually taken to Massachusetts and remained confined until 1778, when he was permitted to embark on a vessel for Martinique. Church and the ship were never heard from again.

Although Gage's spy network was extensive, and the intelligence timely and accurate, it did not mean that it would produce wise decisions. On the contrary, no matter what information he received, his actions were being directed from London by superiors who had no knowledge of local conditions. On November 2 he wrote again to London about the need for reinforcements, this time to Barrington. "A large force will terrify, and engage many to join you," he said, "a middling one will encourage resistance, and gain no friends." Gage added that Britain had never more need of "wisdom, firmness, and union than at this juncture."

The kind of force that Gage wanted was an army of at least twenty thousand regulars, supplemented by a large contingent of irregulars such as German Huntsmen (troops) and loyal Canadians, plus three or four regiments of light horse, as well as a good and sufficient artillery. A tight naval blockade was necessary as well. Establishing an effective blockade would have required a fivefold increase in the fleet already in American waters, from 24 to 120. That would have amounted to a sizable percentage of the entire Royal Navy, which had 170 warships of various types.

Unfortunately for Gage, London was more influenced by reports of the Powder Alarm than they were by his pleas for help. If Gage went on offense, His Majesty thought, Massachusetts would submit in short order, and so would the rest of New England. Lord Sandwich, of course, found the request for a much larger fleet preposterous. He had long been convinced that a few men-of-war preying on defense-less towns would terrify the colonials and force their submission.

Gage would have been surprised to learn that his friend Barrington did not agree with him, either. Nor did Barrington agree with the king, with whom he had good relations personally, or with Lord Sandwich. Barrington thought it was madness to fight the hordes of Americans on the ground. He did not believe the colonies could ever be conquered that way, and he was an experienced secretary at war. He wrote to Dartmouth:

> Our disputes with North America have not at present the foundation of interest; for the contest will cost us more than we can ever gain by the success. . . .
>
> I am against employing troops to conquer that country for the following reasons.
>
> First. I doubt whether all the troops in North America . . . are [able] to subdue [Massachusetts]; being of great extent and full of men accustomed to fire arms. It is true, they have not hitherto been thought brave, but enthusiasm gives vigor of mind and body, unknown before. If . . . Massachusetts (with whom the inhabitants of Connecticut and Rhode Island are said to have made common cause) were conquered, they must be kept under by large armies and fortresses; the expense of which would be ruinous and endless.
>
> Second . . . the most successful conquest that can be imag-ined, must produce the horrors and bloodshed of civil war.

As an alternative, Barrington proposed a strictly naval war, not in the sense that Sandwich and the king envisioned, but a massive blockade designed to smother colonial trade. The idea was as wildly unrealistic as ordering Gage to snuff out the rebellion with the force he had. The Admiralty did not have the ships to carry out such a strategy. Sandwich and the king would have dismissed it out of hand.

———

Although no official communication had yet been received from Philadelphia, by the end of November London was well acquainted with not only the Suffolk Resolves but most of the work of the Continental Congress. As the news came in, it produced an overwhelmingly negative reaction—the exact opposite of what the congressional delegates had hoped. On October 31, Hutchinson wrote in his diary, "Every ship from America brought alarming news; yet, not only the Ministry then in power, but the Opposition—indeed, every Englishman felt that the honor and the dignity of the nation were at stake, and rejected all idea of making concessions to a colony that was literally in a state of open rebellion."

By November 12, Lord North had concluded that violence appeared inevitable. As far as he could determine, and he was the best political analyst in the capital, Parliament could not give in; there was no support for it in the country. The Suffolk Resolves and the list of rights and grievances had shocked too many of his colleagues. They would never agree to use them as a basis for negotiations.

North was not surprised that Congress had voted to impose non-importation, nonconsumption, and nonexportation, and in response, he promised to retaliate by cutting off all American trade with every other country, as well as closing the fishing grounds on the New-foundland banks. His feeling was that if the colonies were not going to trade with Great Britain, they would be prevented from trading with anyone else. This bit of bravado, which the king subscribed to as well, showed again how utterly unrealistic the assumptions under-lying British policy were. The notion that the Royal Navy could restrict colonial trade in this manner was a fantasy. The navy had no way of enforcing anything like what North wanted, yet the idea met with wide approval among Britain's leaders.

North was upset with the patriots for not understanding the political situation in Britain. He was well aware that an uncompromising king, with strong support in the cabinet and in Parliament, was bringing on a war, but for him that was a political given. He didn't expect them to bend. He had hoped that the colonists would, since he took it for granted that British arms would prevail in any military showdown.

When the evidence coming from Philadelphia showed that the colonies were not going to submit, he foresaw only a bloody conflict. In other circumstances, he would have tried to orchestrate a grand compromise, of which he was an acknowledged master. But he did not have the political support he needed. He might have resigned in protest, but instead, he remained the king's man, dutifully supporting His Majesty's dream of a quick triumph in Massachusetts.

Above all, although North often declared otherwise, he wanted to remain Britain's first minister. If he had placed the country ahead of his personal ambition, he might have found the courage to organize a great compromise, but he let his opportunity pass. And as more time went by, his chances of doing it grew slimmer and slimmer.

18

Chatham's Opposition

A VOICE and character much stronger than Lord North's now reentered the lists, determined to change the king's American policy—that of William Pitt, 1st Earl of Chatham. Insisting that Parliament had the right to tax the American colonies had always appeared misguided to Pitt. He had opposed the Stamp Act in 1766 and every attempt to tax the colonies thereafter.

Had his health been better when the king, with great reluctance, asked him to lead the government again in 1766, the Great Commoner would have guided policy along a path that would have made America a contented part of a thriving empire again. The problems with Massachusetts never would have arisen. No tea tax or any other tax would have disturbed relations. The whole attempt to tighten control of the colonies from London would never have been attempted.

Pitt's health did not allow him to dominate the government as he had during the Seven Years' War, however. The result was that the king was able, more and more, to determine policy, and Lord

North, who became first minister in 1770, managed the government for him. Of course, North was far from being a cipher. He deftly handled crises with Spain and Ireland, as well as the national debt. He was a master of compromise, admired by the Commons for his debating skill and wonderful sense of humor.

North was nevertheless at a loss when it came to America. By the fall of 1774 Pitt had become so concerned at how mismanaged American policy had become that, sickness or not, he felt an urgent need to do something. He was infuriated by the king's mindless reliance on the threat of violence to cow Massachusetts. Americans were not going to be easily intimidated, in which case the king would have to carry out his threats and engage in a war that he was unprepared for, and that Britain could never ultimately win. Stumbling into a fight with America was the height of folly, in Pitt's view. Pretending that Americans were cowards, and not the stout fighters they had proven themselves to be in the French and Indian War, could only ensure a calamity. Watching his beloved empire needlessly torn apart was more than he could stand.

After Pitt had spoken in the House of Lords in May of 1774 about the stupidity of the Coercive Acts, he had not been heard from; his fragile health prevented him from surfacing. By the beginning of August, however, he had become so apprehensive that he could remain silent no longer. One of the first things he did was arrange to have a long conversation with Benjamin Franklin, someone he had long admired. He sensed that Franklin had the best interests of the empire at heart and was not working for American independence, although many had accused him of doing so.

Pitt doubtless recalled that in 1766 he and Franklin had played important supporting roles in helping Lord Rockingham, the leader of the opposition, to win repeal of the Stamp Act. Franklin and Pitt had worked independently, yet they could not help but notice the effect the other was having. Pitt, the most powerful debater of his generation, argued against the law in the Commons, while Franklin, at the invitation of the Speaker, stood for four hours in the House on February 3, 1766, answering members' questions. Perhaps Pitt and Franklin, remembering their success against the Stamp

Act, were hoping to produce the same result this time against much greater odds.

Pitt did not know what mood Franklin would be in after the verbal beating Wedderburn had administered in the Cockpit back in January, but he wanted to find out. He had been furious with Wedderburn at the time, thinking his assault on Franklin idiotic, and the general approval of the audience even more foolish. As Pitt would soon discover, Franklin was as frustrated as he was with the direction of affairs, and, although the American was still angry about the incident in the Cockpit, he was not going to cease his efforts to prevent the civil war he saw coming.

When Lord Stanhope, a mutual friend, told him that Pitt wanted to talk with him, Franklin jumped at the chance, thinking that maybe Lord Chatham was the leader he had been looking for. Franklin had been hoping for some time that a major figure would emerge to lead the opposition against the king's policy, but none had so far. Pitt had the requisite stature.

At the end of August, Lord Stanhope brought him to Hayes, Pitt's estate in Kent, for a long discussion. This was the first time that Franklin had visited Pitt, and he was a bit in awe of him. Although Chatham was old now and feeble, Franklin was struck by his inner strength. He felt, as Lord Chesterfield was purported to have said, that Chatham "carried with him, unpremeditated, the strength of thunder and the splendor of lightning."

The first question that Pitt asked was whether Franklin wanted America to remain in the empire, or if he thought the colonies would be better off on their own. Franklin was quick to respond, assuring him that he did not want independence, and that as far as he knew, neither did America. To be sure, there were a few individuals who would like to separate, but he was convinced that the great majority of people wanted to remain. Franklin was not Sam Adams. He understood the shortcomings of Great Britain better than most, but he thought a civil war was to be avoided at all costs. So did Chatham.

With that critical question out of the way, Franklin outlined for Pitt the grand vision he had of what Britain and America could accomplish together.

I then took occasion to remark to him that in former cases great empires had crumbled first at their extremities from this cause, that countries remote from the seat and eye of government which therefore could not well understand their affairs for want of full and true information, had never been well governed, but had been oppressed by bad governors, on presumption that complaint was difficult to be made and supported against them at such a distance. Hence such governors had been encouraged to go on, till their oppressions became intolerable. But that this empire had happily found and long been in the practice of a method whereby every province was well governed, being trusted in a great measure with the government of itself, and that hence had arisen such satisfaction in the subjects, and such encouragement to new settlements, that had it not been for the late wrong politics (which would have Parliament *omnipotent*, tho' it ought not to be so unless it could at the same time be *omniscient*) we might have gone on extending our western empire adding province to province as far as the South Sea.

These were ideas that Franklin had expressed before at greater length, in the September 11, 1773, issue of the *Public Advertiser*, under the title "Rules by Which a Great Empire May Be Reduced to a Small One." He had published similar views as far back as 1760, in a lengthy pamphlet entitled *The Interest of Great Britain Considered with Regard to Her Colonies and the Acquisition of Canada*.

Franklin went on to tell Chatham that he "lamented the ruin which seemed impending over so fine a plan, so well adapted to make all the subjects of the greatest empire happy; and I hoped that, if his Lordship, with the other great and wise men of this nation, would unite and exert themselves, it might yet be rescued out of the mangling hands of the present set of blundering ministers, and that the union and harmony between Britain and her colonies so necessary to the welfare of both might be restored."

Franklin's thoughts were exactly what Chatham wanted to hear. He hoped to fashion a proposal that would allow the kingdom to find its way out of the present morass and meet the legitimate needs of both colonists and mother country.

Unfortunately, Pitt had little influence left in Parliament. Acquiring more at this point was unlikely. Strange as it might seem, he had never been a political infighter, able to put together majorities in the Commons to support his policies. Although he had dominated the government during the Seven Years' War and led the country to stupendous victories, the Duke of Newcastle had managed domestic politics. They were a team. Pitt was the magnificent speaker and debater who inspired with his great vision, while Newcastle was behind the scenes doing the politicking that produced strong parliamentary majorities.

For many years Pitt's illness had put him in virtual retirement. He had been forced to watch from the sidelines. It would be difficult, if not impossible, for him now to do the kind of coalition building necessary to withstand the tidal wave of anti-American feeling sweeping Parliament. The Duke of Newcastle was no longer there to do that kind of work for him.

Edmund Burke, who wanted the Coercive Acts stopped as much as Pitt, criticized him for not working more closely with Lord Rockingham, who was leading the opposition in Parliament. But that was not Pitt's style. Even so, in spite of his limitations, he intended to do what he could. He was famous, widely respected in both countries, and had a powerful voice. He felt a duty to use whatever influence he still had to keep America part of the empire.

Both Pitt and Franklin recognized that events had gone quite far. Something had to be done soon. They agreed that the most effective way to immediately halt the mad rush toward war was to bring General Gage's expeditionary force home from Boston and repeal the Coercive Acts.

———

After meeting with Chatham, Franklin was far more optimistic about the chances of preventing the impending debacle. He reported to Cushing in the middle of September, "I must not now relate to you with whom I have conferred, nor the conversations I have had on the subject, lest my letter fall into wrong hands; but I may say I have reason to think a strong push will be made at the very beginning of the session [of Parliament] to have all the late acts reversed and a solemn assurance given America that no future attempts shall be made to tax us without our consent. Much depends on the proceedings of the Congress."

Franklin thought there were solid grounds for hoping the government would change course, forced by a combination of Pitt, the opposition in Parliament led by Lord Rockingham, and the boycott Congress was imposing, together with the many pledges from Congress that the colonies wanted reconciliation. Since the policy that the king and his supporters were following was based on an erroneous reading of American political sentiment, and since what the king and his minions were doing was illogical and bound to lead to the very thing they were trying to prevent, Franklin believed that London would at last come to its senses. He hoped that Pitt's powerful voice would finally open the eyes of the ministry, the king, and Parliament. There was every reason, he thought, for them to take what Pitt was saying seriously, reverse course, and save themselves from disaster. From the point of view of just plain common sense, he was optimistic that London would change.

Pitt's proposals were presented in two stages. The first was delivered in a speech to the House of Lords on January 20, 1775, after Parliament had returned from its Christmas recess. Franklin was sitting in the visitor's gallery as Chatham's guest, and beside him was thirty-three-year-old Josiah Quincy Jr., an important Boston lawyer, who was close to Dr. Warren and both Sam and John Adams.

Quincy had arrived in London on November 17. The patriot leaders in Boston sent him to get a sense of where the British government stood with respect to Massachusetts and the colonies in general, and report back. They were uncomfortable relying only on Franklin's reports. Quincy's mission was thus of some importance, which Franklin immediately understood.

Quincy had the idea, encouraged by Arthur Lee, Sam Adams's close friend, that Franklin was lukewarm about the patriot cause.

Franklin made it his business to keep the young man close to him and show him that he was in fact a committed patriot. Quincy was entirely won over, and thrilled to be sitting next to Franklin for Pitt's historic speech. Unfortunately, he had an advanced case of tuberculosis and would never get back to Boston alive, dying within sight of shore. He was never able to tell Warren, Sam Adams, and the others what Franklin's true position was.

Pitt began his oration by calling for an immediate withdrawal of British troops from Boston and approval of the work of the Continental Congress. He told the House of Lords that, among other benefits, a troop withdrawal would immediately calm things down in Massachusetts, if not in the whole country. It would be powerfully symbolic. The political atmosphere would brighten. People would have reason to be optimistic about war being avoided. A withdrawal of troops would also assure Americans that their property would never be taken except by votes of their own elected assembly.

Pitt then went on to point out that Britain could never secure her position in America by pursuing her current policy.

What though you march from town to town, and from province to province, though you should be able to enforce a temporary and local submission . . . how shall you be able to secure the obedience of the country you leave behind you . . . to grasp the dominion of eighteen hundred miles of continent, populous in numbers, possessing valor, liberty, and resistance?

This resistance to your arbitrary system of taxation might have been foreseen: it was obvious. . . . [A] glorious spirit of Whiggism [liberty] animates three millions in America. . . . To such united force, what force shall be opposed?—What, my Lords?—A few regiments in America, and seventeen or eighteen thousand men at home!—The idea is too ridiculous to take up a moment of your Lordships' time. . . . We shall be forced ultimately to retract: let us retract when we can, not when we must. . . . These violent, oppressive acts . . . must be repealed— you will repeal them. . . . I stake my reputation on it:—I will consent to be taken for an idiot if they are not finally repealed.

Avoid then, this humiliating, disgraceful necessity. . . . Make
the first advances to concord, to peace and happiness.

Pitt also pointed out something that everyone knew but preferred not
to think about: France and Spain were observing, he warned, "waiting for the maturity of your errors."

Unfortunately for Pitt and Franklin, the proposal was met with
derision and was soundly defeated, by a vote of 68 to 18. Minds were
already made up. There was deep anger at Americans, and a determination to put the upstarts down, coupled with an unshakable belief
that it could be easily done.

Had Pitt's simple remedy been applied, it had the power to stop the
resistance in Massachusetts, which, in turn, would have checked the
clamor for war in Britain. It might well have prevented the American Revolution altogether. A decisive moment was missed, one that
could have prevented the deaths of tens of thousands and the loss of
the American colonies.

The defeat of his first proposal did not stop Pitt. He persevered,
as he always did, and on February 1 he proposed a bill for settling
all disputes with America. He began by insisting on parliamentary
supremacy throughout the empire, but then went on to propose recognizing the Second Continental Congress when it met on May 10
and offering to suspend the Coercive Acts and the Quebec Act. This
wide-ranging proposal also met with an icy reception.

Franklin, who was again present as a spectator in the House of
Lords with Quincy, described what happened next. Lord Dartmouth
was the first to reply, and he

rose, and very properly said, it contained matter of such weight
and magnitude, as to require much consideration, and he
therefore hoped the noble earl did not expect their lordships
to decide upon it by an immediate vote, but would be willing
it should lie upon the table for consideration. Lord Chatham
answered readily that he expected nothing more. But Lord
Sandwich rose, and in a petulant, vehement speech opposed its
being received at all, and gave as his opinion that it ought to be

immediately rejected with the contempt it deserved. That he could never believe it the production of any British peer. That it appeared to him rather the work of some American; and turning his face towards me . . . said, he fancied he had in his eye the person who drew it up.

Lord Dartmouth was taken aback. Noting how opposed the House of Lords was to Pitt's proposal and how much in sympathy it was with Lord Sandwich, he immediately reversed himself and sided with Sandwich, withdrawing his motion to have the proposal lie on the table. Franklin noted that this behavior was typical of the spineless American secretary.

The lords rejected Pitt's second proposal by a vote of 61 to 32. Franklin was crestfallen. He wrote to Charles Thomson:

Lord Chatham's bill, tho' on so important a subject, and offered by so great a character, and supported by such able and learned speakers, as Camden [the Duke of Richmond, the Duke of Manchester, and others] was treated with as much contempt as they could have shown to a ballad offered by a drunken porter. It was rejected on a slight reading: without being suffered even to lie on the table for the perusal of the members. The House of Commons, too, have shown an equal rashness and precipitation in matters that required the most weighty deliberation, refusing to hear, and entering hastily into violent measures: and yet this is the government whose supreme authority we are to have our throats cut if we do not acknowledge, and whose dictates we are implicitly to obey, while their conduct hardly entitles them to common respect.

Franklin was appalled at the way these hereditary rulers handled this supremely important issue.

[T]o perceive the total ignorance of the subject in some, the prejudice and passion of others, and the willful perversion of plain truth in several of the ministers; and upon the whole to see it so ignominiously rejected by so great a majority, and so hastily too, in breach of all decency and prudent regard to the character and dignity of their body as a third part of the national legislature, gave me an exceedingly mean opinion of their abilities, and made their claim of sovereignty over three millions of virtuous sensible people in America, seem the greatest of absurdities, since they appeared to have scarce discretion enough to govern a herd of swine. . . . [T]he *elected* House of Commons is no better, nor ever will be while the electors receive money for their votes, and pay money [by which] . . . ministers may bribe their representatives.

19

Lords North and Dartmouth Secretly Search for Peace

THE ministry had already been moving toward its momentous decision on war or peace before Pitt made his first speech to the House of Lords. Their lordships planned to make their fateful choice when Parliament reconvened in January.

It appeared that Lord North was paying no attention to when Pitt intended to speak or what he might say. And yet privately North and Dartmouth shared his anxiety about the drift toward civil war. They were anxious about the decision the ministry and monarch were about to make with respect to America. Their concern was not as great as Pitt's, but it was there, and it had been since December.

During the second week of December, North had become so concerned that he suggested to the king that a royal commission be sent to America to resolve the controversy. The response from the palace was swift. His Majesty thought that such a proposal would show weakness, which was the opposite of what he wanted. North quickly dropped the matter, but he and Dartmouth were still worried, and their concern grew as the ministry's January deadline for a final decision on America approached. Publicly, they remained staunch supporters of the king's hard line, but at the same time they initiated a secret search for peace.

It was more than a little odd that the two figures in charge of the government's policy, men who publicly supported a tough line on America, were at the same time, seeking—albeit in great secrecy—to find a grand compromise that would avoid a civil war. Unfortunately, their attempt remained hidden. Rather than fight in the open, they searched covertly for an agreement that would satisfy both sides, something that had already been shown to be immensely difficult, particularly when they would not support it themselves publicly unless they had strong political support, which they did not have.

Since Franklin was close at hand, the two lords quietly sought him out and asked for his help, which, after all that had happened, he was still willing to provide. Time was running out. Franklin naturally had misgivings. Even if indirect talks conducted through intermediaries with these key figures produced an agreement, there was little chance it would be carried out. The king and his supporters in the ministry had the country with them, and they saw no reason to compromise. If anything, they appeared to welcome a war.

Given this attitude, whatever Franklin worked out with North or Dartmouth stood no chance of being accepted. And making it even more difficult, neither would openly support it himself. So Franklin's efforts were bound to fail, even if, by some miracle, he found common ground with North and Dartmouth, which itself was doubtful. Nonetheless, he tried; the stakes were too high not to.

A friend of Lord Dartmouth's, Thomas Villiers, Baron Hyde, initiated the negotiations late in November 1774. He suggested to David Barclay, a wealthy merchant and Quaker who made his money trading with America, and Dr. John Fothergill, Dartmouth's doctor and Franklin's longtime friend, that they act as intermediaries for North and Dartmouth and begin a discussion with Franklin. Barclay approached him just as the new Parliament was convening at the end of November, long before the ministry made its final decision on war in January. He began by noting the dangerous situation with respect to American affairs. Franklin agreed, and the conversation began. Franklin told them that, although he was willing to talk, he failed to see how the conversation could lead to a positive result. As far as he could determine, there was not the "least disposition in the ministry to an accommodation." He saw instead a great deal of malice, such that the cabinet "wished to provoke the New England people into an open rebellion, which might justify a military execution" of Whigs and dissenters in both countries, along the lines of what had been done to the Jacobites in the 1740s.

Barclay and Fothergill were quick to deny any such malice. They admitted that some individual ministers fit that description, but said that there were others who were troubled by the way things were going, just as they were, and presumably as Dartmouth and North were.

More meetings followed, and, at their urging, Franklin produced a list of requirements he thought were needed to heal the breach. Dr. Fothergill, who saw Dartmouth regularly, promised to show him the American's proposals, which he thought might be an incentive for Franklin. It was just the opposite. It did not matter, in Franklin's view, what Dartmouth thought; he could never move the ministry or the king. In fact, as far as Franklin was concerned, having Dartmouth as American secretary at this critical juncture was a great tragedy. Yet if Dartmouth was replaced, it was more than likely that a cruder and more hostile character would take his place, someone like George Germain, a member of Parliament who had had a long, agreeable association with the king and shared his views on using military force to control the American colonies.

After Franklin's views were presented to Dartmouth, and presumably to North, more discussion followed, but in the end, Franklin's initial impression proved to have been correct. The parties were so far apart that no grounds for compromise existed, particularly when the ministry and the palace were so anxious to have it out with the Americans. The king was the hardest of hard-liners. No amount of logic was going to sway him.

It eventually became apparent that more negotiations were a waste of time, and Franklin assumed that he had heard the last of them. But he had not; they continued on and off until the middle of February 1775.

Fothergill did not finally write to Dartmouth until February 6, explaining that there was no point continuing. Barclay did not admit defeat until ten days later. Franklin had known from the beginning that it would have been a miracle if they had succeeded.

Interestingly, Fothergill and Barclay were not the only intermediaries who approached Franklin. Another friend of Baron Hyde, Admiral Lord Howe, used his sister to initiate a dialogue at the end of December. Franklin must have been anxious to speak with him, for Howe was a unique figure, in that he had a special personal relationship with the king. Howe's mother was widely known in London society as the sometime mistress of the king's grandfather, George II, such that her son could well be related to His Majesty. There was enough of a physical resemblance between the two that the rumor did not seem farfetched.

Lord Howe was also Great Britain's premier fighting admiral, perhaps the finest naval leader in British history, ranking on a par with Admiral Horatio Nelson. Howe was a parliamentarian as well, and took political matters seriously. He and his family were known as friends of America. His brother, George Augustus Viscount Howe, who was killed at Ticonderoga in 1758, had been a hero in the French and Indian War, and was still a beloved figure in the colonies. The Massachusetts General Court paid for a memorial to be erected to him in Westminster Abbey.

For all these reasons, Howe was worth having serious discussions with, far more so than the other intermediaries. The talks with the admiral went nowhere, however, which Franklin must have feared. At least he tried. One odd thing did happen, which struck Franklin as inappropriate, not to mention insulting. During their discussions, Howe tried to bribe him, thinking, no doubt, that Franklin had far more influence in America than he actually had.

Their final talk occurred on February 19. Howe made one more attempt to bribe Franklin, which this time, drew an angry response.

That aside, Franklin's proposals to the admiral, which were similar to those of the Continental Congress, never had a chance of being accepted by North because of the political climate in the Commons, the Lords, the Cabinet, and, above all, at the Palace.

———

While Chatham and Franklin had been laboring to bring Britain and America together, and North and Dartmouth had been searching for some compromise behind the scenes, the king had been doing just the opposite. He remained committed to making Massachusetts submit to the Coercive Acts.

In his speech opening the new Parliament on November 30, he had clearly indicated what his American policy would be. It had not changed. He pledged that strong action would be taken to restore British authority in the Bay Colony. He found the situation there deplorable and promised to rectify it by making sure the Coercive laws were obeyed. He left no doubt that the supremacy of Parliament would be maintained by whatever means were necessary. "You may depend upon my firm and steadfast resolution," he promised, "to withstand every attempt to weaken or impair the supreme authority of this legislature over all the dominions of my crown." His remarks were loudly applauded. Rushing headlong into a war with his own people had broad support.

Lord Chatham took exception. He told the House of Lords that "instead of suppressing the opposition of the faction in Boston, these measures [the Coercive Acts] had spread it over the whole continent. They have united the whole people, by the most indissoluble of all bonds—intolerable wrongs."

On December 5, North told the Commons that matters were in a "state of suspense" until they heard from Congress, even though he had been receiving reports on what Congress was doing ever since it convened.

It was whispered around London that Galloway, and even John Jay, were sending secret intelligence about the American Congress to North. Although Jay was certainly not doing this, Galloway was a likely source. He seemed desperate to ingratiate himself with the ministry.

The House of Commons did not need to wait and hear what Congress had to say. The king's policy was ratified immediately. On December 5, the House, after a perfunctory debate, voted 264–73 to support whatever measures His Majesty deemed necessary for America. It was the response the king had been working for ever since he told a surprised North to prepare for new parliamentary elections back in August. The king now had a clear path to carry out his program to ensure submission in Massachusetts.

As expected, His Majesty ignored the petition from the Continental Congress when it arrived, nor did he find time to read the list of rights and grievances.

He also had no need to pay attention to the Rockingham group in Parliament, which was the main opposition. Not only were they few in number, but their leader, Lord Rockingham, appeared more interested in the pleasures of country life than in legislative battles. His appearances in the House of Lords were few and his speeches short and barely audible. He worked primarily through Edmund Burke, who was a force in the House of Commons, but he could only do so much against the tsunami of anti-American feeling among his colleagues.

And to make things easier for His Majesty, Pitt was not working with the Rockingham group. There was nothing new in this. Pitt had always been something of a political loner. Even though he shared Rockingham's views, he did not go out of his way to work with him.

Edmund Burke wished that Pitt would work directly with them, and was very critical of him for not doing so. Burke believed that if Pitt had done so, the parliamentary opposition might have been more potent, and the king forced to pay more attention to their frequent warnings, but as it was, Chatham remained a lone actor, in part because he did not have a high regard for Rockingham. He did meet with him briefly on January 7, but nothing of consequence came from it.

In spite of Chatham's political isolation, His Majesty still had to be concerned about him. He had had a long relationship with Pitt and a visceral dislike for him that stretched back many years. Having Pitt oppose him on American policy was on the one hand unwelcome because of Chatham's still enormous talent, but on the other, defeating him would be gratifying. And, more importantly, it would solidify support for a hard line on America.

20

The Decision for War

THE king's American policy was confirmed during three critical meetings of the ministry, on January 12, 16, and 21. Gage's plea for a vastly expanded military presence had long since been rejected. Unaware of that, and fearing that it would be, he had sent his aide Colonel (soon to be Brigadier General) Robert Prescott to London in December to explain the situation in Massachusetts directly to the king and the cabinet. He knew that the ministry would be making its decision about America when Parliament reconvened after the Christmas holidays. Admiral Graves kept the transport *Charming Nancy* ready to sail for London at a moment's notice, and on December 16, Colonel Prescott was aboard, headed from Boston to London, ready to convey Gage's thoughts bluntly to the cabinet. He arrived ahead of the crucial January meetings.

Admiral Graves, who had even less influence with the ministry than Gage, had a letter aboard for Philip Stephens pleading for more warships. Graves also sent a letter from Captain Wallace, the aggressive skipper of HMS *Rose*, the warship assigned to Narragansett Bay, explaining the measures Rhode Island was taking to prepare for possible conflict in the spring of 1775.

Shortly after arrival, Colonel Prescott met with the cabinet at Lord Rochford's office on Cleveland Row, across the street from St. James's Palace. Rochford was the senior secretary of state. On January 14 Colonel Prescott met with the king in what is now Buckingham Palace but was then the Queen's Palace. Having Prescott brief His Majesty and the ministry on the situation in the Bay Colony was a case of the blind leading the blind. Although Prescott undoubtedly conveyed Gage's thinking accurately, and perhaps his own (there is no record of the conversations), neither he nor Gage had any idea of what the real situation was. When civil war finally broke out in earnest at Lexington and Concord on April 19, Gage and his officers were as surprised by what happened as their superiors in London.

As the cabinet met on the sixteenth, the sloop of war *Falcon* stood by at Spithead, the famous anchorage off Portsmouth, to rush new orders to Gage. Lord North and his colleagues finally committed themselves to settling matters with the colonies by force. They also reaffirmed their decision not to send the troops that Gage so desperately wanted. They remained convinced that their commander in North America could do the job with what he had.

Although the defensive preparations advocated by the Continental Congress and being carried out by the Massachusetts Provincial Congress were viewed by the ministry as preparations for an aggressive war, the members did not believe they would present a challenge that Gage couldn't deal with.

At the cabinet meeting on the sixteenth, Lord North also unexpectedly brought out a conciliatory resolution that he intended to introduce in the Commons, to go along with declaring war on Massachusetts. He wanted to offer an olive branch to accompany the sword, and pretend that he was giving Massachusetts and the other colonies a choice between war and peace. As it turned out, the war resolution he later introduced was clear and unequivocal, while the supposed peace offering was vague and confused, and lacked support in the House, although it was dutifully passed, on the assumption that it was going nowhere.

North wasn't fooling anyone. This clumsy sleight of hand was unworthy of him. He was a master at constructing legislative compromises. The only thing his peace offering showed was that he had a bad conscience. He knew that he had let the country down by allowing the war party to gain control of policy when he might have fashioned a grand compromise that secured peace.

Once the ministry had made its decision, Lord Dartmouth wrote his famous dispatch of January 27, 1775, giving Gage his final orders, which led directly to Lexington and Concord. Never did the ministers, sitting in the evening with their French wine, imagine that their decision would have the consequences that it did. They were working on the assumption that they were merely lighting a fire under an overly cautious theater commander.

———

While George III and the North ministry were shoring up political support for crushing resistance in Massachusetts, patriots in Boston had their attention drawn to Fort William and Mary, in Portsmouth, New Hampshire, where a large cache of munitions was stored. The royal governor of New Hampshire, John Wentworth, had informed Gage that Fort William and Mary, near the mouth of the tidal Piscataqua River, was in danger. Rebel militias in southern New Hampshire were expanding, and the governor thought they would attack the fort, which had only a miniscule garrison, and seize the weapons.

Gage responded immediately. In the middle of December, he organized a large detachment of regulars to send to Portsmouth by sea. He kept his plan secret, of course, but the patriots were paying such close attention to his every move that they soon got wind of what he was about to do. Merchant William Cooper, Boston's town clerk, and a member, along with his brother, the Reverend Samuel Cooper, pastor of the Brattle Street Church, of the patriot inner circle, sent for Paul Revere. Cooper gave him a letter addressed to Samuel Cutts, head of Portsmouth's committee of correspondence, telling him what Gage was planning, and hoping that Cutts would act quickly before the British regulars reached the fort. Cooper also told Cutts that Admiral Graves would, in all likelihood, send a potent warship or two as well, which would make attacking the fort impossible.

Revere moved fast. He went immediately to Province House and obtained a pass so that he could ride out of town over the neck. After the Powder Alarm, Gage had had a guard station built at the entrance to the city. Everyone needed a pass to leave. Revere was off at daybreak on December 13 and rode the sixty miles to Portsmouth over icy terrain, delivering the message to Cutts that afternoon. Cutts went to work immediately, summoning the patriot militia in Portsmouth and the surrounding towns, including Exeter and Durham, which had particularly strong contingents. Major John Sullivan was the leader of Durham's militia.

After Cutts had a quick conversation with the Portsmouth committee of correspondence, they decided to attack Fort William and Mary the following day. A force of over four hundred militiamen gathered at dawn and sailed from Portsmouth's waterfront two miles to the fort, where they began their attack around three o'clock that afternoon.

Captain John Cochrane, the fort's commander, had only five men to defend it. The defenseless state of this important military facility showed how pathetically weak the Tories were in Portsmouth, and in New Hampshire generally. In spite of being vastly outnumbered, Cochrane was not going to give up without a fight. As the patriots approached, his men fired one round from three 4-pounders (cannon) before the militiamen overwhelmed them.

Cochrane was a brave officer, but he was also realistic, and as the patriots poured over the walls of the fort, he quickly surrendered, saving both his men and himself.

The militiamen immediately began hauling away over one hundred barrels of precious gunpowder, loading them in the gondolas they had arrived in, and hiding them in a place they thought Governor Wentworth didn't know about. As it turned out, they were right.

While the fort was being captured, patriot John Langdon of Portsmouth alerted Major John Sullivan in Durham, who quickly assembled seventy men for additional work at the fort the following night, December 15. After dark, they took gondolas back to the fort and removed sixteen cannon, cannon shot, and sixty muskets, hauling them over the water to Durham, where they hid them near Sullivan's house.

All during this time—ever since Paul Revere rode into Portsmouth—Governor Wentworth was doing his utmost to put together a Loyalist militia to help Cochrane and save the munitions, but he could not get anyone to serve. The patriots had hundreds turn out in a few hours, while Wentworth could not recruit a single person.

Portsmouth was not the only place patriots were seizing munitions. They were doing it anywhere they could. In Rhode Island they raided Fort George, overlooking Newport Harbor, and brought cannon, gunpowder, and an assortment of weapons to a secret place in Providence. It was a major undertaking. Forty-four cannon were seized, some as large as 24-pounders.

———

The assault on Fort William and Mary had a larger impact on events than the participants realized. Reports of the attack reached London the last week of January. The king, and, indeed the whole government, were infuriated. Since the ministry had just made its final decision for war, hearing the news from New Hampshire confirmed their belligerent views. The orders for Gage to go on the offensive had already been written (although not actually sent). The die was cast. The time for talk was over.

———

While the ministry was making the final decision to use force against Massachusetts, the king decided to do something he had been contemplating for some time—replace General Gage, who remained very unpopular in London. Supporters of the Coercive Acts still blamed him for letting the uproar the laws had caused get out of control. The king had made no secret of his unhappiness, openly referring to Gage as "his mild general."

Finally, in January His Majesty, fed up with Gage's temporizing, asked fifty-eight-year-old General Amherst to replace him. His Majesty seemed to think that Amherst's reputation would produce enough fear to frighten colonists into accepting the Coercive Acts.

The king was aware of the close ties between Gage and Amherst. He planned to overcome the natural reluctance Amherst would have to replacing a close friend by creating a novel command structure in Massachusetts. Under the new arrangement, Gage would be kept on as governor of the colony and continue to draw his pay as commander in chief of the army, but Amherst would be in charge of all land operations.

The offer had no appeal for Amherst, however, and he unexpectedly turned the king down, which wasn't easy. There's no reliable record of what was said. Amherst's refusal may have been based on a number of factors, including his close personal ties to Gage. He surely did not want his friend to be humiliated in this fashion. Probably the biggest factor was the king's unwillingness to send a far larger army to accomplish his goals. America was a vast country, as Amherst knew quite well; it was not going to be subdued by a small army.

It must have been obvious to Amherst that the king and his supporters in Parliament were not prepared to make the sacrifices necessary to accomplish their goals. Blaming Gage was much easier. Amherst refused to become the goat himself. The thought of going back into the political maelstrom in America could not have been appealing, either.

The refusal of England's most distinguished general to accept this assignment, even when the king offered it to him personally, might have prompted another monarch to reexamine his policy, but not George III. Instead, he brushed aside the qualms of one of his most knowledgeable strategists, as if they were of no interest.

21

Parliament Votes for War

O N February 2, 1775, Lord North proposed that the House of Commons make an address to the king proclaiming that a state of rebellion existed in Massachusetts, supported by other colonies, and urging His Majesty to take immediate action to secure obedience to English law and sovereignty. The motion was approved by the lopsided vote of 296–106.

Approval from the House of Lords soon followed. The vote was 104–29. To all intents and purposes, this was a formal declaration of war. The king wrote to North on February 8, telling him how pleased he was with Parliament's decision.

North now moved to pass the Restraining Act, another piece of legislation designed to punish New England. He had had this law in mind ever since receiving word that Congress had initiated nonimportation, nonconsumption, and nonexportation of all British goods. The new law restricted the trade of the New England colonies to Great Britain, Ireland, and the British West Indies and, at the same time, prohibited the same four colonies from fishing on the banks of

Newfoundland. It also prohibited coastal trade between the colonies. On February 10 the act was approved with little dissent, and less thought, 261–85.

Those who voted their approval assumed that the Royal Navy had the resources to carry out what was potentially an enormous undertaking. It became even bigger when soon all the colonies were brought under the act, after they refused to abandon New England. The original bill had been directed only at New England, in the hope that it would split the colonies, but that failed, and the bill was extended to include all of America, expanding the task of the Royal Navy to the point of absurdity. The Admiralty did not begin to have the resources necessary to enforce the law. America, with its long tradition of smuggling and hundreds of miles of coastline, could easily circumvent it.

On February 20 Lord North introduced in the Commons something he called the Conciliatory Resolution. It came just after Parliament and the king had declared war on America. The law purported to offer the colonies a way to stop the bloodshed before it got started—a way to escape the consequences of their disobedience. North claimed that he wanted to offer them a choice between war and peace. His proposal was apparently what he had distilled from the clandestine discussions with Franklin, but if that was the case, he hadn't learned much. The law was a caricature of the substantial proposal that Chatham had made and Franklin had endorsed.

In essence, it promised that Parliament would not impose internal taxes on any colony that undertook to tax itself at a level that met the approval of Parliament. Not surprisingly, no colony found this formula attractive. Franklin said of it, "I cannot conceive that any colony will undertake to grant a revenue to a government that holds a sword over their heads with a threat to strike the moment they cease to give or do not give so much as it is pleased to expect. . . . It seems to me the language of a highwayman."

North told doubters in the House of Commons that his proposal might bring peace, but if not, it would divide the colonies. The law passed by a strong majority, 274–88, and was quickly forgotten. Nobody thought it would be taken seriously on either side of the

Lord Viscount Howe

Comte de Vergennes

Abigail Adams

Dr. Joseph Warren

John Hancock

Samuel Adams

Lieutenant General
Thomas Gage

George Washington

George III

John Adams

Lord Percy

Atlantic, and it was not. More than anything else, it demonstrated that North had serious doubts about the path his country was on.

The government never made a real attempt to negotiate a peace. Britain's leaders wanted to get on with punishing the colonies. There had been plenty of time to consider the decision for war; they were not in the mood for second thoughts. Dartmouth and North felt the tide of opinion, and they dared not stand against it.

Dartmouth had already composed the order to Gage that would begin the war. Although he had written it on January 27, after the three decisive meetings of the cabinet, he did not send it right away. In fact, it did not leave London until February 22 and did not actually depart England until March 13. Dartmouth hung onto it for weeks while North's war legislation worked its way through Parliament and received the king's approval. The delay was not due to weather. Dartmouth wanted the government to have time to give its formal imprimatur to a historic decision. He might also have wanted to see if the negotiations with Franklin turned up anything at the last minute.

When it finally became clear that the government, including the king, the ministry, and both houses of Parliament, and, indeed, the public, had made up their minds on using force, Dartmouth sent his orders to Gage.

———

While this transpired in London, General Gage was marking time, awaiting Dartmouth's new instructions. He was being especially cautious, not wanting to provoke another incident like the Powder Alarm. In February, however, he broke his rule and sent troops to seize some munitions in Salem. He had gotten word that rebels were storing eight stolen fieldpieces near the town's landing place. He thought that among them were four brass cannon that he especially wanted back. In fact, they were nothing of the sort. They were eight old cannon that had been taken from a ship.

Gage dispatched two hundred men from the Sixty-Fourth Regiment, under Colonel Alexander Leslie, to retrieve them. The men were stationed at Castle William. They could move without being observed in Boston. On Sunday February 26, the four companies were loaded on a transport and taken fourteen miles to Marblehead, where they sat until two o'clock in the afternoon. This was the time when Colonel Leslie judged that the townspeople in Marblehead and Salem would be at their meeting houses and unlikely to give him any trouble.

He landed the troops at Holman's Cove, five miles from Salem. Without Leslie being aware of it, Marblehead patriots were instantly alert to what was happening and spread the alarm. Marblehead major John Pedrick was out in front of the others, racing to Salem. As soon as he got there, the bell in the meeting house, which was full of people, began ringing.

Militia colonel David Mason quickly assembled some men and brought the eight cannon over North Bridge to a blacksmith shop in nearby Danvers. Leslie was right behind him and soon reached the town square, where he halted his column next to the meeting house. John Sargent, a Loyalist, came up to Leslie and told him that the cannon he was looking for had been taken to Danvers over North Bridge. Leslie moved in that direction but found that the bridge was a drawbridge that Mason had thoughtfully raised after crossing to Salem on his way back from Danvers.

Leslie demanded that the draw be lowered, and threatened to fire on people randomly if it wasn't. This was an obvious bluff, and the patriots defied him. They couldn't imagine that Leslie had orders to initiate another Boston Massacre.

As tension and tempers rose, the Reverend Thomas Barnard Jr., the town's young minister, tried to settle things down. At the same time, Colonel Mason warned Leslie that expresses had been sent to arouse the countryside and soon hundreds of armed militiamen would be appearing, and he would be forced to either surrender or fight. Leslie took the warning seriously. He decided to accept a face-saving offer to have the draw lowered, in return for a promise to only march ninety feet and then turn back. He had no alternative. The draw was lowered, and he marched a few troops over and back and then returned to Marblehead and his transport, which was soon on its way back to Castle William without the cannon. He had escaped just in time, as minute men from Danvers and the surrounding towns began arriving in Salem. They would have quickly forced Leslie to surrender.

What General Gage would have done then isn't clear. He might have asked for the return of Leslie and his men, but the patriots might have refused and defied him. There would have been little Gage could have done. He was still waiting for new orders from London, and he did not have anywhere near enough troops to challenge the rebels.

Earlier in February Gage had written to Barrington, telling him that he was expecting new orders, and that he anticipated that they would require him to act offensively. He then added ominously, "[T]o keep quiet in the town of Boston only will not terminate affairs; the troops must march into the country." Leslie's experience gave Gage an indication of what might await him if he were forced to go on offense. However, as later events would show, he learned little from this incident.

Nonetheless, Gage prepared for a potential thrust into the countryside by sending troops on regular marches outside the city. The exercises were usually round-trips of fifteen miles. The men welcomed the chance to get away from their daily frustrations in Boston. Major Pitcairn and his marines appeared especially pleased.

22

The Country People

WHEN Parliament and king formally committed Britain to war against Massachusetts, little thought was given to the country people they would have to fight. Although the farmers and artisans of the Massachusetts countryside were 90 percent of the population, and would comprise almost all of the patriot army, Britain's rulers had little appreciation of who they were, and acted as if it didn't matter. London policymakers would not have been surprised if the country people never fought at all—if their courage failed them when the prospect of battling British regulars armed with the latest weapons, including field artillery, became a reality. Talk was one thing; facing professional fighters on the battlefield was something else.

Disparaging colonial fighters was not only common among London's political leaders; it also had a long tradition in the British army and navy. General James Wolfe famously described the New England men who fought and died under him during the French and Indian War as "the dirtiest, most contemptible, cowardly dogs that you can conceive. There is no depending on them in action. They fall down dead in their own dirt and desert by battalions, officers and all." Wolfe, who never spared himself, died a hero's death on September 13, 1759, while leading his troops to victory over the formidable French general Louis-Joseph de Montcalm during the decisive battle of the French and Indian War on the Plains of Abraham outside the massive walls of Quebec City. The name Wolfe would be forever associated with that great battle.

His observations on the quality of colonial fighters were not made in anger, to be regretted later; rather, this was his settled opinion, and it carried great weight. The aristocrats who officered his army shared his views. They rarely had anything good to say about American soldiers. Lieutenant Alexander Johnson's opinion of provincial troops was typical of most British officers. He told Lord Loudoun that they were "obstinate and ungovernable people, utterly unacquainted with the nature of subordination." Loudoun, the commander in chief in North America at the time, could not have agreed more.

The dirty, contemptible dogs that Wolfe and Loudoun found ungovernable were independent farmers like John Parker, of Lexington, Massachusetts, who fought at Quebec and would be elected captain of the town's militia in 1774, a distinction that in military terms meant a great deal. His men, who knew him intimately, were willing to trust him with their lives. For Wolfe and Loudoun to vilify Parker and the thousands of Massachusetts men who fought with them was so divorced from reality that it was impossible to understand, unless one considers that the colonial fighters never behaved as trained animals, the way Wolfe and Loudoun expected them to—the way the rank and file of the British army did.

Calling intrepid fighters like Parker cowardly dogs was evidence of the deep annoyance Wolfe, Loudoun, and their officers felt at how independent-minded colonial troops could be. They were universally derided as gutless for refusing to be treated as cattle. The same cast of mind was common among the British officers who arrived in Boston in 1774 and 1775.

The disdain for colonials was fully reciprocated. The Massachusetts men who watched British officers in action during the French and Indian War came away with a high appreciation of their short-comings. They found nothing remarkable about them. The notion that they might be afraid to fight them was a dangerous miscalculation. The opposite was the case. The provincials would bring great confidence to the battlefield on the day of Lexington and Concord. The widespread belief among British officers that American fighters, particularly those from New England, were a breed apart was hard to refute. They were indeed, but not in the way that Wolfe and his colleagues imagined.

One of the distinguishing characteristics of all armies is that they reflect the society they come from. This was certainly the case with the British enlisted men and their American counterparts during the French and Indian War. Their differences were profound, just as the societies that produced them were. To begin with, Massachusetts men—every one of them—could read and write. Universal education was a priority in the Bay Colony, going back to the Puritans, who were middle-class Englishmen from East Anglia with a deep commitment to literacy and learning, including higher education. Massachusetts militiamen were well acquainted with the issues of the day from the newspapers that were readily available to them at home. Britain's soldiers, on the other hand, were illiterate to a man, entirely ignorant of the larger questions that brought them to the battlefield. It made a big difference.

British soldiers left no written accounts of what their life was like during the French and Indian War, and recorded no observations of American fighters. Massachusetts men, on the other hand, left plenty of evidence of what their experiences had been, including opinions of their opposite numbers in the British army, and of their officers.

The illiterates who populated the British army came from the lowest rung of a hierarchical society, in which order and custom were of supreme importance, and always imposed from above. They were men who looked up to their betters, and would never presume that they had a right, or the knowledge, to participate in governance.

The army was their life. They had nothing to go back to at home. They were marginal men in a society that used them for menial labor. They became soldiers for a variety of reasons, some just to have ample food. Others were attracted by enlistment bonuses. Many were criminals of one sort or another, their sentences commuted when they joined the army. Still others were tricked into joining after imbibing too much in a tavern and then trapped. And there were those who were simply impressed, as seamen were, under some guise. For most, having a uniform and plenty to eat, as well as the chance to plunder, were attractions enough to leave home and risk their lives. Perhaps 10 percent of them were volunteers.

They had no power, economic or political, in their communities. None of them owned land or had any way of acquiring any, and, of course, they had no way to participate in politics, even if they wanted to. Their circumstances before entering the army were not exceptional. There were plenty of potential recruits like them. The king could always depend on a pool of similar men being available for service.

British soldiers were also patriotic, devoted to king and country in a way that the farmers of Massachusetts would find difficult to appreciate. Enlisted men in Britain's army were not unhappy with their local lord and master, or their betters, as they fancied them. They were comfortable in an ordered society, where social mobility was not considered desirable. Being uneducated, powerless, and poor kept them happily in their place.

At the same, it didn't surprise the patriots that so many of General Gage's foot soldiers deserted when they had the chance, even though, if caught, they could be, and often were, executed. Although they were uneducated, they were not stupid or lacking in courage. They could see how much better ordinary people lived in America, and for many of them, that attraction proved strong enough to risk the penalties for desertion.

The young soldiers from the Bay Colony had been impressed when they first encountered the king's officers in their splendid uniforms during the French and Indian War. It wasn't long, however, before they saw their lack of humanity. The aristocratic officers never associated with the men in the ranks. They maintained a great distance, and showed no respect for them. The manner in which they disciplined ordinary redcoats was shocking. The brutal treatment inflicted for even minor offenses made a lasting impression. Monstrous punishments, administered routinely, included lengthy beatings that resulted in death. It often appeared that the officers imposing these punishments came from a different planet. Gibson Clough, one of the disgusted colonials, noted in his journal that British soldiers "are but little better than slaves to their officers."

The distance rigidly maintained between officers and men in the king's army did not exist among the provincials. In fact, the opposite was the case. Officers stayed close to their men, exhibiting the very kind of behavior that repulsed the British. The colonial officers knew that they could not be effective otherwise. They led by example, and their courage inspired.

If the British officer corps had compensated for the coldhearted treatment of the rank and file by brilliance on the battlefield, perhaps their callousness could have been excused to some extent, but what the Massachusetts men found instead was incompetence at all levels that resulted in the unnecessary deaths of thousands. Ordinary soldiers were treated simply as cannon fodder. The provincials understood the need for discipline in the army, but they demanded, and received, respect. Officers could not treat soldiers any way they pleased.

The colonial fighters even found the personal habits of the king's officers obnoxious, particularly their callous disregard of simple moral principles. The men from Massachusetts were deeply religious. They took their faith seriously and practiced it every day. At home, they attended church on Sunday, spending many hours there. British officers ignored the Sabbath, often passing the day gambling on races they organized. Their constant cursing also offended the colonials, as well as their ill-use of camp followers. The large number of women who followed the infantry were not necessarily prostitutes, although some were. Most of them worked hard for the regiments, doing a variety of essential tasks, particularly laundry.

The behavior of His Majesty's officers left an impression of British society that was impossible to erase. It wasn't surprising that the colonial fighters who returned from the war were determined to resist any attempt by London in the 1760s and 1770s to impose stricter controls on them, or to go further and undo the past by remaking Massachusetts society in Britain's image.

———

Unlike the absurd caricature of the colonial fighters imagined in Whitehall and Parliament in 1774, Massachusetts was filled with tough combat veterans, both officers and men. Exact numbers aren't known, but probably 60 percent of the men in Massachusetts who were eligible to serve in the French and Indian War did so. Ten thousand alone fought in 1758. The total eligible male population that year was around forty thousand.

Massachusetts had been on a war footing during most of the French and Indian War. In one way or another, the fighting touched every household. The farmers and their families worked hard to support the war effort. They would have been angry, and not a little puzzled, by General Wolfe's description of their fighters.

The young men from Massachusetts, although not professional soldiers, were nonetheless familiar with military life. Ever since the earliest Puritan immigrants landed in Massachusetts Bay under John Winthrop in 1830, war had been a constant feature of American life. The farmers were not strangers to combat. If they had been the simple peasants that London imagined, Gage would have had an easy time intimidating them. Instead, he was confronting a militia army of veterans and younger men being trained by them. All the men, veterans or not, were, as Lord Barrington liked to point out, "accustomed to fire arms." They were brought up with them and knew how to use them. More importantly, the success they had had in the French and Indian War instilled confidence. Even with inferior weapons, the Massachusetts militiamen had no doubt that they could defeat the king's troops.

The number of combat veterans among the country people far exceeded the size of Gage's army. Any Massachusetts male in his thirties or forties had likely been a soldier. Most of the men in the ranks of the British army in Boston in 1774 had never fought in a war before. They looked pretty on parade in their stylish uniforms, but they were green. Britain had been at peace for twelve years. Her foot soldiers were an unknown quantity. Their lack of combat experience made it impossible to predict how they would perform against the veterans training in the towns.

It was an article of faith among British army officers that the severe discipline they imposed on their inexperienced enlisted men would suffice to make them perform up to standard, which they assumed would be enough to crush the provincials. Among the things missing from their calculations was that Massachusetts militiamen had something to fight for, and the green recruits sitting in barracks in Boston did not.

The country people did not intend to give up a society that was egalitarian and affluent. Unlike the soldiers in the British army, Massachusetts fighters like John Parker were economically well-off, and politically potent. A large percentage of them owned their own land. The landscape of the Bay Colony was a patchwork quilt of small towns and modest farms, owned by the families that worked them. Nothing like them existed in Britain.

Economic opportunity was widespread, and upward mobility common. There was an abundance of land. Anyone willing to work hard could accumulate the money to buy enough acreage for a farm, which was the key to a prosperous life. It goes without saying that the farmers of the Bay Colony were respected in their communities, which they governed democratically.

Service in the army was a duty they fulfilled, but it was not their vocation. They had a fine life to go back to. Very few liked being in the army. It was a sacrifice they endured for the good of the community.

23

The Country People Find
Many Supporters

AMONG the many things that surprised and concerned London
was the support the country people of Massachusetts were
receiving from the other colonies, especially in the South.
The differences among the provinces appeared so large that it was
hard to understand how they could unite. Yet the tobacco barons of
Virginia and the great rice and indigo planters of South Carolina were
solidly behind Massachusetts, even to the extent of being willing to
take up arms.

The royal governors of colonies outside New England had
encouraged the king's skepticism about the ability of Americans to
work together by sending a continuous flow of reports to Dartmouth
explaining that there was actually a striking division of opinion
among the provinces, in spite of the Continental Congress's pretending otherwise. The governors knew how pleased His Majesty would
be with this intelligence. In spite of overwhelming evidence to the
contrary, he took their reports seriously and clung to the notion that

Gage could impose the Coercive Acts with few troops if he had a mind to.

His Majesty would soon discover that the governors' reports were worthless. When it came to opposing the Coercive Acts, unity prevailed among his diverse colonies. He had intended the legislation as a warning to all of them, not just Massachusetts, and he had succeeded, only his warning brought them together. It did not drive them apart.

What the king and his supporters in Parliament failed to appreciate was that as different as the colonies were, they still had something in common that was of immense importance—prosperity. They were all, in their own way, economic success stories. The Coercive Acts endangered the prosperity they had built up over decades. They were not willing to give up their standard of living for the certain impoverishment that Britain was threatening.

Although southern planters had developed a society markedly different from New England's, the Coercive Acts imperiled the planters as much as they did the farmers in Massachusetts. A sudden closing of ports, discarding old charters, and drastic changes in methods of governance all indicated that London was bent on gaining a degree of political dominance that would inevitably affect every other aspect of society. Threatened with a loss of control, the great planters united with their countrymen in the north and the middle colonies to resist.

No agricultural society in the world was as prosperous as that of the country people in the Bay Colony. And the 10 percent of the Massachusetts population not engaged in agriculture was just as successful. The province's seaports were flourishing, just as those all along the Atlantic coast were. The largest—Boston, New York, Philadelphia, and Charleston—were bursting with activity, and so were medium-sized and smaller ports.

Boston appeared to be stagnant because its population wasn't expanding, but this was misleading. The city itself had not been growing, although it was still important, but among the thriving smaller seaports in Massachusetts were Newburyport, Salem, Gloucester, Marblehead, Plymouth, and New Bedford. Much of their trade was in agricultural products made in Massachusetts and sold in the West Indies. Even ice packed in sawdust was regularly brought from New Hampshire and the Maine District of Massachusetts to the West Indian islands.

Taken together, the seaports of Massachusetts were as vital a part of the empire's economy as ever. They were among the leading shipbuilders in the world, and they could build warships. In combination with the other colonies, they had an abundance of the natural resources necessary to build ships of the highest quality, something even Britain lacked. America had the potential to easily become the dominant power on the high seas.

When the other important New England seaports, including Newport, Providence, New London, New Haven, and Portsmouth, New Hampshire, were added to the Bay Colony's, their contribution to the empire's growing wealth was immense. In Boston alone, over a thousand ships cleared from the port every year.

All of this had been accomplished under Britain's mercantilist system. Since passage of the first navigation act in 1660, an economic relationship had developed between England and America that was part mercantilist, part independent, and part illegal. The mercantilist portion placed restrictions on colonial manufacturing and commerce that were principally for the benefit of England but turned out, whether intended or not, to have important advantages for the colonies. The carrying trade, for instance, was confined to British or colonial bottoms, giving Massachusetts an enormous incentive to build ships, which entrepreneurs took full advantage of. Shipbuilding boomed.

Over three thousand merchant vessels were required to handle Great Britain's worldwide trade. After a hundred years of the navigation acts, most of those ships were being built in American yards. New England, particularly Massachusetts, had a large share of the business, including ownership of the vessels. Massachusetts merchants, the most notable of whom was John Hancock, did a vast amount of trading out of the province's seaport towns in ships built there.

Not only was New England prospering, but the South, which had an entirely different economy, was as well, despite being handicapped by its uneconomical slave-labor system. And the middle colonies were also thriving, as evidenced by the rapid growth of seaports like Philadelphia and New York. Both were larger than Boston in 1775. Philadelphia had a population of 25,000; New York, 22,000; and Boston, 17,000. If the other major seaports in Massachusetts were included, the population of all of them together was much larger than either Philadelphia or New York, and so was their shipbuilding. Outside of the British Isles, Massachusetts continued to be the shipbuilding capital of the empire.

There were also strictures in the navigation laws against colonial manufacturing, but these were not oppressive, either, even if strictly enforced, which they were not. It was obvious that the colonies, particularly in the north, would at some point develop industries that could successfully compete with the mother country. The king and his supporters were increasingly concerned about this.

The eighteenth century, even under Britain's trade laws, was one of steady economic growth in every colony. To be sure, Massachusetts, along with the rest of America, and the mother country, felt the adverse effects of the periodic downturns that beset all large economies. Progress was interrupted from time to time by a variety of adverse events, including war and the hardships that accompanied changing from a wartime to a peacetime economy. Growth had been curtailed for a limited period, but over time, there was steady progress, until together, and even separately, America and Britain were the most economically advanced countries in the world. They had been able to adapt and innovate far better than any rivals.

Far more important to the economic success of the colonies than lax enforcement of the navigation laws were the basic rights enshrined in the English constitution: freedom of speech and of the press, trial by jury, and the rule of law. Literacy and near-universal education were also critical underpinnings of rapid economic growth.

Perhaps the most puzzling aspect of the grand dispute Britain was having with her colonies was why London would press so hard in 1774 and 1775 for fundamental changes in a relationship that had been so successful over many decades. One would have thought that the wisest policy would have been to leave well enough alone instead of rushing into an extensive restructuring. This is what Edmund Burke and Lord Chatham argued so cogently.

Rather than glorying in the success of the colonies, Britain's leaders appeared to fear them. They seemed afraid that America would unite and become so large and powerful that the mother country would lose control. Ironically, it was the prosperity of the colonies that appeared of most concern to Britain's rulers. They had come to see them as a potential rival, their economic success a long-term danger that should be addressed sooner rather than later. The longer they waited, the bigger the problem could become.

Without realizing it, His Majesty subscribed to Franklin's vision of what the empire could be if Britain and America remained together. Only the king was afraid that, rather than Franklin's dream of compatible interests being fulfilled, America would, at some point—perhaps in the not too distant future—become the more powerful partner, dominate the North American continent and the West Indies, and be Britain's foremost rival, instead of a contented part of an empire that was greater than Rome or Spain or China at their height.

Seeing the Americans working together in the Continental Congress added enormously to the concern felt in London. The fear of a united America was precisely why the king and his followers believed that something had to be done right away to impose tighter controls, before Americans went their own independent way.

With only a vague, simplistic understanding of history and economics, George III believed that the empire might unravel in the following way: If America was free from the constraints of the navigation acts—if, in other words, America became independent—he was convinced that the West Indies would want to follow "not to independence, but [because they] must for [their] own interest be dependent on North America: Ireland would soon follow the same plan . . . then this island would be reduced to itself, and soon would be a poor island indeed, for reduced in her trade, merchants would retire with their wealth to climates more to their advantage, and . . . manufacturers would leave this country for the new empire."

Massachusetts, the worst of the colonies from the king's perspective, was a case in point. Both the farmers and the city dwellers were examples of great economic success, and they were defying Britain politically. They might be proclaiming devotion to the empire, but they were acting independently. His Majesty had been observing their ways ever since ascending the throne in 1760. By the time of the Tea Party, thirteen years later, he believed that cracking down hard was vital before Massachusetts got more independent-minded and had undue influence not only on the rest of New England but on the colonies to the south.

This was the reason he was so desperate in 1774 and 1775 to remake Massachusetts society and use the new model to strike fear into the rest of the colonies. He saw their prosperity not as a tribute to the success of the empire but as the most serious threat to it, even eclipsing that from other European powers.

Not only was America's prosperity a concern, but the leveling tendencies in politics that were so prevalent, particularly in Massachusetts among the country people, also portended trouble.

24

Tensions Mount

T HE arrival of spring in New England was ordinarily a time of hope and renewal, but in 1775 the people of Massachusetts were dreading the approach of April. It was the traditional time that eighteenth-century armies took the field. Throughout the colony, patriots were bracing for the long-awaited clash with General Gage. They were expecting him to march into the countryside before the end of the month. Militias were drilling in every town, preparing. Even in the sparsely populated Maine District of Massachusetts men were getting ready. The total number of New England militiamen was unknown, but Gage estimated them to be in the thousands, perhaps as many as twenty thousand or more.

On October 30, 1774, he wrote to Dartmouth, "They confide in their numbers, and a small force rather encourages resistance than terrifies; and if I may venture an opinion in matters of such consequence, I would take the liberty to tell your Lordship that I am confident, if these misunderstandings proceed to the last extremitys, that to begin with an army of twenty thousand strong, will in the end save Great Britain both blood and treasure."

An increase of this size in Gage's army would have to have come from overseas, but in 1774 and 1775 that would not have been easy. Britain was diplomatically isolated. She could not look to the other great powers for aid. Russia, Prussia, and Austria were neutral, enjoying the spectacle of the mighty English sinking deeper into a morass of their own making. Spain and France, her traditional enemies, were also delighted with the fix that Britain had gotten herself into.

Frederick of Prussia was particularly adamant about remaining neutral, and Catherine of Russia, who was a great admirer of Frederick's, followed his lead. There were, of course, hundreds of smaller German states other than Prussia, particularly Hanover and Hesse, where Britain could find troops—Hanover because it was comparatively large and George III was its ruler, and Hesse because, like most German principalities, its profligate prince was constantly in need of money.

The king was not seeking foreign help, however. He remained blissfully ignorant of the real situation in Massachusetts, and was simply waiting to hear the good news that the recalcitrant colony had finally come to its senses and submitted to the Coercive Acts without further exertion from him. In a remarkable exchange of letters between Lord Dartmouth and Gage during the winter and spring of 1775, the American secretary showed again how utterly unable he and the king were to understand the actual conditions that Gage faced.

Dartmouth wrote his letter on April 15, just when Gage was receiving the orders that would trigger the Battle of Lexington and Concord. Dartmouth was replying to a letter that Gage had written to him back on January 18, when Gage knew the government was making its final decision on American strategy. "The eyes of all are turned upon Great Britain," Gage had written, "and it is the opinion of most people, that, if a respectable force is seen in the field, the most obnoxious of the leaders seized, and a pardon proclaimed for all others, government will come off victorious, and with less opposition than was expected a few months ago."

Dartmouth's response read as if he had never received any intelligence or policy suggestions from his field commander: "I observed, that in your letter of the 10th of January . . . you say, that if a respectable force is seen in the field, the most obnoxious of the leaders seized, and pardon proclaimed for all others, government would come off victorious. The two first of these objects are already provided for . . ."

Dartmouth would soon find out that "a respectable force" had not already been provided for. How he could brazenly declare that there already was one in Boston was remarkable. Every communication from Gage had reported just the opposite. How Dartmouth, an intelligent man, could write something as uninformed as this in April of 1775 is indicative of the extent to which London made policy based on a fantasy of a colonial world that didn't exist.

In the face of London's determined stupidity, Gage remained at his post and kept doggedly pleading for a change of policy, instead of abruptly resigning and bringing matters to a head. By procrastinating, he was allowing Britain to court a disaster that he would inevitably be blamed for.

———

While Gage waited over the winter for new orders, he did his best to avoid a large-scale fight prematurely. He pursued a policy of watchful waiting until new instructions arrived. He never expected they would be so long in coming, however. At the end of March, he still had not received any. He knew the government had made up its mind in January, but he had heard nothing from London.

As matters stood on the first of April, the king was still expecting him to force perhaps as many as twenty thousand or more armed citizens to submit to the Coercive Acts, when Gage had an army of fewer than four thousand men.

———

Gage was being given no credit for keeping the lid on in Boston through the summer, fall, and winter. Maintaining control of his frustrated army, especially the officers, during the long New England winter had not been easy. Angry soldiers and hateful townspeople were a volatile mix. Preserving the peace, preventing them from slitting one another's throats, was a constant preoccupation. Yet, thanks to Gage, none of the numerous small incidents that took place every day had grown into anything larger. This precarious state of affairs could not go on indefinitely. At some point, there would be an explosion, with unpredictable results. The soldiers were well armed, but so, too, were the townspeople.

One of the officers, forty-four-year-old Lieutenant Frederick Mackenzie, wrote in his diary on January 24, 1775, "The commander in chief [Gage] is determined to make the strictest inquiry into the conduct of all officers concerned in quarrels or riots with the townspeople, and try them if in fault." Gaming and drinking often were the occasions when fighting broke out, and Gage kept them under strict control.

In spite of the obstacles, he had preserved peace in the city for almost a year, and he was proud of that record. His superiors, however, viewed it as cowardice.

At the end of March Gage reported his achievement to Dartmouth:

> The winter has passed over without any great bickering between the inhabitants of this town and His Majesty's troops. Some quarrels now and then happen though of no very great consequence. . . . I have been at pains to prevent any thing of consequence taking its rise from trifles and idle quarrels, and when the cause of Boston became the general concern of America, endeavored so to manage that administration might have an opening to negotiate if anything conciliatory should present itself, or be in a condition to prosecute their plans with greater advantage.

He added, "Government is so totally unhinged, and the people so possessed with the notions instilled into them, that all authority is derived from them, that it may be doubted whether government can ever revert again into its old channel without some convulsion."

———

Since the king never accepted Gage's excuses, he continued thinking about a replacement. After Amherst had turned him down, he
decided to give Gage one more chance to force the rebels to submit,
while at the same time sending his replacement to Boston in case
he failed. Major General William Howe was his potential successor.
Howe was one of Britain's heroes from the Seven Years' War and a
favorite of the sainted General Wolfe. Many of the king's supporters wondered why Howe had not been sent to replace Gage long
before now. Accompanying Howe to Boston would be two more
well-regarded major generals, Henry Clinton and John Burgoyne.
It was quite clear that the king was responding to Gage's pleas for a
vastly expanded army by sending three more generals.

This decision was made in December and January. The three generals departed England for America on April 20 and would arrive on
May 25. By the first of April, Gage was aware that a new set of orders
were on the way, as well as his replacement, should he falter.

25

Still Waiting

WHILE expecting new orders to arrive at any time, Gage decided on a novel way to communicate with the ministry. He asked fifty-three-year-old marine major John Pitcairn to attend a meeting he had called to frighten Boston's leading politicians and make himself look tough to his superiors. He had invited the rebels and the major to his office on March 2. Pitcairn recounted the entertaining scene to Lord Sandwich, as Gage knew he would.

Although Major Pitcairn had scant knowledge of Boston or its leaders, he had a good understanding of what Lord Sandwich wanted to hear, just as Gage did. Pitcairn reported, "Some of the great Whigs, as they are called here," were summoned to Province House for a meeting with General Gage. He told them "that if there was a single man of the king's troops killed in any of their towns he would burn it to the ground. What fools you are, said he, to pretend to resist the power of Great Britain; she maintained last war three hundred thousand men, and will do the same now rather than suffer the ungrateful people of this country to continue in their rebellion."

The major seemed to think that this absurdly high figure would have an impact on the assembled bumpkins. He went on to observe: "This behavior of the general's gives great satisfaction to the friends of government. I am satisfied that one active campaign, a smart action, and burning two or three of their towns, will set everything to rights. Nothing now, I am afraid, but this will ever convince those foolish bad people that England is in earnest. What a sad misfortune it was to this country, the repealing of the Stamp Act; every friend to government here asserts in the strongest terms that this has been the cause of all their misfortunes."

His reference to burning towns was but another indication of the king's wish, as well as Sandwich's, that the navy be used to firebomb towns without warning, making no distinction between Loyalists and rebels. Pitcairn observed that the colonists behaved as he supposed the lower classes would ever do, making "great noise when there is nobody to oppose them, but the moment they see us in arms and in earnest they will talk very differently." He added, "Orders are anxiously expected from England to chastise . . . [these] very bad people."

Although his observations were meant to please the first lord, there's no reason to doubt that they were a true expression of his own convictions. They were in no way indicative of how the patriots were receiving Gage's scolding, however. Pitcairn implied that they were moved, but the opposite was the case. Far from being intimidated, they remained firm, watching the country people steadily build the patriot army, and waiting for Gage to make a move. Pitcairn, on the other hand, with no experience in Massachusetts, but with all the prejudices common to naval officers, thought Gage was making an impression that would give the rebels pause. His judgment was no better than his superiors' in London. He had no idea who exactly the rebels were; nor did he feel he needed to know. He was simply telling Sandwich what he wanted to hear.

His greatest concern at the moment was the inactivity of his marines. They were swilling rum all day and dying from it. They needed some action. He reported to Sandwich, "I have lived almost night and day amongst the men in their barracks for these five or six weeks past, on purpose to keep them from that pernicious rum. I would not have your lordship think from this that we are worse than the other battalions here, the rum is so cheap that it debauches both navy and army, and kills many of them. Depend on it, my Lord, it will destroy more of us than the Yankees will."

Major Pitcairn also spoke in his report about the difficulty he was having with Admiral Graves. The aging admiral was in Boston primarily to line his pockets before retirement. The first lord did not believe the business in Boston required one of his best sea officers. Sandwich had such a low opinion of colonial fighters that the last consideration in appointing Graves had been his fighting ability. The major had trouble with Graves because the admiral was reluctant to release marines for shore duty. He made money off them when they were aboard ship. Graves had a habit of keeping Pitcairn's best marines aboard—men who were volunteers. There were fifty of them. The major counted on them to be an example to the other men. Graves allowed only four hundred men of the marine battalion of five hundred ashore, and the volunteers were not among them. Graves was a problem for Gage as well. Five hundred marines had been sent to him as reinforcements that he desperately needed. Holding a hundred of the best aboard idle warships infuriated him.

Gage and Graves seldom worked well together. Pitcairn at times got caught between them. When Graves ordered him to send more marines back on board, Pitcairn declined. The major needed Gage's approval, but the general refused to give it, knowing that it was only for the purpose of fattening the admiral's purse.

After an incident like this, Graves would take it out on Pitcairn, who reported one such occasion to Sandwich: "It is needless for me to tell your Lordship how he [Graves] talked to me and what he said." Having written this, Pitcairn immediately assured Sandwich that in spite of Graves's dressing-down, he remained in full control of his emotions and addressed the admiral with the utmost civility.

Gage's frustration with Graves was constant. Just getting passes for supply vessels coming into Boston Harbor could be a problem, since it involved paying Graves's secretary a fee. Gage was going to need close cooperation from the admiral in the days ahead, but that did not appear likely.

———

While Gage waited for word from London that would give him a clearer sense of direction, the patriots moved ahead rapidly with arming and drilling. Dartmouth's delay in sending Gage his orders turned out to be a great help. On February 21 the Committee of Safety voted to buy enough military supplies for an army of fifteen thousand.

Every militiaman had his own musket, powder, and ball. So potent had the militias become by early spring that representatives from the more radical counties in the western part of the province, like Berkshire County, were pressing for an immediate attack on Gage's army before it could be reinforced. Hancock and the other leaders had to restrain them. A premature attack would be a political disaster. A hasty offensive against Gage risked losing the support of the other colonies, who had agreed to act only on defense.

It could also unleash Admiral Graves. The patriots had no defense against the warships. They might have had one if they had developed sea militias, similar to the land militias, but there was no tradition of this, and it would inevitably involve acting offensively. In any event, it would bring Graves into play. Until now, Gage had prevented him from doing something politically foolish, like burning down Charlestown or Cambridge.

———

Waiting endlessly for Dartmouth's new orders exacerbated the army's morale problems, which were even larger than the one Pitcairn had with the marines. Gage continued dealing with the problems by keeping his men busy doing practice marches. On March 30 he ordered Lord Percy to conduct the largest one.

Percy was happy with the assignment, and so were his troops. On the appointed day, he marched his thousand-man brigade over Boston Neck to Roxbury and Brookline, and headed toward the Great Bridge over the Charles River in South Cambridge. The patriot alarm system was quickly activated, large numbers of minute men appeared, and the planks on the bridge were torn up in case the battalion intended to cross and march west toward Concord via the Lexington Road.

That was not Percy's plan, however. He turned at the Great Bridge and marched for seven miles along the left bank of the Charles River toward Watertown and another bridge. He did not cross that one, either. Instead, he turned toward Jamaica Plain and marched back to Boston without incident. The Cambridge minute men who had gathered in such significant numbers on the opposite bank of the river just watched. They were not going to take any aggressive action, but they did get some excellent practice at mobilizing.

Percy concluded from the exercise that the regulars, marching smartly in full battle gear, had intimidated the provincials, something Gage desperately wanted to believe. Percy and his officers were now certain that they could overawe the rebels. Just the sight of the regulars, they thought, would be enough to send them running.

It was the wrong conclusion to draw. The patriots were committed to acting on the defensive. They were also committed to being ready in case of an attack. They had proclaimed both things, again and again, and they meant them. Since all Percy did was march around, the militiamen just watched.

The Provincial Congress took special notice of the march, however, and made more explicit what would trigger its extensive alarm system. It soon adopted the report of a committee, which said "[t]hat whenever the army . . . to the number of five hundred shall march out of the town of Boston with artillery and baggage, it ought to be deemed a design to carry into execution by force the late acts of Parliament . . . and therefore the military force of the province ought to be assembled, and an army of observation immediately formed, to act solely on the defensive so long as it can be justified on the principles of reason and self-preservation."

As April approached, John Hancock—still president of the Provincial Congress—grew more apprehensive. On March 30 he issued a somber warning to the Commonwealth's "several towns, as well as individual inhabitants," to be on their guard. "Any relaxation," he declared, "would be attended with the utmost danger to the liberties of this colony, and of all America. . . . our implacable enemies are unremitting in their endeavors, by fraud and artifice, as well as by open force, to subjugate this people."

His warning was an accurate description of the current state of affairs, and people took it seriously. In the meantime, Gage was trying to decide what he was going to do in case he received minimal reinforcements or none at all, or, as he prayed, a large enough army to crush the incipient rebellion. Worcester was on his mind. On February 22 he sent a party of three to reconnoiter the roads leading to the town, forty-eight miles west of Boston, in case he wanted to send a sizable column to destroy the big arms depot there. He was still hoping to receive a substantial reinforcement.

The three men were Captain John Brown, Ensign Henry De Berniere, and Brown's sergeant. Gage ordered Brown and De Berniere to scout and map the countryside between Boston and Worcester. He told them to "go through the counties of Suffolk and Worcester, taking a sketch of the country as you pass; it is not expected that you should make out regular plans and surveys, but mark out the roads and distances from town to town, as also the situation and nature of the country; all passes must be particularly laid down, noticing the length and breadth of them, the entrance in and going out of them, and whether to be avoided by taking other routes."

The men stopped at Brewer's Tavern in Watertown for refreshment and were shocked when a black waitress identified them as British spies in spite of their disguises. She didn't hide the fact that she recognized them. Momentarily flustered, they gathered themselves and left abruptly. Brown was more careful for the rest of the trip. He sought out only known Loyalists for places to rest.

He was aware that even though rebels dominated the countryside,

Loyalists were scattered about. He had a list that Gage provided. Some had been roughly treated, but for the most part, as long as they were a small minority, they were tolerated, albeit grudgingly.

Meanwhile, the observant waitress spread the word that spies were about. But that didn't hinder Brown. The trio made their way to Worcester carefully and returned to Boston with maps, sketches, and a report.

Along the way, Loyalists apprised them of deserters hiding in various places, indicating what a big problem desertion continued to be. For the men of the army and navy who attempted it, the patriots, in overwhelming numbers, were there to help, but getting away was still difficult and extremely dangerous.

On March 22 Gage sent Captain Brown and Lieutenant De Berniere on a similar mission to Concord, ordering them to make a detailed survey of the possible routes for a fast column to take. Gage would have much preferred marching on Worcester, but it was too far. Concord seemed a better place to attack. Of course, he personally would not lead any expedition. That would be left to a subordinate who could be blamed if things went badly.

On their way to Concord, Brown and De Berniere traveled through Roxbury, Brookline, Weston, and Lincoln. Their report noted, "The town of Concord lies between hills that command it entirely; there is a river runs through it, with two bridges over it." They provided exceptional details of military supplies and topography in the town, given to them by Concord's most prominent Loyalist, Daniel Bliss.

They enjoyed the hospitality of this friend of government, who fed them a splendid dinner. Afterward, he went with them to Boston for protection. Even though Concord patriots had shown great tolerance for Bliss, he was now in fear of his life. He had become a traitor, willing to take up arms against his own people.

On the return trip, Brown and De Berniere seemed to have had blinders on. They went by way of Lexington and Menotomy (now Arlington), along the Lexington Road, instead of by way of Weston. Their report described "the road [as] very good almost all the way," which later proved to be exactly the opposite.

On April 5 Gage sent two other spies to Worcester to have another look. One of them was Lieutenant Colonel Francis Smith; the other was John Rowe. On the way they stopped at Brewer's Tavern in Watertown, and the same black patriot recognized Smith, even though he had on a disguise. She even called him by name. He was so shocked he returned to Boston, keeping off the main road whenever he could. Rowe continued to Worcester and later reported to Gage that sending a column there would be disastrous. The militia were ready for him. Rowe also reported that sending any column anywhere would be foolhardy. The rebels were waiting in great numbers for just this kind of move. It might be possible for five hundred cavalry to race to Concord and back, Rowe thought, but he wasn't enthusiastic about that, either. Even cavalry could be in trouble when they stopped to destroy whatever munitions were there.

Gage paid little attention to Rowe. He had been thinking about marching to Concord for some time, and had already told his friend Barrington, the secretary at war, that in order to succeed he had to march into the country. When Brown and De Berniere returned, he concluded that if the new orders from London forced him to, he would make a quick strike on Concord using the Lexington Road.

This is not what he preferred, but after waiting so long for new instructions, he had to be prepared for the worst, which was that he'd be required to take action without the necessary resources. If this was the case, a surprise attack on Concord, although not ideal, looked doable.

Although Gage was thinking seriously along these lines, it doesn't appear that he had discussed his possible strategies with any of his military colleagues. Lord Percy was certainly in the dark about his plans. On April 8 Percy wrote to the Reverend Thomas Percy, noting that the rebels, as far as he could determine from their activity in Boston, were preparing for a fight. They were forming an army to set fire to Boston "and attack the troops before a reinforcement comes." He lamented that on "our side no steps of any kind can be taken as yet," because no orders had arrived from London.

Percy had no idea that Gage, depending on the orders he received, was thinking seriously of sending a column into the countryside. If given a chance, Percy probably would have questioned the wisdom of doing it. He thought that the rebels would most likely attack the city in coordination with their supporters in it. He had observed for some time that "they [the rebels] are every day in greater numbers evacuating this town, and have proposed in Congress, either to set it on fire and attack the troops before a reinforcement comes, or endeavor to starve us."

———

As both London and the patriots were aware, the French were following events closely. Vergennes, who was emerging as a powerful player in Paris, was receiving intelligence regularly. He could not have been more pleased to see the disaster that the English were inflicting on themselves. He was watching for ways that France could take advantage. Already, he was allowing American shippers to land their cargoes in France, which was a violation of Lord North's recently approved Restraining Act. Justifications were invented, and British protests turned aside. The French pointed out that they were not obliged to enforce British law or turn away ships in distress.

———

Before Gage's new orders from Dartmouth arrived, he tried to elicit Graves's help with a quick march to Concord, if that turned out to be the only action he could reasonably take. He wrote to the admiral, "I shall . . . be obliged to you for your opinion of the number of troops that the boats belonging to your squadron in the harbor would be able to take on board should I have occasion to make application to you for their assistance."

General and admiral then had a conference on April 6 at 10:00 a.m. in Gage's office at Province House to go over details, which made it appear that they were working well together, although nothing could have been further from the truth. Nonetheless, Graves wanted it to look as if he was on top of things. He reported separately to the Admiralty some of what he was doing for the cause, as well as the difficulties he was operating under. "I have placed [the *Somerset*] where the *Lively* and *Canceaux* [two smaller warships] formerly lay, between Charlestown and Boston," he reported to Philip Stephens. "It is very likely that in this situation she will be of considerable service."

Graves also complained that the fleet in Boston continued to be short of men from death and desertion. And he reported that the pilots for the harbor, if they served the Royal Navy, were subject to awful retribution from the rebels.

———

While Gage was mulling over the details of a possible run on Concord, he was weighing the possibility that the country people, when it came right down to it, might not actually oppose him, for one reason or another. In spite of all the evidence to the contrary, he still had a sliver of hope that they wouldn't dare attack regular troops. He also entertained the possibility that any attempt at mobilizing the town militias into something larger might simply fail.

As he explained to Governor Josiah Martin of North Carolina, who had sent an urgent request for munitions, "This province has sometimes been, and now is, in the newfangled legislature termed a provincial congress, who seem to have taken the government into their hands[;] what they intend to do I can't pretend to say, but they are certainly much puzzled how to act. Fear in some and want of inclination in others will be a great bar to their coming to extremities, tho' their leaders use every measure to bring them into the field."

26

Fateful Orders

Early on the morning of April 14, 1775, Lord Dartmouth's long-awaited orders arrived in Boston aboard the 20-gun sloop of war HMS *Nautilus*. Her passage from Plymouth, England, had taken only thirty-three days.

As Captain John Collins eased her alongside Long Wharf, twenty-six-year-old army captain Oliver DeLancey Jr. appeared on deck in full uniform and made his way down a hastily arranged gangplank with a waxed cotton packet tucked under his left arm. Inside was a secret dispatch from Lord Dartmouth containing the critical instructions that Gage had wanted for so long.

Dartmouth had sent two warships with identical documents. The other would arrive shortly. It was not uncommon in the age of sail to send two, and even three, ships with important messages in case one foundered. Duplicate orders had been entrusted to Captain John Linzee, skipper of the 20-gun sloop of war HMS *Falcon*. He had departed Torbay on March 13 and arrived in Boston on April 16.

It did not take Captain DeLancey long to reach headquarters at

Province House on Marlborough Street. General Gage received him cordially. DeLancey was a member of a powerful New York Tory family, and a cousin of Mrs. Gage. After delivering his dispatch, the young captain quickly took his leave.

One can only imagine Gage's thoughts as he looked at DeLancey's packet. Did it contain instructions that would finally allow him to bring ends and means more closely into alignment? The date on the orders, January 27, 1775, suggested that he would be disappointed. Dartmouth had obviously hung on to them for weeks before sending them, suggesting indecision, which could well mean a continued unwillingness to send him the troops he needed.

Just two weeks before, Gage had written to Barrington asking, once more, for something different. "[I]t appears to me," he said, "that you are now making your final efforts respecting America. If you yield, I conceive that you have not a spark of authority remaining over this country. If you determine on the contrary to support your measures, it should be done with as little delay as possible and as powerfully as you are able, for it is easier to crush evils in their infancy than when grown to maturity."

By delaying sending the new orders, Dartmouth had caused the loss of perhaps as much as a month and a half of valuable time for Gage to employ his troops, while it gave the rebels critical time to prepare. The American secretary had no idea his delay might complicate Gage's task.

Immediately after the general began reading, his worst fears were confirmed. Instead of giving him truly new orders, London was insisting that he carry out the old ones. Dartmouth informed him that there would be no substantial increase in the army. He did promise a small one, but he ordered Gage not to wait for it.

Dartmouth rubbed more salt in the wound by insisting, once again, that the rebels were merely "a tumultuous rabble, without any appearance of general concert, or without any head to advise, or leader to conduct that could render them formidable to a regular force led forth in support of law and government." This misperception was based on the powerful impression that the Powder Alarm had made in London. It did not reflect what had happened since.

During the succeeding weeks and months, the rebels had created a militia army filled with experienced officers and combat veterans. They were anything but a leaderless mob.

For months, Gage had been reporting that he was not facing a rabble. As far back as September 2, he had written to Dartmouth, "Tho' the people are not held in high estimation by the troops, yet they are numerous, worked up to a fury, and not a Boston rabble but the freeholders and farmers of the country. A check anywhere would be fatal, and the first stroke will decide a great deal. We should therefore be strong and proceed on a good foundation before anything decisive is tried, which it's to be presumed will prove successful."

On September 25, 1774, he had written to Barrington, "Affairs here are worse than even in the time of the Stamp Act, I don't mean in Boston, but throughout the country. . . . From appearances, no people are more determined for a civil war, the whole country from hence to New York armed, training and providing military stores. Every man [Loyalist] supposed averse to their measures [is] so molested and oppressed, that if he can get out of the country[side], which is not an easy matter, he takes shelter in Boston."

Later in his dispatch Dartmouth did admit that perhaps things had gotten out of hand in Massachusetts, and he insisted that "the honor and safety of the empire" required that "force shall be used to repel force." At the same time, he reiterated that only a tiny reinforcement was necessary. If more men were needed, Dartmouth suggested that Gage recruit Loyalists, or "friends of government." From the general's point of view, this was putting the horse before the cart. Months before, he had explained to Dartmouth that the Loyalists would not come out in support of the government until "a respectable army is seen in the field." Only then "would numbers declare themselves and join the king's troops." At the moment, they were thoroughly intimidated.

Whether Gage himself believed that Tories were out there in impressive numbers just waiting for him to command a larger army was questionable. The king thought that vigorous action on Gage's part with the troops he already had was the key to bringing them out.

Although a respectable force would not be forthcoming, Dartmouth, who knew nothing about military tactics, felt no inhibition about giving Gage instructions on how to use his troops. "It appears that your object has hitherto been to act upon the defensive," he observed, "and to avoid the hazard of weakening your force by sending out detachments of your troops upon any occasion whatsoever, and I should do injustice to your conduct, and to my own sentiments of your prudence and discretion; if I could suppose that such precaution was not necessary."

He ordered him to put that strategy aside and go on offense. To begin with, he was to return to Salem. "It is hoped however," Dartmouth said, "that this large reinforcement to your army will enable you to take a more active and determined part, and that you will have strength enough, not only to keep possession of Boston, but to give protection to Salem, and the friends of government in that place, and that you may without hazard of insult return thither if you think fit, and exercise your functions there, conformable to His Majesty's instructions."

A more ludicrous instruction, given the circumstances in Massachusetts, would have been hard to imagine. Gage must have been appalled reading it. He must also have wondered where the "large reinforcement" was.

Dartmouth then went on to tell Gage that since the rebels in Massachusetts Bay, Connecticut, and Rhode Island were determined to "cast off their dependence upon the government of this kingdom, the only consideration that remains is, in what manner the force under your command may be exerted to defend the constitution and to restore the vigor of government."

Leaving aside the facile, erroneous, and indeed dangerous assumption that the New England colonies wanted independence, Dartmouth's demand that Gage use the troops he had to conquer New England must have appeared bizarre. Dartmouth even hinted that Gage lacked courage, which, after decades of fearless service, must have struck him as outrageous.

More nonsense followed. Dartmouth told Gage again that in his opinion, "those who have taken up arms in Massachusetts Bay, have appeared to me as the acts of a rude rabble without plan, without concert, and without conduct, and therefore I think that a smaller force now, if put to the test, would be able to encounter them with greater probability of success than might be expected from a greater army." He argued that it would be better to strike now before the rebels had "form[ed] themselves upon a more regular plan, to acquire confidence from discipline, and to prepare those resources without which everything must be put to the issue of a single action."

Dartmouth's characterization of what Gage would face when he took the field was so divorced from reality that it must have been especially disheartening. The dispatch then went on to tell Gage "that the first and essential step to be taken towards re-establishing government would be to arrest and imprison the principal actors and abettors in the Provincial Congress (whose proceedings appear in every light to be acts of treason and rebellion)." Dartmouth appeared unacquainted with the fact that the military strength of the rebels lay in the thousands of committed militiamen out in the country. Even if Gage arrested Adams, Hancock, and a few others, the armed country folk would still be there. And they had plenty of able leaders unknown to London.

Dartmouth continued his instructions by insisting that if fighting did erupt, "it will surely be better that the conflict should be brought on, upon such ground [as now exists], than in a riper state of rebellion." Having said this, he characteristically relieved himself, the cabinet, and the king of all responsibility for a defeat resulting from his orders and placing all blame squarely on Gage. "It must be understood, however," he told him, "after all I have said, that this is a matter which must be left to your own discretion to be executed or not as you shall, upon weighing all circumstances, and the advantages and disadvantages, on one side, and the other, think most advisable."

Later in the dispatch he reiterated the same point. "In a situation where everything depends so much on the events of the day, and upon local circumstances, your conduct must be governed very much by your own judgement and discretion." He added, "With regard to the state of America in general, affairs there are now come to a crisis in which the government of this country must act with firmness and decision."

The small increase in troop strength that Dartmouth promised would come from Ireland—four regiments of foot, the Twenty-Second, Fortieth, Forty-Fourth, and Forty-Fifth, totaling fewer than two thousand men. At the moment, London wasn't worried about an Irish uprising.

Dartmouth had assured Gage that these troops would be forthcoming immediately, but that was not the case. They did not depart Ireland until March, and, even then, they were diverted to New York, where they arrived after the Battle of Lexington and Concord. Even if they had reached Boston in time, they would have only increased Gage's army to a little over five thousand.

27

Gage's Decision

WHAT was Gage to make of these new instructions? They were ordering him to attack the rebels, yet leaving it up to him to decide if the time was right, and then telling him that the time was indeed right. However ludicrous the orders were, he had to find some way to make it look as if he was carrying them out. The king was sending a clear message—take the field. Marking time while hoping that London would adjust its thinking to reality was no longer possible.

Gage had to make a move, even though he had no viable strategy. He already knew that three major generals were on their way. They would leave Portsmouth on April 20 aboard the 28-gun frigate *Cerberus*, under Captain James Chads. William Howe, the senior of the three, would be Gage's replacement, should he decide to resign, or if the king relieved him, or if he took the kind of action Dartmouth was ordering and suffered a defeat. The three generals could arrive as early as the end of May.

Gage had had plenty of time to consider what he might do under these circumstances. He might have decided that since there were no good alternatives, he would await the arrival of General Howe and, under one pretext or another, turn command over to him. A timely illness that forced him to return home might provide a way out. He must have considered this seriously, but in the end chose to take action, as the orders were demanding. He had already made up his mind that, under these circumstances, a lightning raid on Concord was the best alternative.

The potential size of the rebel militia army and the fact that he was getting almost no support from Loyalists made whatever Gage did risky, and the risks increased by the day. Yet if he coupled a successful strike on Concord with the seizure of Sam Adams and John Hancock, London might be appeased for a time. This would in no way solve Britain's American problem, and it could well exacerbate it, but that was not his concern right now; keeping his job was, and in order to do that, he set aside his qualms and moved ahead.

Even if in some sense a surprise raid on Concord appeared successful, it could only benefit the rebels. Destroying a few supplies, which could easily be replaced, was not going to undermine their morale. It would do just the opposite—infuriate the country people and swell their ranks. Seizing rebel leaders like Sam Adams and John Hancock, although at one point he had advised doing it as part of an overall strategy, would also be counterproductive. It would create two useful martyrs, giving the country people even more reason to fight.

On the other hand, a raid on Concord might succeed if organized properly, and it might mollify London for a time while he awaited the arrival of William Howe. Perhaps something might happen that would improve his situation, although in the middle of April it was hard to imagine what that might be.

General John R. Galvin, in his detailed study of the Battle of Lexington and Concord, thought Gage wanted to conduct "a kind of spoiling attack . . . to set back preparations for organizing and supplying the Provincial army and to put the rebels off balance. It was also calculated to be a show of force to intimidate the Provincial Congress and to attract support for the king."

If that's what Gage expected to achieve, his method of doing it appeared to be that of an inexperienced commander who had no real awareness of his own situation or of his enemy's, and Gage was certainly not that. Given all the information he had about the potential of the militias, and the timidity of the few Loyalists in Massachusetts, his raid on Concord would not intimidate the rebels or put them off balance. It was more likely to strengthen their resolve and add to their ranks. What he was actually doing was initiating an action that made no military sense but might appease his critics at home.

Even though his plan was modest, he was still taking a big gamble. If it was unsuccessful and the rebels overwhelmed his attackers, the rebellion would be strengthened substantially, and not just in New England but throughout the colonies. And he would pay a big political price in London. Calls for his head would mount, and they would be fatal to his career.

No matter what happened, a surprise raid on Concord could never accomplish the king's goal of forcing Massachusetts to submit to the Coercive Acts. Gage's decision was that of a desperate commander being forced to do something—almost anything—in circumstances that called for continuing to mark time while waiting for his successor to arrive.

———

At the time that Gage received Dartmouth's confused orders, he had eleven regiments of various sizes in Boston, totaling around 3,500. The exact number isn't known. British regiments were small and of varying size. They were not intended to be uniform. Sickness and desertion had diminished them.

Admiral Graves had a similar problem. His seamen, many of whom were impressed, deserted in droves when they got anywhere near land, particularly in America. He reported being down 160 sailors, with more likely to disappear as the good weather approached.

In spite of the difficulties, Gage believed that he had enough resources, with the cooperation of Admiral Graves, to make a successful run on Concord, and he began preparing immediately after receiving Dartmouth's dispatch.

———

The patriots, meanwhile, had been getting ready for Gage to make a move. The large arms cache in Concord appeared to Dr. Warren as a likely target. It was within easy reach of Boston. On April 8 he sent Paul Revere to make sure that the town was alert to the possibility of a surprise raid. Townspeople responded by moving some of the munitions to other towns and hiding the rest in Concord, much of it at the farm of Colonel James Barrett, the town's political and military leader.

Although Gage did not make a move right then, the town continued concealing the military stores, believing that the danger was real enough. The Provincial Congress, which was meeting in Concord, also took the warning seriously. It adjourned on April 15, and the members prudently left town.

The patriots were watching Gage's every move, expecting some sort of action, particularly after the sudden appearance of the *Falcon* and the *Nautilus*. Seeing these warships race into the harbor was a sure sign that something was up. A thrust into the countryside aimed at Concord was a likely possibility. It was not hard to figure out. Concord was a shire town of importance, the place where the Provincial Congress met. It was also a large arms depot, and it was close to Boston. No other town combined these characteristics.

Paul Revere described how the patriots in Boston gathered intelligence:

> In the fall of 1774 and winter of 1775, I was one of upwards of thirty, chiefly mechanics, who formed ourselves into a committee for the purpose of watching the movements of the British soldiers, and gathering every intelligence of the movements of the Tories. We held our meetings at the Green Dragon Tavern. We were so careful that our meetings should be kept secret that every time we met, every person swore upon the Bible that

they would not discover [reveal] any of our transactions but to Messrs. Hancock, Adams, Doctors Warren, Church, and one or two more.

. . . In the winter, towards the spring, we frequently took turns, two and two, to watch the soldiers by patrolling the streets all night. The Saturday night preceding the 19th of April, about twelve o'clock at night, the boats belonging to the transports were all launched and carried under the sterns of the men-of-war. (They had been previously hauled up and repaired). We likewise found that the grenadiers and light infantry were all taken off duty.

From these movements, we expected something serious was [to] be transacted. On Tuesday evening, the 18th, it was observed that a number of soldiers were marching towards the bottom of the Common.

The sudden movements caught the attention of the entire town, including the British troops. Lieutenant Frederick Mackenzie wrote in his diary, "It was pretty generally known, by means of the seamen who came on shore from the ships, about 2:00 o'clock [in the afternoon], that the boats were ordered to be in readiness."

28

Crossing the Rubicon

REVERE had it right: "something serious" was indeed about to be transacted. At 10:00 o'clock on the evening of April 18, two critical meetings took place in Boston. One was at Province House, where General Gage gave final orders to the two officers who would lead the secret raid on Concord, Lieutenant Colonel Francis Smith, of the Tenth Regiment of Foot, and Major John Pitcairn.

Lieutenant Colonel Smith was the senior regimental commander in Boston, having served in America for twelve years. A large, heavy-set man, he had a reputation for being brave and unflappable. Pitcairn was commander of the marine regiment, and the ranking major in Boston. He thought of rebel militiamen as peasants and cowards, and was looking forward to teaching them a lesson.

The other meeting was at Dr. Joseph Warren's stylish residence on Hanover Street, where Paul Revere received final instructions to alert the countryside of an imminent attack. He was well known as the patriots' most important messenger.

With Sam Adams and John Hancock hiding in Lexington, Dr. Warren was the patriot leader in Boston. General Gage had made no move to arrest him. Perhaps he thought that doing so would trigger a spontaneous uprising in the city, which would have ruined his plan to raid Concord.

Warren's information about Gage's plans had come from a number of sources, including Revere. There has been speculation over the years that perhaps Warren also received intelligence from Gage's wife, the former Margaret Kemble, who may have been a super spy opposed to British policy. This theory has never been proven, and is highly unlikely, for the simple reason that Warren didn't need her. Gage's plan for a surprise attack on Concord was already well known. And the Gages' marriage was a solid one. Nothing that happened later in their lives would indicate that there was any trouble between them of a kind that would lead her to destroy him.

Revere had been anticipating Gage's move for a long time, and he knew precisely what he was going to do when the moment arrived. He planned to cross the Charles River to Charlestown and race west to the country towns between there and Concord, alerting patriot militiamen along the way, as well as the cadre of alarm riders who would spread the news far and wide.

Neither Revere nor Warren knew for sure which of the two routes the redcoats would be taking out of Boston—across the Charles River (potentially the quickest) or overland via the neck and Roxbury. The boats Gage had been collecting could have been a feint.

To make certain that the countryside was alerted and the patriot mobilization begun, Warren had earlier dispatched an additional alarm rider, William Dawes Jr., directing him to cross the neck and take the road to Concord that went through Roxbury and Cambridge, before joining the Lexington Road. Like Revere, Dawes was instructed to also alert Adams and Hancock.

Dawes was perfect for the job. He was an accomplished actor and had no trouble fooling the guards at the neck. They did not appear particularly watchful. Requiring them to be especially vigilant that night was a small but important detail that Gage had overlooked. It would not be his last.

—

While Revere and Dawes were on their way, Gage was giving Smith written orders and supplementing them with verbal instructions. What he put in writing was of great interest; so, too, was what he left out. The written orders were quite detailed, suggesting that he had excellent spies.

Since Smith's mission was something Gage was doing to please London, rather than part of a well-thought-out strategy, he knew it was fraught with peril and might well miscarry, which led him to be careful about the guidelines he crafted for Smith. Like his superior, Lord Dartmouth, Gage wanted to deflect any blame for failure onto his subordinates. They were not ignorant of the game and would, in turn, report in a way that left them blameless.

The written orders read:

> Having received intelligence, that a quantity of ammunition, provisions, artillery, tents, and small arms, have been collected at Concord, for the avowed purpose of raising and supporting a rebellion against His Majesty, you will march with a corps of grenadiers and light infantry, put under your command, with the utmost expedition and secrecy to Concord, where you will seize and destroy all artillery, ammunition, provisions, tents, small arms, and all military stores whatever. But you will take care that the soldiers do not plunder the inhabitants, or hurt private property.
>
> You have a draught [map] of Concord, on which is marked the houses, barns, &c., which contain the above military stores. You will order a trunnion to be knocked off each gun, but if it is found impracticable on any, they must be spiked, and the carriages destroyed. The powder and flour must be shook out of the barrels into the river, the tents burned, pork or beef destroyed in the best way you can devise. And the men may put balls of lead in their pockets, throwing them by degrees into ponds, ditches &c., but no quantity together, so that they

may be recovered afterwards. If you meet with any brass artillery, you will order their muzzles to be beat in so as to render them useless.

You will observe by the draught that it will be necessary to secure the two bridges as soon as possible, you will therefore order a party of the best marchers, to go on with the expedition for [that] purpose.

A small party on horseback is ordered to stop all advice of your march getting to Concord before you, and a small number of artillery go out in chaises to wait for you on the road, with sledge hammers, spikes, &c.

You will open your business and return with the troops, as soon as possible, which I must leave to your own judgment and discretion.

It's likely that these instructions were supplemented with verbal orders to capture Adams and Hancock, and most importantly, what to do if Smith ran into resistance from the militias. Although Gage instructed Smith to protect private property, he did not specify in writing what to do if the rebels attacked him. It was an odd omission. Obviously, Smith would respond, but Gage wanted to make certain that under no circumstances was he to initiate any fighting. He was only to fire if fired upon.

It was strange to be giving an order not to begin any action to someone leading a column into hostile country to destroy weapons of war. Nonetheless, Gage wanted to be able to say that the rebels were the aggressors—if it came to that. He was hoping that it wouldn't. He was counting on the rebels not being able to get to the battlefield in sufficient numbers to give Smith trouble, either because they did not have the time to get organized, or because, when it came right down to it, they did not have the brass to go beyond words and actually risk their lives against the king's troops.

If Smith did run into trouble, Gage had Lord Percy's thousand-man brigade in reserve. All Smith had to do was dispatch a fast rider or two back to Boston, and Percy would come flying to the rescue. Gage was confident that Percy's men, combined with Smith's, would be enough to defeat anything the rebels could possibly mount against them.

The two keys to success for Smith were, as Gage explained to him, secrecy and speed, yet it was already clear to Gage that the rebels knew all about his plans. Telling Smith in his orders that secrecy was of great importance, instead of warning him that the rebels already knew of their plans, is hard to explain. It certainly was something Smith needed to know.

Gage's unwillingness to tell Smith was even more puzzling, since Lord Percy already knew. Stunned when he first found out, Percy had immediately informed Gage that the rebels were aware of his plan to raid Concord. Percy had discovered it after he visited Gage earlier on the eighteenth for a briefing on what part he was to play in the ensuing action.

Following his meeting with Gage, Percy had been walking through Boston Common and was taken aback when he overheard a group of men discussing the march to Concord. Not quite believing what he was hearing, he demanded to know what they were talking about. To his chagrin, he discovered that they knew the march was about to begin, if it hadn't already, and that the troops were going to Concord to confiscate war materials, particularly cannon.

He rushed back to Province House, where he told Gage that his secret was out. What Percy did not know was that Gage already knew from at least one other source. When Gage had given Percy his orders earlier, he had, for some unknown reason, not informed him that the rebels already knew of the plan.

Since Percy, one of only three brigade commanders in Boston, had an important part in Gage's strategy, it was more than a little strange that this vital information was kept from him. And if Gage didn't tell Percy, it's unlikely that he told Smith.

Gage's behavior was certainly baffling. Knowing that a raid on Concord was to take place that night would give the rebels more time to assemble and reach the battle zone, which could well be the difference between victory and defeat.

Since secrecy was no longer possible, speed became of greater importance. Gage emphasized it in his orders to Smith, but it was never attained, either. Many things would slow Smith down. He was never able to dash to Concord and back, as Gage had hoped. And much of the blame rested with Gage himself. His consistent tactical blundering became a heavy burden for both Smith and Percy.

Gage allotted Smith a force of around seven hundred. The exact number isn't known. It could have been a bit higher. Seventy-four were officers and the rest soldiers of various ranks. The column was calculated to be large enough in case Smith was challenged by rebel militia, but small enough for him to move quickly out to Concord and back before the rebels could organize any serious opposition. If Smith ran into trouble, Lord Percy was in reserve. Gage hoped it would not be necessary to send him to the rescue, but with secrecy being compromised and speed doubtful, his dependence on Percy could become total.

The one thing Gage did not want, above all else, was for Smith to be defeated. He could not imagine that Percy and Smith combined could possibly meet that fate. He was so convinced of it that he made no special plans in the event it happened; nor did he confer with the admiral about the possibility. Dealing with Graves was an ordeal he avoided whenever he could.

Once Gage made the decision to raid Concord, he made another that was also risky. He structured Smith's force in a novel way. The column would be made up entirely of the grenadier and light infantry companies from each of the twelve regiments in Boston. These companies were universally recognized as the best. Each regiment had ten companies. One company was composed entirely of grenadiers, the tallest, most powerful men in the regiment. Another was made up exclusively of light infantry, the fastest and most agile. They would be invaluable as flankers in a countryside honeycombed with forests and stonewalls.

Taking men from twelve different regiments meant that they had never worked together before, which could be a problem, since they would be engaged in an amphibious operation at night that they had never practiced, and in territory that was unknown to them. The men undoubtedly found the arrangement odd, as Smith and Pitcairn probably did, but having been cooped up in Boston all winter, they probably didn't care. They were happy just to be getting out of the city and doing something real against the rebels, whom they had come to despise. Nearly all of them, officers and men alike, had a personal score to settle with the provincials.

Gage never seemed to have considered abandoning the raid. He had a low regard for the capacity of the rebels to form an army on short notice, particularly when this would be their first attempt. Even though speed and secrecy had been compromised long before Smith's column left Boston, Gage remained steadfast, clinging to the hope that Smith would get to Concord and back before the militias got organized.

And Gage still had Percy. Having his brigade (three regiments) in reserve was reason enough to continue. Of course, if Percy was dispatched to save Smith, only 1,500 to 2,000 troops would be left in Boston to put down an uprising. This was doubtless on Gage's mind, but he had orders to make a move, and he was not going to let what he thought was only a slight possibility deter him.

29

Paul Revere

ALARM riders had been on Gage's mind for some time. If he could stop them, it would go a long way toward preventing the successful mobilization of the rebel army. He made what he thought was a workable strategy to capture the key riders, but, like his other plans, it was poorly thought out and badly executed.

When he informed Smith that "[a] small party on horseback is ordered to stop all advice of your march getting to Concord before you," he thought that this was all that was needed to contain the alarm riders. In fact, thirty towns surrounding Concord were alerted within a few hours, and all the others, throughout New England, a short time later.

The "small party on horseback," turned out to be ten poorly disguised but well-armed officers, under the command of Major Edward Mitchell, of the Fifth Regiment. With only a vague understanding of the overall mission, Mitchell departed Boston late on the afternoon of April 18, riding over the neck to Roxbury, where he left two men to watch that exit from the city. Later that night, one of the most important alarm riders, William Dawes Jr., rode right past Mitchell's officers, without them making a move to stop him. He alerted a large swath of the countryside before arriving in Lexington, thirty minutes after Paul Revere.

Meanwhile, Mitchell had carried on. After leaving the two officers at Roxbury, he rode to Cambridge, where he posted two more men on nearby Charlestown Common. From there they could observe riders coming over Charlestown Neck. Paul Revere was planning to take this route.

Mitchell then rode slowly with the rest of his party along the main road to Lexington, arousing suspicion in a countryside already nervous about what the redcoats intended to do when April and the good weather came. Plenty of people noticed the heavily armed riders. Among them was eighteen-year-old Solomon Brown, a minute man from Lexington. He saw Mitchell's party while he was returning home from a market in Boston.

Thinking something was up, he hurried to Lexington, where he arrived around sundown, and went immediately to Munroe Tavern, expecting to find William Munroe, first sergeant of the Lexington militia. Brown was in luck. Munroe was there and very interested in what he had to say. Munroe thought that what Brown saw was a British patrol heading toward Lexington. He assumed they were after Sam Adams and John Hancock.

Munroe wasted no time warning both men. They were staying, or rather hiding, nearby at the parsonage of Congregational minister Jonas Clarke, leader of the Sons of Liberty in Lexington. Munroe placed an eight-man guard outside the parsonage and remained there himself. At the same time, he sent a message to forty-five-year-old John Parker, elected captain of Lexington's militia, warning him of the suspicious activity. Parker took the warning seriously. He was two miles away at his farm, and came to the town center soon after Revere arrived around midnight. Parker made his way to Buckman's Tavern, where he found forty minute men. They had been gathering ever since Solomon Brown's alert.

Parker was a tall man with a commanding presence and extensive combat experience. He also had tuberculosis, which would kill him in seven months. He undoubtedly suspected that his illness was serious, and he probably intended to use the time that the Almighty had allotted him to serve his community, as the other militiamen were doing. And like his comrades, he certainly planned to pass on to his children and grandchildren the legacy of freedom he had enjoyed. The Lexington militia had no intention of allowing a tiny coterie of British aristocrats to take their farms and turn their progeny into peasants.

During the French and Indian War, while serving alongside the king's soldiers, Parker had seen for himself how his counterparts were treated by their aristocratic officers. That experience spoke to him more loudly than words. He passed this on to Lexington's younger militiamen. Older veterans were doing the same in every Massachusetts town.

Sergeant Munroe's suspicions were confirmed a little later when he noticed Mitchell and his party cantering through Lexington during the night. This made him even more apprehensive. He sent Solomon Brown and two others, Elijah Sanderson and Jonathan Loring, to trail the riders and find out what they were up to.

Meanwhile, farther along the road to Concord, Mitchell's party happened on Josiah Nelson, a Lincoln minute man, who thought they might be alarm riders. He soon found out differently when Mitchell, reacting reflexively, smacked Nelson on the head with the side of his sword and rode on, as Nelson stanched the blood running from his wound.

Mitchell's thoughtless action was exactly the kind of thing that Gage hoped to avoid. To make matters worse, Nelson's wife, Elizabeth, bandaged the wound enough to enable him to ride to Bedford and alert the minute men there. In the meantime, she told her neighbors what had happened, and they in turn aroused theirs. As word passed through Lincoln and Bedford, the first stirrings of the incipient patriot army began, thanks in part to Major Mitchell.

———

Long before Gage finished giving Lieutenant Colonel Smith his orders at Province House, Paul Revere had been on his way to alert the town militias and start the alarm riders fanning out across the countryside. After leaving Dr. Warren, he had moved with impressive speed, meeting first with his neighbor, twenty-three-year-old Robert Newman, telling him to hang two lanterns from the belfry of nearby Old North Church, the highest point in Boston—a little over 190 feet. With the help of vestrymen John Pulling and Thomas Barnard—also Revere's neighbors—Newman climbed the belfry steps of Christ Church and briefly displayed the lanterns.

They were signaling Charlestown's Committee of Safety that the British column was traveling west toward Lexington and Concord across the Charles River, instead of marching over Boston Neck to Roxbury, then to Brookline, and crossing the Great Bridge over the Charles River at Cambridge. The boats that were assembling off Boston Common were not a feint.

Boston at that time was almost an island. The only thing connecting it to the mainland was the neck, a half-mile-long, 120-foot-wide isthmus. On either side were mudflats. During the high tides that accompany a full moon, the mud and isthmus were submerged, making the city an actual island.

Newman's signal to the Charlestown patriots would not only alert them to the movement of Smith's column, it also told them that Revere was on his way. A fast horse would be waiting for him when he arrived at Charlestown's municipal dock.

Arrangements had been made for the signals and the horse on April 16, the previous Sunday. Revere had stopped in Charlestown on his way back from Lexington. He had gone there to warn Adams and Hancock about the likely movement of British troops on Concord, and the possibility that they would arrest them when they reached Lexington, if they went that way. They might also go by way of Weston. It would be faster, but also provide less protection from snipers than the Lexington Road.

The signaling to Charlestown's Committee of Safety would make it possible for another patriot to ride in Revere's place, in case he did not make it across the river. No other alarm rider would be as effective as Revere, because he was so well known, but he had to prepare for the possibility that he wouldn't make it to Charlestown.

In fact, there was an excellent chance that he would not. A serious obstacle was in his way: the 64-gun battleship HMS *Somerset*. Admiral Graves had recently stationed her in the ferry way between North Boston and Charlestown. She had been there for a few days, taking the place of the *Canceaux* and the *Lively*. Revere assumed that she was there to block communication between Boston and Charlestown, and prevent alarm riders from getting out of the city.

Actually, Graves had this powerful warship positioned there to intimidate Charlestown. He did not want the rebels installing artillery on Bunker Hill or Breed's Hill and threatening his fleet. On the night of April 18, however, Revere had to assume that the *Somerset* would be on high alert, watching for alarm riders, which is why his signaling system (the lanterns at Christ Church) was so important.

He planned to row across the mouth of the river to Charlestown in a small boat that he had hidden in a clump of bushes at the beach in North Boston. Two companions, Joshua Bentley and Thomas Richardson, would accompany him. After depositing him in Charlestown, Bentley and Richardson would row back to Boston immediately and report to Dr. Warren.

Their plan placed them in great peril. If lookouts on the *Somerset*, or her guard boats, which circled the giant ship every night to prevent desertion, caught sight of them, they could easily pick them up. If that happened, they would be unceremoniously thrown into a tiny brig that was nothing more than a wooden cage. Merciless interrogation would follow. And after that, they could well find themselves in chains in the hold of a ship bound for England, where they could be tried for treason and hanged. Alternatively, they could be impressed into the *Somerset*'s crew, where their chances of survival would be slim as well.

Regardless of the danger, Revere and his companions wrapped themselves in surtouts, hurried to the edge of the Charles River in North Boston, and dragged Revere's 20-foot skiff over the sand to the water's edge. He couldn't help but be worried. "It was then young flood," he recalled many years later, "the ship was winding [on single anchor] and the moon was rising." There was no way the *Somerset* could miss them.

The trio set aside their fears, and bravely rowed with muffled oars six hundred yards across the mouth of the river to the town dock in Charlestown. The *Somerset* paid no attention to them. She was not on high alert, as Revere had anticipated. Her skipper, Captain Edward Le Cras, had no orders to stop alarm riders. Even the regular ferry between Boston and Charlestown was allowed to operate. As improbable as it sounds, Revere could have gone to Charlestown on the regular boat.

When he arrived at the public dock, Charlestown's Committee of Safety was waiting. Several members had seen the signals from Old North Church, and they had a fast horse ready to be saddled. Revere remembered that "while the horse was being prepared, Richard Devens, Esq., who was one of the Committee of Safety, came to me and told me that he came down the road from Lexington after sundown that evening; that he met several British officers, all well mounted, and armed, going up the road."

Grateful for the warning, Revere mounted Deacon Larkin's horse, which was originally his father's, and reputed to be the fastest in the county. Revere was soon on his way to rouse the countryside, cantering across Charlestown Neck at around eleven o'clock.

Unaware of their exact location, he was heading straight for the two officers that Major Mitchell had stationed at Charlestown Common. As he got closer, his eyes went automatically to an iron cage he had seen many times before. The sight was familiar but horrifying. Hanging chained in the cage was the carcass of a slave named Mark. His cadaver had been strung from a gibbet twenty years ago, punishment for murdering his brutal master, a sea captain named John Codman. Mark's putrefied remains were on permanent display.

Codman had treated his slaves so badly, and for so long, that Mark and his wife, Phyliss, also Codman's slave, poisoned their tormentor in a fit of rage. After suffering under his tyranny for years, all they wanted was a better master. It was not to be. Mark's body became a symbol—an affirmation of slavery in Massachusetts.

Revere and Mitchell's two officers spotted each other almost at the same time. Remembering what Devens had told him, Revere turned right and raced for the Medford Road with the officers chasing after him. One of them tried to cut him off by getting ahead of him, while the other went straight for him. Larkin's horse was faster than theirs, and they were unacquainted with the area. Revere outran the one coming behind him and raced to outdistance the other. While he was galloping as fast as he dared, he looked over and saw that the second officer had driven his horse into a clay pond, coming to an abrupt halt and flying over the animal's head.

Revere continued to Medford, where he awakened the captain of the minute men, and then moved on, alerting almost every house until he reached Lexington at midnight. He knew the town well and went directly to the Hancock-Clarke parsonage, where he found Munroe and his guards. Munroe didn't know who Revere was and was suspicious, but soon Hancock poked his head out of a second-story window and reassured the vigilant sergeant.

As Revere walked through the front door, he found the entire house astir. Sam Adams came down from an upstairs bedroom to get the latest news, as did the Reverend Jonas Clarke. Clarke, a Harvard graduate, was a powerful advocate in the community, telling his congregation every Sunday to stand up for their rights, whatever the cost.

Nearly all the pastors in Massachusetts were Congregationalists and patriots. Their support was critical. Every week, in every town, pious sermons were preached on the righteousness of the fight to preserve freedom, especially religious freedom. The danger of having the Anglican Church established as the official church in Massachusetts was very real to the pastors and their parishioners.

When Revere first arrived in Lexington, he was hoping to find Dawes, but when he discovered that Billy wasn't there, he assumed that British officers on patrol had picked him up. Since Dawes had departed Boston long before Revere had, it was natural to suppose that he had been captured. Luckily, that wasn't the case. A half-hour later, Billy rode into town, much to Revere's relief. Dawes was tired but otherwise in good shape, ready to go on to Concord.

Meanwhile, the bell in the tower next to Lexington's meeting house had been ringing, and Captain Parker's men were turning out. One can only imagine what was going through their minds when they heard that bell.

As the militiamen were assembling, Captain Parker sent a scout down the Lexington Road to see where the British were and whatever details he might find. In less than an hour, the scout returned. No British were in sight. Parker sent his men home and told them he would summon them at the right time by the beat of the drum. Not all of them went home; some lived too far away. Many adjourned to Buckman's convivial tavern, where Parker would later make his headquarters.

No one seemed to have questioned why the Lexington men were gathering. The British column that was coming would be many times the size of Parker's company. Opposing them would be suicide. It was a time for cooler heads to prevail. Instead, John Hancock, the president of the Provincial Congress and the head of its Committee of Safety, was insisting on personally standing in line on Lexington Green with musket and sword, along with the rest of the militia.

Sam Adams was appalled. He told Hancock that the idea was romantic nonsense. Hancock's job was to travel to Philadelphia and the Continental Congress, which was scheduled to meet again on May 10 and would have important business to attend to.

Neither Hancock nor Adams told Parker to wait for the militias from surrounding towns to gather and then join them before confronting the British. Since they knew that Revere and the alarm riders were out, they could be certain that the militias in the other towns would be assembling. Hancock had worked hard to shape the alarm system that was now going into effect. Surely it was his responsibility at this crucial moment to advise Parker on how to proceed. Inexplicably, he did not.

The militias assembling in the other towns would soon outnumber Smith's column. Parker could easily have waited until they appeared, and then become part of the larger army that was building.

This is what Hancock should have advised. Instead, Parker was left on his own to figure out what to do. It was a grievous dereliction of duty on Hancock's part, one that would lead shortly to a great tragedy on Lexington Green.

———

Meanwhile, Revere and Dawes were racing toward Concord. Accompanying them now was twenty-three-year-old Dr. Samuel Prescott of Concord, who had been in Lexington that morning visiting Lydia Mulliken, a young woman he had a special interest in. The Mullikens' house was south of town, directly across the Lexington Road from Munroe Tavern.

When Prescott was riding through town on his way home, he had spotted Revere and Dawes on the green and, after a brief conversation, joined them with great enthusiasm. Revere described the young doctor as a high son of liberty. Indeed he was, and anxious to help rouse the countryside. The three rode off together, intending to alert Lincoln and Concord. When they were halfway to Concord (three miles), Prescott and Dawes stopped at Bull Tavern to warn the patrons, then went to a house nearby, where Lincoln minute man Nathaniel Baker was courting a young woman. Baker immediately went off to alert whoever had not gotten word yet.

Revere had continued on and suddenly ran into part of Mitchell's patrol—two well-armed officers. In moments, Prescott and Dawes were visible, and the two officers shouted for support. Four more officers quickly appeared with other prisoners. One of them was Solomon Brown; the others were Sanderson and Loring, the men Munroe had sent to trail Mitchell.

Prescott reacted instantly, turned his horse, and rode into a field, where he jumped a low stone wall and sped off into the backcountry, which he knew well but the British patrol did not. He escaped and hurried on to Concord, while Dawes turned his horse around and raced back toward Lexington. Revere was the only one captured.

The resourceful, quick-witted Revere soon had the attention of Major Mitchell. He told him that a large number of militiamen were gathering on Lexington Green and were about to waylay Smith's column; that at least five hundred had already assembled, and that more were on the way from surrounding towns.

He was convincing. Mitchell now felt that his first duty was to race back toward Boston and warn Smith. With a new sense of urgency, he led his party, including Revere, back toward Lexington, intending to continue south down the Lexington Road until he ran into Smith. When Mitchell's party was within sight of Lexington's meeting house, a few minute men for some unknown reason fired a volley, which unnerved Mitchell, making him more anxious than ever to get to Smith before it was too late.

Revere and the other prisoners were now an encumbrance. He had to get rid of them. After taking Revere's splendid horse and exchanging it for another, Mitchell released all his prisoners and galloped down the road to warn Smith. Not wanting the rebels on Lexington Green to capture him, he remained so far away that he never got close enough to determine just how many were there.

While Mitchell went off in search of Smith's column, Dr. Prescott alerted more Lincoln militiamen. One of them was the captain of the town's minute men, William Smith, Abigail Adams's brother. Smith gathered his men quickly, and they were soon on the march to Concord, where they would be the first outside company of fighters to reach the town. Their arrival was a big morale booster.

Immediately after being released, Revere raced back to the Hancock-Clarke parsonage and urged Hancock and Adams to leave, which they did, heading toward Woburn. Revere and John Lowell, Hancock's clerk, went with them. When they reached the house of Captain James Reed of the Woburn militia, Hancock suddenly remembered that he had left a trunk containing sensitive records of the Provincial Congress at Buckman's Tavern. Revere and Lowell immediately turned back to retrieve the trunk.

While they did, the mobilization of the patriot army was under way, as alarm riders spread the word to the thirty towns surrounding Concord. Militiamen hurried to village greens in preparation for a march to the battle zone. As they gathered, more alarm riders alerted towns farther away—within hours, all of New England would be aroused and assembling. It would take some of the more distant militias over a day to reach the battle area between Boston and Concord, but they were coming. And, as it turned out, their presence would be of enormous help to the patriots after the initial battle on the nineteenth.

30

The British March to
Concord Bogs Down

A T 8:00 on the evening of April 18, the regimental commanders from ten of Gage's eleven regiments arrived at Province
House to receive their final instructions. The general ordered
them to have their respective grenadiers and light infantry companies
on the beach at the foot of Boston Common by 10:00 p.m. with one
day's provisions in their haversacks and no knapsacks. Armament was
severely limited—only thirty-six rounds for each man and no supply
wagons on the other side of the Charles River.

The grenadiers and light infantry companies in all eleven regiments had been taken off duty and prepared to move three days
earlier, something the patriots could not help but notice. The men
were to march from their barracks on the eighteenth to the place of
rendezvous in small parties so as not to attract attention, and use the
countersign "patrole" if challenged.

They were told, generally, what they were about, but only when
it was time to march, although it's hard to imagine that they had no
idea before then. Gage was taking great pains to keep their move-

ments secret, which, in the close confines of Boston, was patently impossible. John Ballard, a stableman who worked at Province House, overheard someone remark, "Tomorrow, there will be hell to pay." Others heard similar suspicious remarks and passed them on.

Nonetheless, difficult or not, Gage was determined to go ahead with his plan. Sergeants awakened men quietly in the barracks and led them out the back door to prevent their comrades from knowing what was happening. They walked through the streets in silence. If a dog barked they bayoneted it. Considering that the secret had long since been out, these elaborate precautions appeared bizarre.

The grenadiers and light infantry of the Twenty-Third Regiment, the Royal Welch Fusiliers, were the first to arrive at the place of parade in the most remote part of the beach. Their encampment had been the one closest to it. They could see the small boats from the men-of-war and transports that the patriots had noticed being prepared earlier. When the officers, including the regimental adjutant Lieutenant Frederick Mackenzie, saw the number of boats, they must have been surprised, if not flabbergasted, and not a little chagrined that only twenty were there.

The high command had never calculated exactly how many would be needed. Graves could have easily provided double that number. The fact that he didn't, and that Gage did not insist on it, meant that the officers of the Twenty-Third were in for a long night. If no more boats were coming, at least two trips would be necessary to take Smith's column across the Charles River. The distance was about a mile and a quarter. The paucity of boats would at least double the amount of time necessary for the entire column to cross, making the chance of succeeding with the mission far more difficult, if not ruining it altogether.

The oversight might have been explained by the poor relations between Gage and Graves. But this was not a valid excuse. If Gage had made a determined effort to coordinate closely with Graves, he could have secured the right number of boats. There is no evidence that he made the attempt.

By order of the admiral, the boats in question had been assembled alongside the *Boyne*. Lieutenant John Bourmaster was in command of the operation. He had no idea what the proper number of boats should be; nor had he had any experience with an amphibious operation of this kind. Graves later wrote in his journal, "The boats of the squadron, by the desire of the general, were ordered to assemble alongside the *Boyne* by eight o'clock in the evening, and their officers were instructed to follow Lt. Bourmaster's direction."

It sounded as if the general had determined how many boats were needed. Graves, like Bourmaster, probably had no idea. Underestimating to the extent that Gage did was remarkable, considering how vital it was to get the number right.

Another important oversight was that no general officer was on the beach directing the embarkation. Neither Gage nor Major General Haldimand, the commander of troops, was on the scene, and the three brigade commanders were not, either. Men were coming from many different regiments, and the operation had the potential to be confused, with time lost sorting things out. In addition, reassembling the companies after landing on the other side of the river could cause further delay if they were not loaded into the boats properly.

Having the commander in chief personally supervising the operation would have been only prudent. Things would have been far less chaotic. One thing Gage had in his favor—and it was of great importance—was the weather. The river was calm and the moon bright.

Lieutenant Colonel Smith would now need at least two trips to get his men across the water and on the road to Concord. It's not clear when Gage found out about this ruinous delay, but he was ignoring it. Smith would also find, to his surprise, that neither Gage nor any of his officers had reconnoitered Phip's Farm (Lechmere Point), on the other side of the Charles River, where they were to land. It appeared to have been chosen because of its location on a map, and the fact that the owner was a strong Loyalist. As it turned out, the landing place was not suitable, and caused more delay.

Naval officers got the soldiers from the Twenty-Third Regiment, the first to arrive on the beach, into the available boats quickly, and towed them a short distance off shore. When the rest of the companies arrived, the naval officers put as many as would fit into the boats, while the others remained on shore. The navy planned to tow the boats over to the landing area at the farm on Phip's Point in East Cambridge.

Around this time, Smith and Pitcairn arrived from their meeting with Gage. The boatloads of men could not depart for the other side of the river until the two commanding officers were on the scene. Once they were, the boats were towed to the landing area at Phip's Farm. Major Pitcairn went with the first group, while Smith remained on the beach with the rest. It took an hour and a half to cross, land the troops, and return.

The entire operation, including the transport of all seven hundred men, might have consumed only an hour if everything had been planned properly. Instead, it was not completed until well after midnight—after Revere had already arrived in Lexington.

All of the *Somerset*'s boats were employed moving the troops, which meant that the guard boats, which normally were deployed around the great warship during the night to impede desertion, were absent this evening, allowing Revere and his two companions, in their passage from North Boston to Charlestown, to row in front of the battleship and not be picked up. Gage had given no thought to confining alarm riders within Boston. He was relying entirely on Major Mitchell to stop all of them.

Once the initial boatloads were under way, they crawled past the warship HMS *Nautilus*, which was stationed off Magazine Point, and then landed in the extensive marsh area at isolated Phip's Farm. The large house and several barns stood high on a remote hill away from the swampy area at the water's edge.

When the troops landed in what was known as Cambridge Marsh, they encountered more unforeseen problems. No progress was made until Smith got to the marsh in the second wave of boats. It was a chilly night, and the men in the first round of boats unexpectedly found themselves wet up to their knees as they slogged through the marsh to a dirt road.

Once the second round of troops were landed, men had to go back to the boats for supplies and the officers' horses. When the supplies finally arrived, most of them were thrown away, the men having brought some with them. After this, the column started their march by "wading through a very long ford up to their middies."

Smith did not actually get his men on the solid dirt road to Lexington until two o'clock in the morning. The speed that Gage was counting on, and which was never more than a slight possibility, was now impossible to attain. The only thing left for Smith to do was pray that the rebels would be delayed getting their militias to the battle zone, and that Percy would be ready the moment he needed him.

Frustration in the ranks was mounting, as Smith's soaking-wet men marched along what is now Somerville Avenue to Union Square in Somerville onto the Lexington Road (Massachusetts Avenue).

Smith grew increasingly concerned with the time. It was well after 2:00 when he entered Menotomy. As he approached this small crossroads town, he heard what he hoped he wouldn't—noise, and plenty of it. Bells were ringing from the belfry of the meeting house, and signal guns were going off, indicating that the town and countryside had been alerted. Indeed they had. Revere and Dawes had aroused them hours before.

Smith's column marched down the main street (Lexington Road) and approached the Black Horse Tavern, where prominent patriots Elbridge Gerry, Azor Orne, and Charles Lee had spent the night. The trio were shocked by what they saw coming down the road and managed to escape. The previous day, they had been meeting with their colleagues on the Committees of Supplies and Safety.

As Smith's column moved toward Lexington, his men captured every helpless civilian on the road. Two were from Woburn, heading to market in Boston, and two were Lexington farmers, also going to market. All four would be dead before the day ended. Smith was becoming alarmed by how late it was. He decided to send Pitcairn on ahead to Concord with six companies of light infantry to seize the two bridges that Gage had specified in his orders. Concord Loyalists Daniel Bliss and his brother-in-law Daniel Murray accompanied Pitcairn's detachment and acted as guides. Bliss, who had been a respected member of the Concord community, had allowed his political leanings to turn him against the people he had lived happily with for years. One can imagine how torn he must have been. Whatever his feelings, he would survive the upheavals of the day and make it back to Boston.

After Pitcairn departed, Smith grew more concerned about all the guns going off and the bells ringing. He thought that the whole countryside must be aroused against him, and with great reluctance he decided to send a fast courier back to Boston to tell Gage that reinforcements were necessary. With Pitcairn off, Smith could not retreat. His only option was to press on and hope that Percy would arrive in time. He had never anticipated sending for reinforcements so soon, but he did not want rebel militiamen to overwhelm him.

Gage had already been thinking about getting reinforcements prepared. Since it took Smith's column hours more than he had anticipated just to cross the Charles River, he had to adjust his strategy to some degree. At four o'clock in the morning, an hour before Smith's courier arrived, Gage ordered Percy to get ready.

When Smith's courier reached Province House at five o'clock, Gage immediately got the rest of his troops prepared for a possible uprising in the city. What he did not do was make sure that Percy had received his previous communication. It was one more critical detail that he did not personally attend to. He just assumed that Percy had received it. But he had not, which caused another inexcusable delay that Gage remained unaware of for some time.

The reason that Percy did not get Gage's original message was that it was not carried directly to him but to the quarters of his brigade major, Thomas Moncrieff, who was not there at the time to receive it. When Moncrieff returned, he failed to see the message, which a servant had placed on a tray.

While Gage's order lay unopened, the urgent message from Smith reached Province House at five o'clock. Percy was still asleep. An inquiry was then made and the error discovered. By six o'clock a portion of the brigade was on parade, but had to wait for the marines.

The marine units failed to appear, however. No message had been sent to them at their barracks. It had been sent to Major Pitcairn, who, of course, wasn't there.

Straightening all of this out meant that Percy's actual time of departure was delayed until nine o'clock, which nearly caused Smith's outright defeat and surrender.

31

A Massacre at Lexington

As Major Pitcairn and his six companies of light infantry made their way along the Lexington Road toward Concord, they, too, captured everyone they found. Two men, Ashel Porter and Josiah Richardson, were from Woburn; another, Simon Winship, was from Lexington. Pitcairn was two and a half miles from Lexington Green when his men seized Winship. Half a mile farther on, one of the redcoats took another man, Benjamin Wellington, who was a member of Parker's militia company, but he wasn't found out, and was released after surrendering his musket.

Pitcairn was unaware that another rider, Thaddeus Bowman, whom Parker had sent to scout, had caught a brief glimpse of the leading edge of the British detachment, wheeled his horse around, and raced back to town, galloping toward Buckman's Tavern, yelling for Parker. While Pitcairn continued marching, the Lexington militia began assembling on the green. Captain Parker had ordered his young drummer, William Diamond, to beat the call; the bell in the tower next to the meeting house clanged out its message, as did several alarm guns. Militiamen poured out of Buckman's with their weapons, while others left from their homes, rushing to the green. The British were now only minutes away.

Two strangers joined the Lexington men, Sylvanus Wood, from Woburn, and his friend Robert Douglas, of Maine. Douglas was visiting his father. Both had their weapons. Parker was glad to have them. Another member of the militia company on the green was a slave named Prince Estabrook, a familiar figure in town. A certain number of slaves would fight for the patriots during the Revolution, hoping to secure their freedom.

Estabrook succeeded. After being wounded in the fighting at Lexington, he recovered and went on to soldier throughout the War of Independence. At the end of it, he was given his freedom. Of course, liberty for a person of color always had to be qualified; in Massachusetts, as everywhere, prejudice was a persistent evil that would never go away, even for someone like Estabrook, who had fought so nobly for his country. He always had to be careful where he went. He could be reenslaved at any time—grabbed off the street, placed in chains, and sold.

Shortly, at least seventy-seven of Parker's militiamen were assembling on the village green with their muskets. Lexington men living farther away were hurrying to get there as fast as they could. In minutes the British would be visible, wearing splendid uniforms and carrying the latest muskets, with gleaming bayonets attached.

Parker must have been concerned, seeing his friends and relatives in the open with no protection. If the redcoats attacked, it would be disastrous. There was a chance they wouldn't. It was generally known that they were bound for Concord. Perhaps they would take a left at the fork in the road just in front of the meeting house and continue down what was known as the Concord Road and leave Lexington alone.

Actually, that's exactly what Gage wanted them to do. But Major Pitcairn, given all that he had told Lord Sandwich, was interested in administering a lesson to the farmers. Perhaps this was his chance. He did not know yet what awaited him on the green, but if circumstances allowed, it's unlikely that he would pass up the opportunity.

Parker, on the other hand, had no intention of initiating a fight. He had no orders from any higher officer to begin an action, and he certainly would not have done so, orders or no orders, when the redcoats outnumbered his men to the extent they did. Parker was an experienced, level-headed officer with a deep regard for his troops. Firing on the British would have been suicide, and he was not about to order anyone to do that. He later described what happened: "I . . . ordered our militia to meet on the common in said Lexington to consult what to do, and concluded not to be discovered, nor meddle or make with said regular troops (if they should approach) unless they should insult or molest us; and, upon their sudden approach, I immediately ordered our militia to disperse, and not to fire."

General William Heath, in his memoirs, written many years later, thought that assembling the militiamen and situating them close to the road was a bad idea. "Bravery, when called to action," he wrote, "should always take the strong ground on the basis of reason." A native of Roxbury, Heath was thirty-eight at the time of the battle and would play a leading role in directing the patriot town militias.

In retrospect it was easy to see that Parker never should have assembled his men until the British column had passed. He should have waited, then collected his militia and joined the patriot army, which was organizing faster than General Gage ever thought possible. But that was hindsight. Parker was responding reflexively to the approach of a hostile force heading for the heart of Lexington. He had a duty to summon the militia and consult them about what should be done. Of course, a discussion wasn't possible at this point. The situation was confused, and an unknown number of redcoats, in full battle gear, were bearing down. Their intentions were unknown, but they certainly looked threatening.

Had Sam Adams and John Hancock been there right at this moment, Parker undoubtedly would have sought their advice, but they were not. He was on his own and had to act fast without knowing anything about what was happening generally. Given that, his decision to disperse seemed eminently sensible.

———

Pitcairn, at the moment, was separated a good distance from Smith, and close enough to Lexington Green to hear the bell in the bell tower next to the meeting house clanging, and the alarm guns firing to summon Parker's company. He even heard William Diamond's drum.

None of this should have concerned him, except that he had been badly misinformed about what awaited him on Lexington Green. He had been told that the rebels were far more numerous than they actually were. Only a short time before, Major Mitchell and his party had appeared with the latest news from Lexington. Since Mitchell had just come from there, Pitcairn paid close attention to what he had to say. Other informants had told him what the situation was in the town, but Mitchell's assessment carried the most weight.

With no basis for saying so other than what Revere had told him, Mitchell claimed that at least five hundred militiamen were assembled on Lexington Green with their weapons, and that they looked hostile. A short time later, Pitcairn halted his companies and had them load their guns.

Lieutenants William Sutherland and Jesse Adair, who were part of a small advance party that included Daniel Bliss and Daniel Murray, also reported hostile townsmen ahead. They described how a militiaman had attempted to shoot them, but that his weapon had misfired. His hostile intent was real enough, they said.

Pitcairn felt the need to be ready. His six companies numbered at most 238 men. If the Lexington militia had five hundred fighters on the green, the prudent course would have been to wait for Smith to come up. Since this would be contrary to Pitcairn's orders, and he professed to have no respect for the farmers, he marched on. He was in full command now, able to deal with the rebels in the way he wanted. It was nearing five o'clock; visibility was improving as the sky began to illuminate between false dawn and sunrise.

———

While Parker's men were assembling and Pitcairn was close to a mile from the meeting house, Paul Revere and Hancock's aide, John Lowell, reached the green and raced to Buckman's Tavern to retrieve Hancock's trunk. In an upstairs room, Revere looked out the window and saw Pitcairn and his men marching down the Lexington Road. Fearing that a battle was about to break loose, he and Lowell hurried from the tavern with Hancock's papers, passing close enough to the militiamen to hear Parker say, "Let the troops pass by and don't molest them, without they begin first."

Revere pushed on but had not gone far when he turned around and saw what he called the "Ministerial Troops" at the side of the meeting house, where they had halted. The road they were now on was the Bedford Road, not the Concord Road.

Approximately where the famous Minuteman Statue now stands on Lexington Green, the Lexington Road divided. To the left, it became the Concord Road; to the right, the Bedford Road. Lexington Green was between the two roads. It was much larger than the present green. Parker's militiamen were assembled closer to the Bedford Road than the Concord Road.

There was no reason for the redcoats to be on the Bedford Road, except that Parker's company was closer to it. They could see clearly that the militia force was much smaller than theirs, which must have produced a surge of energy as they contemplated teaching the farmers a lesson with minimal risk to themselves.

Their positioning indicated that they meant to attack. There was no other reason for them to be situated where they were. They had nothing to fear from the pitifully small number of militiamen in front of them.

While Pitcairn's men were ready to attack, he was curiously absent. For no apparent reason, he had separated himself from his men and taken the Concord Road. With him were Major Mitchell and five others, including Sutherland. As a result, Pitcairn and his small entourage were momentarily out of sight of and out of contact with his troops. Their officers were with them, however, apparently in full control.

Marine lieutenant Jesse Adair was leading them. He knew that General Gage had given Pitcairn strict orders not to fire first—not to precipitate an engagement unless absolutely necessary. Nonetheless, this is exactly what Adair's detachment was poised to do. It's impossible to believe that neither Pitcairn nor Smith had passed General Gage's instructions on to their officers, particularly the command to act only on the defensive.

At this moment, however, with the odds so much in their favor, Adair and his fellow officers must have felt that they had Pitcairn's approval to ignore that order. In any event, whether they did or not, it would be fairly simple afterward to invent a rebel or two firing on them from behind the ubiquitous stone walls, or from Buckman's Tavern.

Suddenly Revere heard a gun fire. It sounded like an officer's pistol. "I heard the report," he wrote, "turned my head, and saw the smoke in front of the troops. They immediately gave a great shout, ran a few paces, and then the whole fired. I could first distinguish irregular firing, which I supposed was the advance guard, and then platoons."

The redcoats, with their officers in the lead, shouted wildly as they ran at the militiamen, who were scrambling to get out of harm's way. A few were able to fire at the attackers, but with no effect. Parker had already ordered his men to disperse. Seeing over two hundred hostile redcoats beside the meeting house about to attack gave him no other choice.

While the Lexington men were dispersing, Pitcairn's officers kept up a full-scale attack, their overwrought troops shooting and stabbing everyone they could. Militiaman Jonathan Harrington Jr., like the rest of his comrades, was running away when he was shot in the back. He instinctively staggered toward his home on the other side of Harrington Road, which abuts the green. His wife was watching from an upstairs window, horrified, praying that he'd get back alive. Racing downstairs, she opened the front door, only to have him expire in her arms, his warm blood seeping through the hole in his chest onto her dress.

Jonas Parker, the captain's older first cousin, was determined to stand his ground against this onslaught, and was shot before being bayoneted. While he bled to death, his son, Jonas Parker Jr., who was not far away, managed to escape unharmed.

William Tidd and sixty-two-year-old veteran Robert Munroe weren't so lucky. They were shot in the back as they hurried toward a stone wall, following the order to disperse. The veteran Tidd was second in command of the militia. Munroe was third. He died, but Tidd survived.

The British officers, to a man, later claimed that the militiamen fired first and that the infantrymen responded. They maintained, again in unison, that the regulars got overwrought and were soon out of control. Their story was that a shot or two from behind a long stone wall triggered the vicious assault. They did not initiate it, they claimed, or have any way to stop it.

What else were they going to say, when their orders prohibited precisely this kind of behavior? They were never going to admit having initiated and led what turned into a riot. Yet they were seen leading their men, and doing nothing to impede their wild assault.

In a sworn deposition given six days after the event, militiamen from Captain Parker's company told a completely different story. These were deeply religious men who would never lie under oath. They recalled the following: "about five [o'clock]; formed on the parade; we were faced toward the regulars then marching up to us, and some of our company were coming to the parade, with their backs toward the troops, and others on the parade began to disperse, when the regulars fired on the company, before a gun was fired by any of our company on them; they killed eight of our company, and wounded several, and continued their fire until we had all made our escape."

The Lexington men who told this story on April 25, 1775, were Nathaniel Parkhurst, Jonas Parker Jr., John Monroe Jr., John Winship, Solomon Pierce (who had been wounded), John Muzzy, Abner Mead, John Bridge Jr., Ebenezer Bowman, William Munroe 3rd, Micah Hagar, Samuel Sanderson, Samuel Hastings, and James Brown.

At the same time that the redcoats began their attack, Pitcairn had come around the side of the meeting house on the Concord Road and rushed toward the militiamen yelling for them to "lay down your arms, lay down your arms." He claimed later that he saw two hundred rebels. How he could do an accurate estimate in the midst of all the confusion was a mystery.

Pitcairn's shouted commands had no effect. His men, and their officers (on horseback), were running at the militiamen, while the patriots were hurrying to get away. In the midst of this uproar, hearing Pitcairn, much less doing what he said, was impossible, particularly when he was doing nothing to halt the deadly attack in progress.

By this time the redcoats had morphed into a mob, killing and wounding with abandon, chasing down every militiaman they could. Pitcairn did not stop the slaughter; neither did his officers. Pitcairn or Adair could have gotten a drummer to beat ceasefire, but they allowed the massacre to continue. Nothing was done to halt the bloodshed until Lieutenant Colonel Smith finally arrived with the rest of the column.

Realizing that this wild melee was precisely the kind of rampage that General Gage did not want, the colonel's first instinct was to stop it. The wanton killing had gone on for so long, however, that he had difficulty bringing it to a halt. The redcoats were heading, as fast as they could, for the nearby houses, like the Harringtons', seeking plunder. Anyone who stood in their way would have been killed.

Luckily, Lieutenant Sutherland soon came within shouting distance. Smith ordered him to find a drummer and have him beat ceasefire, which finally brought the massacre to an end. Pitcairn, had he wanted to, could have done the same thing.

Eight militiamen were dead and nine wounded—a horrendous, 22 percent casualty rate. No redcoats were killed or even seriously wounded. Nonetheless, Pitcairn and every one of his officers insisted that the outnumbered, retreating militiamen had fired first. Their reports differed markedly on where the initial shots came from, but they were all certain that their side did not fire first.

To make their claims credible, Pitcairn had to contend that his own men had suffered to some degree. If the militiamen, as he claimed, had fired first, if they were the aggressors, it would look strange if they were the only ones to suffer casualties. He maintained that one of his men was slightly wounded, which was true.

Since a scratch on a single soldier did not seem sufficient evidence, Pitcairn claimed that his own horse was grazed, not once but twice. This was the same horse he rode the rest of the day until it threw him and ran away.

Pitcairn was insisting that the rebel militiamen, who had grown up with weapons and used them all the time—many of them former soldiers with reputations as marksman—suddenly could not shoot straight. As it turned out, Pitcairn really didn't need an excuse. Even though an unprovoked massacre of retreating militiamen was the exact opposite of what General Gage had intended when he gave Smith and Pitcairn their orders at Province House, no one was held to account.

The reason was political. What transpired was exactly what Pitcairn had told Lord Sandwich he intended to do, knowing that the powerful first lord of the Admiralty would highly approve. Above all, it was precisely what the king wanted. Indeed, an action of this type had been specified in Lord Dartmouth's orders to Gage, the ones he had received only days before.

When His Majesty was informed about Lexington, he wrote a personal note to Lord Sandwich. "Your letter accompanying those received from Major Pitcairn is just arrived: that officer's conduct seems highly praiseworthy. I am of his opinion that once those rebels have felt a smart blow, they will submit; and no situation can ever change my fixed resolution to bring the colonies to a due subordination to the legislature of the mother country or to cast them off." The part about casting them off was something he liked to say but was not meant to be taken seriously, as he would demonstrate later beyond any doubt.

Even though the high command in London approved of the Lexington massacre, it did not have the result they expected, just as none of their decisions directed at forcing Massachusetts to submit did. Instead, the wanton killing energized the rebels and fueled the mobilization that was in progress.

———

There was a good chance that had the British held their fire, the Lexington militia would never have fired on them, and Smith would have been allowed to go on to Concord unmolested. Had Parker's men been allowed to disperse, they certainly would have done so, and left the more numerous redcoats alone. Had Pitcairn had control of his companies, or had he wanted to, he could have gone on to Concord without a fight.

But that was never possible. The political bile that had been spewing from London since the Tea Party got focused here, as out-of-control redcoats became the unwitting instruments of their masters' revenge against mere farmers for standing up to them. That, of course, is not what Major Pitcairn wrote when he made his report to General Gage on April 26. He claimed that his account was delayed because "my time at present is so much employed." He used the same excuse to explain the brevity of the account, which was the most important, since he was in command when the massacre occurred. He implied that "a more particular narrative" would be forthcoming when he had the time, but that was the last thing he wanted to do, and it was forgotten.

What General Gage was most concerned about later was learning who fired first. Even though His Majesty was not in the least concerned about it and in many ways would have been happy to hear that his men had initiated the fight, Gage was fixated on being told that his men did not fire the first shot. They, of course, picked up on the commander's attitude and told him what he wanted to hear. On this point, Pitcairn assured him that the rebels were indeed the aggressors and had fired first. Gage got identical assurances from every officer. They had obviously colluded.

Pitcairn wrote in his report that when his six companies of light infantry were about two miles from Lexington it was three o'clock in the morning. It was then that he had received the intelligence from Major Mitchell that five hundred rebels, and perhaps more, had assembled on the village green. Pitcairn told Gage that the rebels were "in arms . . . determined to oppose the King's troops, and retard them in their march." Based upon that information, he led his men toward Lexington Green. On the way, two of his officers, Adair and Sutherland, "informed me, that a man of the rebels advanced . . . [beyond] those that had assembled [on the Green], had presented a musquet and attempted to shoot them, but the piece flashed in the pan. On this I gave direction to the troops to move forward, but on no account to fire, or even attempt it without orders."

He claimed that when he first saw the assembled rebels, they numbered two hundred. He continued to advance.

> When I came within about one hundred yards of them, they began to file off towards some stone walls on our right flank—The light infantry observing this, ran after them—I instantly called to the soldiers not to fire, but to surround and disarm them, and after several repetitions of those positive orders to the men, not to fire &c, some of the rebels who had jumped over the wall fired four or five shots at the soldiers, which wounded a man of the tenth, and my horse was wounded in two places, from some quarter or other, and at the same time several shots were fired from a meeting house on our left—upon this, without any order or regularity, the light infantry began a scattered fire, and continued in that situation for some little time, contrary to the repeated orders both of me and the officers that were present.

This was the extent of Pitcairn's brief report, except for a final word. He told Gage: "It will be needless to mention what happened after, as I suppose Colonel Smith hath given a particular account of it." Gage couldn't help but wonder how Smith was going to give a fuller account when he hadn't been there for the most important part of the massacre.

It is sometimes pointed out in Pitcairn's favor that he could not have left a large group of hostile soldiers behind him at Lexington while he went on to Concord. Yet this is exactly what Smith did in the end. He did not capture and disarm Parker's company. After the massacre, the British column marched on to Concord and left the Lexington militia where they were, with their weapons.

And where they were was bitter and angry. Revenge was on their minds. Their captain would soon use this to bring them together again and become part of the incipient patriot army. The Lexington men would have their revenge later that day and play an important part in the patriots' ultimate victory.

———

The massacre never would have happened had Parker not assembled his men in the first place. The problem wasn't Parker's, however. The patriot army simply wasn't well enough organized to send him word not to confront the British column but to let it pass and only attack later, when the militia army had had time to mobilize and his men could become part of it.

The confusion occurred because there was no higher officer to give Parker direction. The Lexington militiamen found themselves part of an army just being formed, and as a result, their captain did not know enough about the broader picture to send them home. No one was to blame for their being in the exposed position they were. If there was to be any blame, John Hancock bore more responsibility than anyone else, but somehow, his role and culpability have been ignored.

Historians bent on assessing blame have looked elsewhere. Harold Murdock, after careful study, became convinced that Sam Adams was counseling Parker, and he concluded that "Parker acted under orders; that the post he took was not of his choosing. Samuel Adams, the great agitator, had been a guest of Parson Clark's for days, and he was the dynamo that kept the revolutionary machinery in motion . . . and now did he feel that the time had come to draw once more the British fire?"

Arthur B. Tourtellot came to the same conclusion, and John Hancock supported him. Hancock recalled that Adams was in favor of Parker's confronting the redcoats at Lexington. He remembered that while he and Adams were on the way to Woburn, Adams, knowing that an uneven clash of arms was likely to take place on Lexington Green, had declared, "O! What a glorious morning is this." Hancock maintained that they were still within earshot of the guns going off in Lexington.

The weather happened to be particularly fine that morning, but Hancock did not think Adams was commenting on the weather. What Hancock was suggesting was that Adams's need for martyrs was being satisfied by the killing and maiming of the innocent men of the Lexington militia. In fact, Hancock remembered Adams adding, "I mean, this day is a glorious day for America."

We have only Hancock's word for Adams's declarations, and the relationship between the two men was not always close or cordial. They were often political rivals. Adams was not Parker's superior in a military sense. He could not order him to do anything. In fact, Parker had no orders. What he did was regrettable, but that did not mean he was operating under Adams's direction.

If Adams actually said what Hancock claimed, he was probably referring to the many militiamen who passed them on their way to join their companies in Woburn center. Adams could not help being inspired by young patriots hurrying to give their all for a cause he had been promoting for a very long time.

Allen French, after years of study, concluded that Adams did not order Parker to sacrifice his men; nor did French believe that Parker would have done so had he received such a command.

What these accounts leave out is Hancock's responsibility. They imply that he was Adams's underling, which was far from the case. As leader of the Provincial Congress's Committee of Safety, he was the person who should have counseled Parker, not Adams.

32

The Road to Concord

THE scene of carnage on Lexington Green—the blood, the dead, the screaming wounded—sickened Reverend Jonas Clarke, as it did the rest of the town and would the Commonwealth and every other colony.

Lexington was a small community of 120 families, with a total population of around 900. The disaster would deeply affect every one of them. The suffering would be worse than anything they had experienced since the French and Indian War. Clarke's heart ached when he thought of the dead men's families and their permanent suffering. Defying the British colossus had consequences. The words in support of liberty that he had spoken so often, on and off the pulpit, suddenly took on a whole new meaning. He was further horrified when he witnessed the celebratory ritual the redcoats performed after the bloodletting. They were in formation on Lexington Green when they enacted a scene that turned his stomach. Smith had them under control again, and under his supervision, they fired a volley in commemoration of their victory.

Clarke considered the ceremony sacrilegious. The militiamen they had skewered were their own people. To make matters worse, the redcoats then shouted three huzzahs, and with fife and drum playing marched off toward Concord, six miles away, in a celebratory mood.

Not all of Smith's officers were eager to go on to Concord. Some urged him to return to Boston while he could. Given what had happened, the Concord militia, which was certain to be much larger than Lexington's, would have had time to assemble, as would other towns' militias, all of which could mean a brutal fight ahead—the opposite of the cakewalk in Lexington.

Smith's response was unequivocal. He had his orders, and he intended to carry them out. He had no appreciation of how dramatically the massacre would change the military equation. Accounts of the slaughter would grow in the telling and produce a reaction that galvanized the patriot army. Instead of the few dozen men Pitcairn ran over in Lexington, Smith could be facing thousands, well prepared and highly motivated.

Ignoring the warning from his officers, he pushed on. The massacre had inspired more hope than fear. If anything, he appeared rejuvenated. The easy victory meant that his mission in Concord would be speedily accomplished and he would be back in Boston before nightfall. He was in a much better frame of mind than he had been in Menotomy, when he had sent for Percy. He may even have regretted calling for reinforcements. If the Lexington militia was any indication, he had nothing to fear from the farmers.

Not long after the British column disappeared down the road to Concord, Lexington patriots captured five British stragglers and took their weapons. These men were doubtless deserters who were waiting for their opportunity to disappear. Sylvanus Wood captured a sixth while he and his friend were trailing far behind Smith's column.

The handling of the prisoners was exemplary. They were welcomed as if they were potential converts, which most of them would become. This was in sharp contrast to the brutal treatment the British handed out to their prisoners during the long war that followed.

Thousands would die in captivity, many from starvation. Where all this hatred came from was hard to understand, but it was certainly there.

While Smith moved slowly toward Concord, the patriots were rapidly mobilizing under the loose direction of the Provincial Congress's Committee of Safety. Neither Smith nor Pitcairn appreciated the potential size of the rebel army. Middlesex County alone could field six thousand fighters. Unaware of this looming disaster, Smith continued on, passing as he went a thinly populated section of Lincoln. A few militiamen were visible in the hills. Some even fired at the column. Smith sent flankers out on both sides of the road, and the militiamen disappeared.

The people of Concord knew the redcoats were coming. Dr. Prescott had long since alerted them. After escaping from Major Mitchell midway between Lexington and Concord, he had raced over fields he knew well, and had come back out on the Concord Road at the house of Samuel Hartwell, a sergeant in the Lincoln minute man company. Hartwell wasn't home, but his wife, Mary, was. Prescott asked her to get word to her neighbors, which she did. One of them was William Smith. Prescott continued on to Concord, rousing everyone along the way. Soon Concord's meeting house bell was ringing and minute men were assembling. It was close to 1:30 a.m. Prescott did not stop there; he kept riding, alerting Acton and Stow. He also got his twenty-six-year-old brother, Abel Prescott Jr., to alert Sudbury and Framingham. When Abel returned to Concord around noon that day, a nervous British soldier shot and wounded him. He would die that summer from the injury.

Around 7:30 a.m., Smith's column reached Meriam's Corner, a mile and a quarter from Concord's town center. His arrival was expected; the people were ready for him. So was their gifted leader, sixty-five-year-old Colonel James Barrett, a veteran of the French and Indian War. Barrett had had lengthy combat experience at Oswego, New York, under William Shirley; at Ticonderoga, under James Abercrombie; and at Crown Point in 1758, with Amherst. The Provincial Congress appointed him colonel of the Middlesex County militia, and Concord made him head of its militia. He was the obvious choice; there were no other candidates with his experience and leadership ability.

Barrett had already sent Reuben Brown, a minute man and harness maker, to Lexington to find out what was happening. Barrett knew that the British column Prescott had warned the town about would be marching through Lexington. Brown returned sooner than Barrett expected with an alarming report. A battle was raging on Lexington Green between redcoats and Captain Parker's militia. Smoke obscured his view, but plenty of shots were being fired. Barrett wanted to know if there was real ball in those British muskets. Brown couldn't tell for sure, but he thought so.

Barrett had been expecting an attack on Concord for some time. Not only was it the shire town (capital) of Middlesex County, but the Provincial Congress met there, and a big arms cache, including cannon, had been hidden within its precincts. Paul Revere had warned the selectmen back on April 6 to expect the regulars to come calling sooner rather than later. Barrett had taken the warning seriously and redoubled his efforts to get the arms and military stores hidden or moved out of town. There was a lot to do, and he had been at it ever since.

The extent of the arms cache was impressive. There had been many suppliers. David Cheever of Charlestown, a member of the Provincial Congress's Committee of Supplies, was one of them. He had delivered 20,000 pounds of musket balls and cartridges, 50 reams of cartridge paper, 206 tents, 113 iron spades, fifty-one wood axes, 201 billhooks, 19 sets of harness, 24 boxes of candles, 14 chests of medicine, 27 hogsheads of wooden ware, 1 hogshead of matches, cords, iron cannon balls, 20 bushels of oatmeal, 5 iron worms for cannon, and rammers and other equipment.

Cheever was just one supplier. There were others in Boston, Salem, Marblehead, and Newburyport. The last items to be moved out of Concord were four brass cannon. They were taken to Groton on Tuesday the eighteenth.

While Barrett was racing to deal with the arms cache, he was wondering how much support he was actually going to get from the county's other towns when the time came. He was reassured when two companies of fighters from Lincoln marched into Concord early on April 19. Captain William Smith's minute man company was leading them. After Mary Hartwell had alerted him, Smith rushed to Lincoln center and assembled his minute men. He also warned Captain Samuel Farrar, leader of Lincoln's militia. Both marched their companies to Concord. When Smith saw Barrett, he confirmed that serious fighting was going on in Lexington.

Two companies of Bedford men soon appeared as well, reassuring Colonel Barrett even more. Josiah Nelson had alerted the town, showing his bandaged head as proof that the British meant business. Two alarm riders from Lexington had also visited Bedford. One of them, Benjamin Todd, would be back on Lexington Green later for the fight. Captain Jonathan Wilson gathered his company of minute men at Fitch's Tavern in Bedford center. At the same time, militia captain John Moore assembled his company, and they both set out for Concord, arriving just after the Lincoln men.

Nine militiamen from Groton arrived in Concord around this time. When the brass 6-pounders had appeared unexpectedly the day before, their curiosity had been aroused, and they marched off to join Concord's defense.

Colonel Barrett decided that the Concord militias, and others from nearby towns, would gather at 200-foot-high Punkatasset Hill, which overlooked the Concord River and North Bridge. They could defend themselves there against a British attack and wait until reinforcements from the surrounding towns gave them a big numerical advantage. The size of the oncoming British column was unknown, but Barrett was confident that the collective town militias would be far bigger. He also decided to remain on the defensive and not fire the first shot under any circumstances.

While he was organizing the town's defenses, he was also hiding the last of the remaining weapons cache at his farm. After making arrangements for the militias to assemble at Punkatasset Hill, he had rushed back home, where his coolheaded wife, Rebeckah, and her family were finishing the immense job of hiding the military stores. She and her children were doing such an excellent job, the colonel remained just a short time before returning to supervise the gathering militias.

By the time Smith's column reached Meriam's Corner, Barrett was prepared. Smith and his men were unaware of the danger. They had marched the five miles from Lexington in high spirits. They were now only a mile and a quarter from Concord's town center.

On the northerly side of the road a string of low hills about sixty feet high began. Colonel Barrett was there with some of Concord's militia to observe. Smith sent light infantry to scatter them and secure the hills.

When the infantrymen reached the summit, they saw militiamen in large numbers pulling back out of range. No shots were exchanged. Barrett was not interested in forcing an engagement at this point, although some in Concord wanted to, most notably the Reverend William Emerson. Barrett prevailed, however, and withdrew over North Bridge to the high ground at Punkatasset Hill, a mile to the west of the bridge. He was expecting huge reinforcements later in the day, and he intended to wait patiently for them. He was not going to make the same mistake that Captain Parker had made.

———

Once Colonel Smith's light infantrymen were deployed on the low ridge overlooking the road into the town center, he continued on with the main body of troops into the village. He was surprised to see retreating before him David Brown's minute man company, which was one of four companies in Concord. Two of them were minute men and two regular militia. Together they amounted to 250 fighters.

Brown had marched up from the town center, and when he saw Smith he calmly turned around and, with fifes and drums sounding, retraced his steps back to the village, announcing to Smith and his warriors that Concord and Middlesex County were ready for them. What Smith and Pitcairn made of this display isn't known, but it should have put them on notice that they were not going to have an easy time of it in Concord.

While Smith led his column into the village, Concord's fighters remained on Punkatasset Hill, waiting patiently for the reinforcements they were counting on. It was now after eight o'clock. Smith didn't know it, but his period of grace was fast running out.

Unaware of the huge number of militiamen converging on Concord, the British began destroying the limited amount of military stores left in the town. The urgent need for speed did not occur to Smith. In fact, he appeared to be taking his time. With Lord Percy about to arrive, there seemed to be nothing to worry about. Smith did not want to push his men too hard; it had already been a long day.

The work in town for the soldiers was relatively easy, seeking out and destroying what military stores the patriots had not already spirited away. Additional stores were hidden at Barrett's farm, however, which made Smith's task more difficult. Spies had warned Gage about the munitions stored there.

Smith sent a man he trusted, Captain Lawrence Parsons, of his own Tenth Regiment, with seven companies of light infantry to cross North Bridge, turn left, and proceed to Colonel Barrett's homestead, two miles from the west end of the bridge. Punkatasset Hill was to the right, so that Parsons would be moving away from the patriots gathering there, not toward them. Gage had supplied Smith with a detailed map, indicating that stores in quantity were hidden at Barrett's, although not precisely where.

Smith did not entrust Major Pitcairn with this important assignment. He kept him in the town center on a tight leash. He did not want the major's recklessness to result in another bungled assignment, as had happened at Lexington. Smith was making it clear that he was holding Pitcairn responsible for the massacre, no matter what was said to the contrary by either Pitcairn or the other officers.

North Bridge was a little less than a mile from the town center. When Parsons got there, he left Captain Walter Sloane Laurie, of the Forty-Third Regiment, with one company to guard the east end, the one closest to town, and then marched five companies across the bridge. He left two of the five on nearby hills to guard that end of the bridge and his path back from Barrett's home. He then took three companies to Barrett's. Ensign Henry De Berniere went with him as a guide. A seventh company was to follow a bit later with engineer's tools.

Captain Laurie positioned his company so that he could keep an eye on the rebels assembling across the river. Although Parsons had not placed him in charge of the two companies guarding the other side of the bridge, he expected them to cooperate. The three companies were close enough to act together in case of an attack from the militiamen on Punkatasset Hill.

At the same time that Smith was securing North Bridge and sending Parsons to search Barrett's farm, he ordered Captain Mundy Pole, of the Tenth Regiment, to guard South Bridge. The two bridges were the only ones over the Concord River. Smith's task was made easier by the departure of every Concord resident who could get out of town. Few people were left. Anyone who could leave did so. Of course, some were left, and Smith's intention was to treat them as General Gage wanted—respectfully.

As Smith's men carried out their orders to destroy all the military supplies in and around the town center, Colonel Barrett's force on the hill grew at a rapid pace. In addition to the men from Concord, Lincoln, and Bedford, companies were arriving from other towns. Some individuals were even coming on their own. Militiamen from Carlisle, which was then part of Concord, appeared; Lieutenant Colonel John Robinson's Westford men did as well. Captain Isaac Davis arrived with three companies from Acton. One of them was Davis's minute man company; the other two were regular militia under Captain Joseph Robbins. Colonel Francis Faulkner led another company of militia from Acton. Soon, in excess of four hundred militiamen had assembled on the hill, with plenty more coming. The three companies of British troops below had only one hundred between them.

Colonel Barrett's patience was being rewarded. He had returned to his farm to check on last-minute preparations for the arrival of Parsons. When he had seen the British companies marching toward North Bridge, he had raced to get ahead of them, reaching the farm well before they did. Once he and his family were prepared for Parsons's arrival, he sped back to his troops via a circular route.

———

While Colonel Barrett's force grew, the larger militia army was expanding rapidly throughout the Commonwealth. Since this was the first attempt by the Provincial Congress to bring the various town militias together into larger regiments, brigades, and even an army, there were plenty of problems. What was remarkable was how well they were functioning in spite of them.

The biggest problem was the lack of a command structure that could guide the whole. There was no general with a competent staff to supervise what had become a wide-ranging enterprise. The Provincial Congress had appointed six generals—William Heath, of Roxbury; Artemus Ward, of Sudbury, who was sick; Jedediah Preble, of Portland, Maine, who refused the honor; Seth Pomeroy, of Worcester, who was gathering men and heading toward Concord but was too far away to be of use on April 19; John Thomas, from Kingston, in Plymouth County, and John Whitcomb, also from Worcester—who would arrive, miraculously, at the end of the day. None of them were able to assert overall control at this point. General Heath, who had been alerted early in the morning, would play a significant role later in the battle. But he was never in overall command, directing with a competent staff.

The building blocks of the patriot army were the town militias. They were divided into minute men companies and regular militia companies, and they were doing exceptionally well under their elected officers. These officers, in turn, had voted for men like James Barrett to lead their regiments, which were groupings of companies from the towns. The regiments were organizing rapidly as well, and would perform on the battlefield that day under experienced men like Barrett. Beyond the regiments, however, the patriot army was not yet a functioning body.

On April 19, the fight against the British would be done by regiments and town militia companies, operating guerrilla-style, at times coordinating in regimental formations and at others acting largely on their own. The towns did an excellent job of getting trained companies with experienced leaders into the fight, and so did the regiments. Even without the guidance of a commander in chief, on April 19 the militia companies and regiments would perform splendidly. And beyond these, the larger army was coming into being hour by hour. The patriots were proving General Gage wrong by mobilizing fast, which was the one thing, above all else, that could be his undoing.

With only newly appointed generals, the patriots' highest-ranking officers on the ground leading the regiments were colonels like James Barrett. He was just starting his job, however. Nonetheless, the sheer number of town militias, even loosely coordinated, made them a potent force when Lieutenant Colonel Smith had fewer than eight hundred men and Lord Percy only a thousand.

In the end, an amazing thirty towns surrounding the battle area responded to the call of the alarm riders and sent men into combat. They were located in four counties: Essex, Middlesex, Suffolk, and Norfolk. Other militias and regiments from counties too far away to get to the battle zone on the nineteenth, like Worcester and Hampton, as well as those from Rhode Island, Connecticut, and New Hampshire, were marching as fast as they could. They would not reach the battle area until a day or two later. But they were on the way—over twenty thousand of them.

33

The Concord Fight

WHEN Smith first arrived in Concord village, the task before him seemed simple enough—destroy all the military supplies and weapons stored around the town. He had a detailed map showing where they were. Dr. Benjamin Church had personally given it to Gage. Although Smith did not know where the map had come from, he expected an easy time of it in Concord, including the possibility of getting in and out without firing a shot. He did not understand what little time he really had. Word of the Lexington massacre was spreading fast.

While Smith was destroying supplies around the village center, Colonel Barrett was back on the scene at Punkatasset Hill, confident that his family would hide the remaining military supplies. Some of the militiamen were for confronting the British at the bridge right then, but Barrett was determined to wait until more reinforcements arrived. He expected them soon. There was every reason to wait, and, of course, since he was in charge, that's what they did. It turned out to be another of his wise decisions. The number of militia companies that eventually appeared were everything the people of Concord could have wanted.

Meanwhile, Captain Laurie and his men were becoming increasingly nervous watching the ranks of the rebel army on the hill swelling. Laurie still had only a hundred men. Parsons had an additional 120 at Barrett's. Laurie and his men got even more concerned when the rebels moved from the hill down to Major John Buttrick's four-acre meadow, which was much closer to the bridge. Buttrick was second in command under Barrett. Buttrick's house was on a low hill above the meadow.

Laurie sent an urgent message to Smith asking for reinforcements right away. A quick answer came back, promising two companies of grenadiers—not nearly enough. Meanwhile, the British 4th and 3rd Companies of light infantry, which had been on the patriot side of North Bridge, were understandably getting more anxious at the approach of the huge rebel force, and they withdrew back over the bridge to Laurie's side. The patriots did not attack them but let them pass unmolested. This was Colonel Barrett's consistent policy. He was committed to remaining on the defensive and not firing first.

At just this moment, militiamen at Buttrick's meadow saw smoke rising from the village center. They were worried that the British were burning the town, which wasn't the case, but it seemed to be. Actually, grenadiers were setting small fires to various things they had come across, including wooden carriages for mounting cannon. As more smoke billowed, some angry Concord men asked Barrett if he was going to let the redcoats burn the town down.

Barrett had to decide if the patriots were going to cross the bridge and attack Laurie, as a prelude to possibly taking on Lieutenant Colonel Smith. Captain William Smith of Lincoln urged him to. Barrett agreed that they could not allow Smith to burn the town, and ordered Acton's Isaac Davis to clear the bridge of redcoats. Davis was eager for the assignment. Barrett told him and the others again that they were not to fire unless fired upon. Barrett did not want to go on the offensive at this point unless forced to. Although his army was growing, he assumed it was smaller than Smith's.

The sight of Isaac Davis and his men coming across the bridge rattled the outnumbered redcoats at the east end. One of them, Captain Charles Lumm, leaped on his horse and galloped back toward town to find out where the reinforcements were. Meanwhile, Captain Laurie ordered every man to back off the bridge. They managed to pull up a few planks as they retreated, but not enough to stop the patriots, who were coming on fast. Laurie and his men hastily formed a defense just off the bridge.

Even though Laurie's force was less than a quarter of the oncoming patriots, he decided to fight it out rather than retreat as fast as he could. It was an odd decision by a veteran officer. Since Smith had not arrived with reinforcements, there was every reason to withdraw, and none at all to remain at the bridge, initiating a fight with a vastly superior force. But that's what Laurie did.

After he had organized his fighters off the end of the bridge, the nervous redcoats inexplicably fired a volley. This came after they had fired three random shots. Luther Blanchard, a nineteen-year-old fifer from Acton, and Jonas Brown, of Concord, were wounded. Blanchard would die a few months later from his wound. The three British companies now fired volleys that killed Isaac Davis and Abner Hosmer, of Acton. Davis's blood splattered on young Thomas Thorp, who would survive that day and go on to fight in Washington's army during the entire War of Independence, never forgetting that warm blood.

Major Buttrick shouted to his soldiers to fire back. They had been drilled for so long on the need not to shoot first that when they were actually fired on they froze, until the major shocked them with his screams: "Fire! Fire!" They did, with good effect.

Laurie fled, his men behind him. So did Lieutenant Sutherland, who was wounded and had taken refuge behind the stone wall in front of the Reverend Emerson's house. Two of the men with him had been killed. The British ran for the town, their wounded hobbling after them as best they could. It wasn't a pretty sight.

They soon ran into Lieutenant Colonel Smith, who was finally coming to the rescue. Smith's grenadiers gave them cover, and they all returned to town. The patriots did not pursue. Some of them ran to higher ground, where they could observe the village center, and

saw a large contingent of redcoats, and also that they were not burning the town.

Casualties in the engagement were two patriots killed and four
wounded. Four British officers were also wounded. One of them
would die later. Three of their men were killed and five wounded. It
had been a brief fight but a bloody one.

Barrett decided to halt and wait for more patriot companies to
arrive before going after Smith. Barrett still did not know how large
Smith's force was; nor, of course, did he have any idea that Percy's
brigade was on the way. It was another wise decision by an experienced commander.

———

Smith did not know it yet, but the tide of battle had now turned
against him dramatically. Having entered the village so confi-
dently just a short time before, he could hardly have imagined that
his entire column would soon be in grave danger. He compounded
his problem by waiting in the village center for Percy. He waited
and waited, but no reinforcements came. And while he waited, the
patriots grew stronger.

Smith could not simply pick up and retreat. He had wounded and
dead to tend to. And his troops, after their early-morning activities,
needed some rest. He had Parsons and his men to consider. What of
them? How did they do at Barrett's, and how were they going to get
back? Smith was stuck in Concord.

As it turned out, Parsons was able to return to Smith's column
without difficulty, thanks to Barrett. Parsons had found very little at
the farm, due to the ingenuity of Rebeckah Barrett and her family.
On the way back, he saw dead redcoats near the east end of North
Bridge, where Laurie had made his brief stand. One of the dead had
had his head split open with a hatchet—the work of a frightened
youth.

No matter, a great deal of propaganda was later made of how the
rebels were "scalping" helpless redcoats, which wasn't true. In fact,
the patriots could have attacked Parsons as he returned to the main

body of Smith's army, but they did not, which was the only reason he got back at all. Barrett did not want a full-scale encounter right then. He still wanted a greater superiority.

———

At noon, Smith finally left Concord center and began the march back to Boston, expecting Percy to arrive at any moment. Light infantry flankers were out searching the ridge that overlooked the main road, but no rebels were sighted. A smaller number of light infantry were sweeping the fields on the opposite side of the road, but they found nothing, either. The infantrymen on the ridge kept pace with the column as it marched the mile and a quarter to Meriam's Corner.

It was a bleak procession. There were no fifes sounding or drums beating. The men were downcast and tired, and they had a long way to go—sixteen miles to Boston. The walking wounded stayed in the middle of the column, while the seriously hurt were on horseback or in a few chaises. The column reached Meriam's Corner without incident, the faces of the redcoats grim.

34

The Bloody Road Back
to Lexington

SMITH suspected that he was going to meet more serious opposition than he already had, but he was only five miles from Lexington, and Percy's brigade and fieldpieces were long overdue. Although Percy had sorely disappointed Smith, he continued expecting him momentarily. He took it for granted that if Percy appeared, all would be well. Smith could not imagine that colonial militiamen would dare attack Earl Percy's brigade.

Meriam's Corner was a crossroads, where the Lexington and Bedford roads met. A small stream known as Mill Brook ran just beyond where the roads came together. Meriam's sprawling, seventeenth-century farmhouse and barns sat on a hill overlooking the brook and the roads.

In order to stay on the Lexington Road, Smith had to cross a small bridge over the brook. Just beyond the bridge, hundreds of militiamen waited, concealed in ditches, behind boulders, stone walls, fences, bushes, and trees on both sides of the road. Their numbers now far exceeded the British column, and they were fresh, compared to Smith's weary troops. Colonel Barrett's remarkable patience was about to be rewarded.

The shooting began after the British flankers had come down from the ridge to join the main column and had squeezed over the narrow bridge with the rest of the troops. Upwards of fifteen hundred well-organized, well-supplied militiamen had converged on this part of the Lexington Road. Others were still coming. Those who had already arrived had concealed themselves. The patriots who had fought at North Bridge were among them. They had raced along the Great Meadow north of the low hills next to the highway, out of sight of Smith's flankers.

Once Smith's troops were across Mill Brook, they came to a halt. Scouts noticed militiamen on the high ground next to the Meriam farmhouse. A squad of grenadiers fired a volley to scare them off. That, in turn, triggered a massive reaction from the hidden patriots.

Twenty-two-year-old Ensign Jeremy Lister, of Smith's own Tenth Regiment, wrote, "Immediately as we [the light infantry] descended the hill into the [Lexington] road the rebels begun a brisk fire but at so great a distance it was without effect, but as they kept marching nearer when the grenadiers found them within shot they returned their fire. . . . It then became a general firing upon us from all quarters, from behind hedges and walls." Lister forgot that his infantrymen had crossed the bridge, and that the grenadiers had fired a volley before the general action commenced.

Patriots from Concord, Lincoln, Acton, Bedford, Billerica, Carlisle, Littleton, and Groton unloaded on the redcoats. So did men from Sudbury, the largest town in Middlesex County—six companies of them. The Sudbury minute men were under Captain John Nixon, a veteran of the French and Indian War who had fought at Fort Ticonderoga and in Canada with General Amherst. The Sudbury militia were led by Captain Aaron Haynes. Other fighters were from Framingham, Reading, Chelmsford, Woburn, and Westford.

Still more angry militiamen were coming. Collectively they would make the next five miles a living hell for Smith. Individual redcoats slipped away and quietly surrendered, but there were only two dozen of these. Not only did the militiamen outnumber Smith, but they knew the lay of the land, and where best to attack him. After being hit hard at Meriam's Corner, Smith stepped up his pace and got some relief. But the patriots kept harassing him from fields off the Lexington Road. Some of these militiamen were themselves attacked by Smith's flankers.

No matter what the difficulty, Smith had to keep his column on the road. If it dispersed into the countryside, he would lose all control, and his men, unfamiliar with the area, would soon be surrendering or dying. After hurrying along under fire for a mile beyond Meriam's Corner, Smith came to Hardy's Hill in Lincoln, where parts of two patriot regiments waited—eight companies of fresh militiamen. They were from East Sudbury (Wayland), under Captain Nathan Cudworth; West Sudbury, under Lieutenant Colonel Ezekiel Howe; and Framingham, under Lieutenant Colonel Thomas Nixon. They were waiting in the woods to batter Smith's men going up and going down the hill.

Once Smith reached the bottom, he had to cross a narrow bridge over Tanner's Brook. On the other side, the Lexington Road began to climb uphill again and make a sharp turn to the left, followed by another to the right that became known as Bloody Angle. Thick woods covered the area, providing excellent concealment. Patriots hit the struggling column hard. It was difficult for Smith's men to see where the fire was coming from. Captain Jonathan Wilson and his Bedford minute men were among the fighters. After delivering a blow at Tanner's Brook, Wilson had raced with his sharpshooters to the wooded area on the hill and waited. Three companies of Woburn militia were strategically placed there as well, under Captains Joshua Walker, Jonathan Fox, and Samuel Belknap. Major Loammi Baldwin, 30, was in overall command of the Woburn men. They also had raced from Tanner's Brook to get into position. Nathaniel Wyman, a minute man from Lexington, was there alone. He had come thinking this would be a good place to get some revenge, even if he had to pay for it with his life. Reading men, under Major John Brooks, 22, were also there.

De Berniere had warned Smith about this particular area, and the colonel was prepared, but it didn't matter. The patriots tore into his ranks. The fighting was fierce. Wilson and Wyman were both killed. Flankers accounted for most of the patriots' dead and wounded. The British column suffered far more. They struggled on, moving as fast as they could. Smith was now leaving his wounded and dead behind. Those who were too tired to keep up fell by the wayside. Smith was desperate. He still had flankers out, and they kept taking a toll of patriots, surprising them from behind, but the flankers suffered as well, as did the rear of Smith's column, where patriots who had fought at Meriam's Corner, Hardy's Hill, and other places along the road continued to hound the battered column.

Smith did not know that Captain John Parker and the Lexington militia were waiting for him, two and a half miles from their desecrated green. They would soon exact their revenge. Parker had recovered from the massacre and mustered his men, every one of them anxious to pay back the redcoats.

One hundred and twenty highly motivated Lexington fighters faced Smith when he crossed the Lincoln line into their town. Captain Samuel Thatcher's militiamen from Cambridge had joined them. Parker had carefully selected the location at a curve in the road between two farms. His men had an excellent view of the road in front of them.

John Muzzy owned one of the farms. He was a member of Parker's company, along with his two sons. A third son, the eldest, was named Isaac. He had been killed on Lexington Green. The other farm was owned by Samuel Hastings, who was one of Parker's militiamen. He was ready with his weapons.

When Smith's lead company came into view, Parker's men waited patiently for more of the half-mile-long column to appear, and then poured heavy volleys into their ranks, wounding Smith and knocking him off his horse but not killing him. Exhibiting great courage, Smith, with considerable help, got back on the horse and led his battered column around the hillock as best he could. But finding that he was still a prominent target, he dismounted and hobbled alongside his weary animal.

As more of the British column came up the road, Parker and his men had to withdraw, but they remained in the fight, joining militiamen from previous encounters who were coming along both the road and the fields. The Lexington men stayed within striking distance, killing when they had the opportunity.

Once Smith got his men beyond the two farmhouses, he began climbing Fiske Hill beyond the bloody hillock. More pain awaited. Parker's men were joined by others, and they kept after the ragged column. Lexington minute men, among them Nathan Munroe, fired on the redcoats as Smith worked laboriously over Fiske Hill and down its side.

The British had still not reached Lexington Green. Smith must have wondered if he ever would. He even had one more hill to negotiate. It was known as Concord Hill and was higher than Fiske. He had no choice but to move forward. His officers and men were running now, throwing off all discipline, every man for himself, continuing to abandon their wounded. Smith tried desperately to create some semblance of order among the devastated ranks but failed. He was now about a mile from Lexington Green and soon would be forced to surrender.

His troops could barely move forward, while the patriots were increasing in strength from fresh militias. At the same time, Smith was running out of ammunition. Lieutenant Barker wrote that the rebels "were so concealed there was hardly any seeing them." And he noted ruefully that they were always increasing in ranks "while ours was reducing by deaths, wounds, and fatigue, and we were totally surrounded with such incessant fire as it's impossible to conceive. Our ammunition was likewise near expended."

Major Pitcairn's horse was shot out from under him. He survived unscathed, wondering, no doubt, what he was going to report about what had happened if he ever got back, which at the moment did not look likely. Smith and his officers and men would not be able to trudge much farther before surrendering. It was either that or be killed by the still "incessant" patriot fire.

De Berniere described the horrific scene: "When we arrived within a mile of Lexington our ammunition began to fail and the light companies were so fatigued with flanking they were scarce able to act, and a great number of wounded scarce able to get forward, made a great confusion. Colonel Smith had received a wound through his leg, a number of officers were also wounded, so that we began to run rather than retreat in order—the whole behaved with amazing bravery, but little order; we attempted to stop the men and form them two deep, but to no purpose, the confusion increased rather than lessened."

By now Smith had given up on Percy. He was resigned to surrendering, and so were his officers and men. They were totally defeated, exhausted. No more huzzahs. They were eating those words. So was Pitcairn. The redcoats were so dazed with fear they were about to run right past Lexington Green.

Their remaining officers made one last effort to get them under control. Somehow, they got out in front of the nearly hysterical foot soldiers, and with bayonets pointed at them, got them to stop their retreat. De Berniere wrote, "At last . . . the officers got to the front and presented their bayonets, and told the men if they advanced they should die: Upon this they began to form under a very heavy fire."

This arrangement wasn't going to last. The officers were about to lose control again, and perhaps be killed by their own men, when suddenly, frenzied cheering rose from the ranks, announcing the arrival of Lord Percy. His two 6-pounders soon brought the fighting to a standstill. The firing ceased for a time. The transformation happened so fast that it appeared as if a benevolent deity had suddenly intervened.

35

Lord Percy to the Rescue

WHEN the wounded, exhausted Smith saw Percy, he knew his column was saved. It was still a long way to Boston, but Percy's fresh troops and their artillery gave him confidence. A huge feeling of relief spread through the ranks.

It had taken Percy since nine o'clock that morning to reach Lexington—five and a half hours. His brigade had marched over Boston Neck to Roxbury and Brookline to Great Bridge at Cambridge, where it was forced to stop. The patriots had torn up the planking. But they left the planks nearby, and the bridge was quickly repaired enough to allow the troops and artillery to get across, but not the supply wagons, which contained critical ammunition and food. Percy's men were not carrying their own food. They were depending on the wagons.

Once over the bridge, Percy marched passed Harvard College along what is now Massachusetts Avenue. With no opposition, he went through Cambridge quickly and pushed on three miles to Menotomy. He was having a hard time believing that Smith could have gotten into real trouble, but obviously he was having serious problems—otherwise he would never have sent for reinforcements.

As the battalion moved through Menotomy, Percy was assuming that he and Smith combined could easily deal with the rebels. The area he was passing through looked strange, however. The houses were closed up, as if they had been deserted. That might mean that the inhabitants had fled, along with the militia. But what it really meant was that the women and children had left. The men remained, preparing for the redcoats to return.

Lieutenant Frederick Mackenzie described the eerie feeling they had as they marched through the unnaturally silent town.

> We went out of Boston by the Neck and marched through Roxbury, Cambridge, and Menotomy toward Lexington. In all the places we marched through, and in the houses on the road, few or no people were to be seen; and the houses were in general shut up as if deserted, though we afterwards found these houses were full of men, and only forsaken by the women and children . . .
>
> When we arrived near Lexington, some persons who came from Concord informed us that the grenadiers and light infantry were at that place, and that some persons had been killed and wounded by them early in the morning at Lexington.

One of the people was Lieutenant Edward Thornton Gould, who appeared between one and two o'clock in the afternoon in a buggy with a foot damaged in the fighting at North Bridge in Concord. Somehow Gould had gotten himself out of Concord and even beyond Lexington without being captured. He told Percy that the rebels had attacked the grenadiers and light infantry around daybreak in Lexington. He also told him that Smith's column was back in Lexington attempting to retreat.

Gould's most useful information was that there were rebels in large numbers ahead, and that they did not hesitate to fire on the regulars. Percy wasn't expecting either the numbers or the courage. He had assumed that the farmers would be both disorganized and afraid. He found it difficult to accept that they were actually forming a serious resistance and were in a position to give Smith's column, and indeed his own brigade—artillery and all—real problems. He remained confident that his reinforcement would crush whatever opposition was still left.

A measure of how little Percy and his officers understood what they were up against was their letting Gould proceed back to Boston in his chaise, not realizing that he had no chance of getting there. After leaving Percy, Gould traveled on Massachusetts Avenue to Menotomy, where he was captured and made a prisoner.

Patriots had earlier captured Percy's supply wagons, when they tried to roll through Menotomy. The wagons had had to wait a considerable amount of time for repairs to be made on the Great Bridge before they could cross. Percy's troops would sorely miss the food they contained—even more than the ammunition.

At 2:15 p.m. Percy began hearing gunfire ahead, and it put him on guard. As he approached the summit of the ridge south of Lexington Green, the gunfire grew louder. Even now, he still had only a vague idea of the trouble Smith was in. At 2:30 Percy reached the top of the ridge, where he stopped to survey the scene below. He could scarcely believe his eyes. A ragged column of redcoats was in full retreat, with rebels swarming all around. He had to move fast to save Smith from total disaster. Acting instinctively, he hurriedly brought up his two 6-pound artillery pieces and put shots through the meeting house and Daniel Harrington's home. The rounds produced enough terror to bring a halt to the firing.

An unnatural silence replaced the cacophony of battle. Mackenzie remembered the scene: "As soon as the grenadiers and light infantry [Smith's column] perceived the 1st Brigade [Percy] drawn up for their support, they shouted repeatedly, and the firing ceased for a short time."

Smith and his exhausted, terrified men were deliriously happy. Lieutenant Barker wrote later: "We had been flattered ever since the morning with expectations of the brigade coming out, but at this time had given up all hopes of it, as it was so late. As soon as the rebels saw this reinforcement, and tasted the field pieces, they retired."

Taking advantage of the sudden lull, Smith's men rushed up the ridge into the welcoming arms of Percy's column, which had formed into a semi-horseshoe to receive them. "We formed on a rising ground and rested ourselves a little while," Barker wrote, "which was extremely necessary for our men who were almost exhausted with fatigue." It was obvious to everyone that Percy had saved Smith's column from destruction. Not a single man would have escaped death or capture. Lieutenant Barker wrote that if Percy had not arrived at precisely that moment, "we must soon have laid down our arms, or been picked off by the rebels at their pleasure."

Percy's semi-horseshoe arrangement allowed Smith's battered troops to pass through to nearby Munroe Tavern, where the wounded could be treated and the rest of his men could find some water and nap, although it would not be for long. Even though they were in desperate condition, Percy could not delay for any length of time before marching back to Boston. Night was coming on, and the rebels were increasing in strength, as well as resting themselves. He understood now that he had grossly miscalculated their strength, and he was quickly adjusting his thinking.

Although Smith's men needed far more time to recover, Percy began his retreat at 3:30. Some of the wounded would have to be abandoned. Fortunately for them, they would receive humane treatment. Before leaving, Percy had the Mulliken house burned to the ground, along with Mrs. Mulliken's shop. The pillaging of homes and burning them afterward was a regular British practice during the retreat, in spite of explicit orders to the contrary from Gage. Fortunately, Lydia Mulliken and her family were not harmed. They had already left.

Young Dr. Samuel Prescott, Lydia's intrepid alarm rider, wasn't there, either, but he continued the fight during the Revolution, becoming, oddly enough, a crew member on a privateer that was captured. He was shipped off, as so many American prisoners were, to the infamous maritime prison at Halifax, where he died. Even for someone with the constitution of Dr. Prescott, surviving the malice and brutality at Halifax proved impossible. Lydia waited a long time for him to return before marrying someone else.

—

Percy's sole objective now became simply getting back to Boston. Smith's mission was already a colossal failure, but if Percy's brigade was forced to surrender, which at the moment seemed a real possibility, the damage would be incalculable. It could well mean that Gage himself would be forced to surrender the army in Boston.

With Percy's brigade out of the city, Gage was vulnerable. An uprising by thousands of armed Bostonians, supported by even more militiamen from outside, could overwhelm him. The basic problem he had had from the beginning of a woefully inadequate army was still there and could be his undoing. If his situation did indeed become desperate, Admiral Graves might use his fleet to destroy the city and any other seacoast town he had a mind to. This would likely become the primary strategy, which, in turn, would ignite an extensive revolution involving all the colonies, as well as Britain's European enemies. To prevent this larger calamity, Percy had to reach Boston.

Fortunately for Gage, Lord Percy was the finest general Britain ever assigned to the American theater. If anyone could prevent this ill-conceived mission from evolving into a catastrophe it was him. Just getting back to Boston was going to be a monumental task, however. Percy's chances did not look good. His brigade now appeared very small in comparison to the hordes of militiamen pouring into the battle area. Smith's column could provide little help. Indeed, it had to be protected.

To make matters worse for the British, General Heath arrived on the scene at about the same time that Percy began his dash for Boston. Heath assumed responsibility for coordinating the various militias and regiments to the degree he could, moving around the battlefield, giving direction. He seemed to be everywhere at once, encouraging, making the patriot fighters feel part of a larger army that could defeat a formidable enemy.

Dr. Joseph Warren was on the battlefield with Heath, further strengthening the patriot army. The presence of both Warren and

Heath, exposing themselves right next to the militiamen, injected great confidence into the ranks. Both men had been at the meeting of the Committee of Safety on April 18 at the Black Horse Tavern in Menotomy with Azor Orne, Jeremiah Lee, and Elbridge Gerry. Heath and Warren remained working until very early in the morning, when Heath left to join his men in Watertown. He went by way of a crossing road to avoid Smith's column coming up the Lexington Road. Warren managed to avoid Smith as well and returned to Boston. Later that day Heath and Warren met near Watertown and rode to the battle zone, which was by then south of Lexington. They remained together for the rest of the day.

Just getting to the battlefield had been something of an adventure for Warren. He had crossed the Charles River that morning on the ferry, which, to his amazement, was still operating on its normal schedule. He traveled right past HMS *Somerset*, as Paul Revere and his companions had the night before. The great warship showed no interest whatever in the ferry. Captain, Edward Le Cras still had no orders from Admiral Graves concerning the ferry. Relations between the admiral and Gage were such that this obviously important matter continued to be overlooked. Allowing Dr. Warren to leave Boston and assume joint command of the rebel army was incomprehensible.

Gage's blundering had reached the point now where not only were the two columns he had sent out from Boston in danger but the army in the city was as well. This state of affairs would have astonished London. Gage had committed so many errors and overlooked so many essential details that one could only conclude that his heart wasn't in an enterprise that clueless superiors had forced him to undertake.

Percy thought he faced in excess of fifty rebel companies, with more appearing all the time. He didn't know the precise number, but he could see that the rebel army was already formidable enough to defeat him if he wasn't careful and luck wasn't with him.

36

A Masterful Retreat

WHEN Percy finally left Monroe Tavern at half past three and was on the road back to Menotomy, he traveled over a mile before the patriots renewed their attack. The heaviest fire, as he had anticipated, was directed at the rear of his column. He had assigned Mackenzie's Royal Welch Fusiliers the tough job of protecting that area. Pitcairn's marines supported them. The major, to his chagrin, had by now discovered the real potency of the rebels, but he was still in one piece, and bravely directing his men.

A vicious running battle developed that would continue until Percy reached Charlestown. Its ferocity surprised and stunned him, but he kept his cool and single-mindedly drove toward the safety of Bunker Hill, where the fleet could protect him. Above all, he wanted to avoid surrendering. If he could do that, he would consider it a victory.

Although it would have appeared inconceivable when Percy left Boston, he now had to prepare Gage for an attack on the city. If

Percy was forced to surrender, the rebel army would pose a real threat to Gage. Before leaving Munroe's Tavern, Percy reported his predicament to Gage and warned that Boston itself was in danger. Gage needed to be told right away that his initiative had turned into a disaster that could well get much worse. He was already aware of the possibility of an uprising in the city being supported by a victorious rebel army outside. This had always been his nightmare. What he needed to know now was that it was a real possibility within the next few hours.

Lieutenant Harry Rooke, Gage's aide-de-camp, would carry the message to Boston. He had been assigned to Percy so that the generals could communicate. Getting through the mass of patriot militiamen between Menotomy and the Charlestown ferry, however, would not be easy. Rooke left Munroe's before Smith and Percy got under way, galloping through the countryside, keeping off the main road, carrying his baleful news swiftly. He reached Charlestown around four o'clock. The rebels had not spotted him. Once in Charlestown, he took the ferry to Boston and delivered his message to Gage a little after five o'clock. The crestfallen general immediately placed his men on alert.

Meanwhile, Percy, after departing Munroe's, placed Smith and his shattered formation in the van. The colonel's painful leg wound forced him to ride in a chaise. Before leaving, a few of his men shot John Raymond, a cripple, and one of Munroe's neighbors who had been serving drinks, while the rum lasted, to Smith's troops. His reward was a musket ball in the chest. The old man's dead body slumped against the back door of the tavern.

Percy marched directly toward Menotomy, the peaceful town he had traveled through without incident just a short time before. The return trip would be different. The heaviest fighting of the day would occur here. Its viciousness would forever be etched in the mind of the thirty-three-year-old nobleman. Among the many things that surprised him were the mounted patriot soldiers who showed up, as well as a number of militiamen who arrived at the battle zone in wagons. Of course, most came on foot, but in numbers that amazed him, and with courage he had never anticipated but grew to respect. The foe he had had such contempt for when he first rode through Menotomy had turned into a worthy opponent.

The shooting and killing that had resumed a little over a mile from Munroe's grew steadily. Pierce's Hill (Arlington Heights) lay between Lexington and Menotomy. The column was soon approaching it. General Heath remembered that even then, "the fire was brisk on both sides." It was so heavy that Percy employed his artillery, but with little success. The blistering patriot attack tore into his column as it descended the hill to the base, an area known as the Foot of the Rocks. Ensign Lister remembered the heavy rebel fire: "I found the balls whistled so smartly about my ears I thought it more prudent to dismount, and as the balls came thicker from one side or the other, so I went from one side of the horse to the other for some time, when a horse was shot dead close beside me, that had a wounded man on his back and three hanging by his sides. They immediately begged the assistance of my horse, which I readily granted, and soon after left him solely to their care."

Menotomy's main street (Lexington Road) was lined mostly with houses. Enough patriot companies had converged on it to make it a major battleground. Over four thousand militiamen were engaged. Half were in Percy's rear and the other half on his flanks and in houses. Thirty-five companies from Roxbury, Dedham, Brookline, Medford, Watertown, Weston, Malden, Norfolk, Gardiner, Needham, Salem, Lynn, Beverly, and Danvers, as well as the men of Menotomy itself, joined the fight. And the patriots who had fought earlier in the day remained in the battle. Percy had less than half their number—sixteen to eighteen hundred.

He sent strong flanking parties out to the left and right of the town, while his main column drove down the middle of the main road. The fighting got much worse as they approached Menotomy center and its meeting house. General Heath described the fighting there as heavy. "In this battle," he recalled, "I was several times greatly exposed, in particular at the high grounds at the upper end of Menotomy and also on the plain below the meeting house; on the latter, Dr. Joseph Warren—afterward, Major General Warren—who kept constantly near me, and then but a few feet distant, a musket ball from the enemy came so near his head as to strike the pin out of the hair of his earlock."

The homes on both sides of the Lexington Road were of particular concern to Percy. They provided perfect cover for the rebels. He gave orders to secure each of them. Enraged redcoats visited every building, thinking nothing of killing anyone who surrendered. One of the bloodiest encounters was at the home of Jason Russell.

Russell was determined to stay and fight it out. After leading his wife and children away to a place of safety, he went back to defend the house. As luck would have it, eleven minute men from Beverly, who were being chased by a large number of redcoats up the main street, sought refuge in the house, where the redcoats attacked them. They stabbed to death three patriots near the front door. One of them was Russell, who had a bad foot. He fell right in his front doorway and was stabbed over and over again by crazed infantrymen when they stepped inside. The rest of the minute men had fled to the cellar. They killed two redcoats trying to get at them before the British gave up and left, taking what silverware they could grab on the way out. When Mrs. Russell returned, she found her husband and eleven militiamen dead.

Seventy-eight-year-old Samuel Whittemore, a grizzled veteran of the French and Indian War, was in his house near Alewife Brook (then the Menotomy River) when he heard Percy's column pass through town on its way to Lexington. He grabbed his musket and two pistols and walked up to Menotomy center and waited, expecting that at some point the redcoats would return. He stationed himself behind a stone wall near the meeting house. His patience was rewarded when Percy's van appeared, and he opened fire, killing three. Percy's flankers were on him quickly, stabbing him, watching the blood spurt from his chest and moving on, assuming the old man was dead. But he wasn't. Against all odds, Whittemore recovered. He did not die until he was ninety-five.

At Cooper Tavern, farther down the road, the redcoats burst in and killed two men, while Benjamin Cooper and his wife managed to reach the cellar and save themselves. The infantrymen remained upstairs, drinking everything in sight, forgetting the two owners below.

Percy's flankers, meanwhile, surprised and killed many unsuspecting rebels, shooting and stabbing them. Percy himself was seated on a splendid white horse in plain view. His bravery was commendable, and his luck extraordinary. How he and the horse survived was a miracle. The only thing he lost was a button from his uniform. A musket ball somehow knocked it away without injuring him. The horse was hit but carried on, while Percy remained unscathed.

De Berniere wrote that the rebels "kept a very heavy fire [from the houses], but our troops broke into them and killed vast numbers; the soldiers showed great bravery in this place, forcing homes from whence came a heavy fire, and killing great numbers of the rebels." He didn't mention the looting that the redcoats were doing, contrary to orders. The earlier looting by Smith's men on a small scale had escalated. Many, if not most, of Percy's men had theft as their primary objective. On balance, it was probably a help to the patriots, as they caught looters in the act and killed many of them. The robbers often stayed too long in homes, so absorbed with finding silver spoons they forgot where they were and were either captured or shot.

———

Percy developed genuine respect for the colonial fighters. "During the whole affair," he wrote later,

> the rebels attacked us in a very scattered and irregular manner, but with perseverance and resolution, nor did they ever dare to form into any regular body. . . .
>
> Whoever looks upon them as an irregular mob, will find himself much mistaken. They have men amongst them who know very well what they are about, having been employed as rangers against the Indians and Canadians, and this country being much covered with wood, and hilly, is very advantageous for their method of fighting.
>
> Nor are several of their men void of a spirit of enthusiasm, as

we experienced yesterday, for many of them concealed themselves in houses, and advanced within ten yards to fire at me
and other officers, though they were morally certain of being
put to death themselves in an instant.

You may depend upon it, that as the Rebels have now had
time to prepare, they are determined to go through with it, nor
will the insurrection here turn out so despicable as it is perhaps
imagined at home.

A mile and a quarter beyond Cooper Tavern was the Menotomy River. Percy drove toward it and crossed. He soon discovered
more patriots waiting. Some were gathered behind a hastily thrown
together defense made up of empty casks near the blacksmith shop
of Jacob Watson. Percy's flankers raced ahead of the main column
and surprised the patriot defenders, killing most of them, including
Major Isaac Gardiner, of Brookline; John Hicks, a participant in the
Tea Party; and Moses Richardson, a carpenter at Harvard College.

Percy's column was now in Cambridge, and he had an important
decision to make. Just ahead was a critical fork. The road to the right
led into the heart of the town; the road to the left ran through what
is now Somerville to Charlestown Neck and Bunker Hill. If Percy
went by way of Cambridge center, he would be going back the way
he had come—down what is now Massachusetts Avenue directly to
Harvard College, and continuing past it to the Charles River and the
Great Bridge he had crossed earlier on his way to rescue Smith.

If he chose to turn left, the distance to Charlestown Neck would
reduce his journey by five miles. On the other hand, a large body of
militiamen from Essex County, led by Timothy Pickering, was fast
approaching. Percy could be attacked by over three hundred fresh
militiamen, led by a competent officer. The redcoats would also have
to deal simultaneously with the growing force of militiamen attacking their flanks and rear.

If Percy turned right, however, he stood a good chance of being
defeated, and forced to surrender. He could expect that the planks
on the Great Bridge over the Charles River would have been taken
up, as they had been before, when he marched out of Boston to rein-

force Smith. And he could anticipate that the rebels would be there in force, just as they had been on March 30, when he led his men on a practice march from Boston along the Charles.

Although Percy didn't know it, General Heath was in charge at the Great Bridge, and he had indeed taken up the planks. He also had a large body of militia on the far side of the Charles ready to contest Percy's crossing. The British brigade could be trapped between the river and Heath's men on one side, and the over 3,500 militiamen continuing to press on his rear. In a short time his exhausted column would be forced to give up.

Had the army and navy been able to work together, Admiral Graves could have sent small warships up the Charles River to aid Percy. In fact, soon after Lieutenant Rooke had reached Boston earlier that day, Gage and Graves could have secured control of the Great Bridge. They would have driven Heath's men away quickly, as well as kept at bay the large rebel force pressing on Percy's rear. No such cooperation existed, however, and Heath remained in control of the vital bridge.

With night fast approaching, Percy decided to take the left fork and fight his way to Charlestown Neck. Once in Charlestown, the fleet would provide protection. The decision was really an easy one. He would still have to fight his way to Charlestown Neck, but it was his only viable option. He later explained in his report to Gage that he took the Charlestown road "lest the rebels should have taken up the bridge at Cambridge (which I find was actually the case) and also as the country was more open and the road shorter."

Going by way of Charlestown would not be easy, however. He might never make it to the neck and the protection of the fleet. He had to pass Prospect Hill next, and the patriots were waiting for him. General Heath had stationed a large contingent there. Percy had to make a turn to the right to get around the hill, and Heath had his men prepared. Percy used his cannon to disperse them, however, and pushed on through what is now Union Square in Somerville, only a mile from Charlestown Neck. Once through the square, he was forced to use his artillery again, which he did successfully.

He was not safe yet. The rebels were still in his rear, perhaps three thousand of them, held at bay by artillery and Pitcairn's marines. Mackenzie's exhausted men had been relieved from duty in the rear.

As Percy got closer to Charlestown Neck and safety, three hundred of Colonel Timothy Pickering's fresh Essex County militiamen were still approaching. Pickering could have had them on the scene much earlier had he wanted to. He had been alerted early in the morning and could have had his troops in the fight long before this, but he dragged his feet. He had no feel for the political situation and thought talking could resolve matters without bloodshed. He wanted a negotiation, having no idea how impossible that was at this point.

Actually, when Pickering arrived, he had fewer than three hundred troops. Some men had gone to fight much earlier. Newburyport, which was the major city in Essex County, had already sent 115 militiamen to fight, and they had given a good account of themselves. Newburyport's most important contribution had come before that day, however. It was from her seamen, bringing war supplies in clandestinely.

Pickering soon occupied nearby Winter Hill and sent word to Heath, seeking direction. Heath responded quickly, warning him not to attack Percy, whose column was still much too strong for the Essex men. Heath also thought that Pickering might be in danger from the *Somerset*'s guns and possibly other smaller warships. The naval guns had a long reach and could be devastating. Whether Percy would try to coordinate with Graves was uncertain, but Heath saw no reason to take the chance, particularly when Percy alone could handle Pickering. Years later, Heath maintained that Pickering had far more men than he actually had, and never contacted him—that he made the decision not to attack on his own. If that was the case, Pickering's decision was a wise one.

The way was now clear for Percy to pass over the neck and reach the safety of Bunker Hill, where he planned to set up a defense and rely on the fleet for protection. He would have HMS *Somerset*'s big guns covering his move across the causeway, preventing the rebels from pushing over the neck. His army could be relieved by other units from Boston and his weary men brought across the water to the city.

Complicating matters was a mass exodus of citizens from Charlestown. They caused a traffic jam on the neck as they struggled to get out of harm's way against a tide of redcoats coming in the opposite direction. Percy also had to worry about rebel snipers shooting from inside Charlestown's numerous buildings. He warned the selectmen that if they did, he would retaliate by burning down the town.

Gage and Graves were both alive to the danger, and also warned Charlestown's selectmen that they would burn down the town if any snipers fired from the protection of the buildings. The selectmen had been afraid right along that Admiral Graves was itching to use the *Somerset* to firebomb the town.

When Graves had received reports of the redcoats retreating to Charlestown, he had decided that he'd better get more involved in the battle. He finally ordered Captain Le Cras on the *Somerset* to stop "all communication between Boston and Charlestown." The politically savvy Le Cras made a note in his log of when exactly he received this important communication, so that he would not be blamed, when the inevitable recriminations started, for having allowed unimpeded passage of boats and patriots from Boston to Charlestown on the eighteenth and nineteenth of April. Graves then ordered all the marines on board his warships to be ready to land in Charlestown at a moment's warning. His order came in the afternoon, after Gage had received Lieutenant Rooke's startling report earlier in the day about the unexpected difficulties Percy was anticipating, after he saved what was left of Smith's column.

Lieutenant James Johnson led the marines into Charlestown to protect Percy's column when it arrived. Graves expected little from Johnson, however. He was relying on the *Somerset*'s guns to stop any rebel advance into the Charlestown peninsula. He wrote: "[I]t was the *Somerset* alone that preserved the detachment from ruin. The vicinity of that formidable ship to Charlestown so intimidated its inhabitants that they (tho' reluctantly) suffered the king's troops to come in and pass over to Boston, who would otherwise have been undoubtedly attacked, and in their defenseless conditions such a proceeding must have been fatal to all the land forces on that side, exhausted as they were with fatigue and without ammunition."

Graves continued with a comment on a nightmare scenario

that was on everyone's mind in the British camp. The result of the destruction of Percy's army, he wrote, "might have been that of the rest of the army in Boston, for had the Charlestown people massacred those poor harassed soldiers just returned from Lexington, there can be no doubt but they would have immediately crossed to Boston, where they were certain to find 19 of 20 willing and ready to assist them in finishing their work."

In view of this ultimate danger, Graves urged Gage to permit him to firebomb "Charlestown and Roxbury, and . . . seize the heights of Roxbury (Dorchester) and Bunker's Hill." He added that it was his opinion, which he expressed to Gage, that their strategy now should be "burning and laying waste the whole country."

Gage was not interested in the navy going about laying waste to every town within reach of its guns, but it was something the king had been suggesting for some time. In fact, when His Majesty found out what had happened at Lexington and Concord, this is exactly what he ordered done immediately. His order would take weeks to reach America, and by that time much had changed. Nonetheless, he remained frustrated that Graves was not using his warships to terrorize America's seaports. His Majesty was coming to the conclusion that Graves was as inactive a warrior as Gage.

———

When it became clear that Percy was going to reach the protection of Bunker Hill between seven and eight o'clock, Heath, who had by this time established a measure of control over the various militias, brought the patriot attack to a halt around Charlestown Common.

After Heath had already stopped the fighting on his side, General Gage sent Brigadier General Robert Pigot over to Charlestown with reinforcements for Percy and more ammunition. Graves then began evacuating Percy's men back to Boston. The toll of redcoats had been grim—73 killed, 174 wounded, and 26 missing. Many of the latter, if not most, were deserters. This was a horrendous casualty rate, when one considers that Smith's original column had between seven and eight hundred men. The patriots had 49 killed, 41 wounded, and 5 missing.

Lieutenant John Barker summed up the planning and execution of the expedition in his diary. It was a scathing criticism, which was deserved, but it contained some obvious errors, and he was very much mistaken in thinking that the expedition would have succeeded had it been done a bit differently.

"Thus ended this expedition," he wrote,

> which from beginning to end was as ill planned and ill executed as it was possible to be; had we not idled away three hours on Cambridge Marsh waiting for provisions that were not wanted, we should have had no interruption at Lexington, but by our stay the country people had got intelligence and time to assemble. We should have reached Concord soon after daybreak, before they could have heard of us, by which we should have destroyed more cannon and stores, which they had had time enough to convey away before our arrival; we might also have got easier back and not been so much harassed, as they would not have had time to assemble so many people; even the people of Salem and Marblehead above 20 miles off had intelligence and time enough to march and meet us on our return. . . .
>
> Thus for a few trifling stores the grenadiers and light infantry had a march of about 50 miles (going and returning) through an enemy's country, and in all human probability must every man have been cut off if the brigade had not fortunately come to their assistance.

37

The Siege of Boston: Part One

WHEN Percy's column reached Charlestown, Gage could breathe a sigh of relief, but only for a moment. He still faced an enormous challenge. The entire British expeditionary force in Boston was in danger, and this included the warships in the harbor. Massachusetts militiamen, whom London's anti-American enthusiasts held in such contempt, were now surrounding the city in large numbers, with more coming. Within days, there would be over sixteen thousand.

A rebel attack on the city could occur at any time, and given the state of his army, Gage would have a hard time defeating it. He had been reduced to around two thousand healthy fighters. If an armed uprising within Boston was coordinated with an amphibious attack from outside, his shrunken force could be decimated. A street-to-street fight could develop that the badly outnumbered redcoats would be unable to cope with. Anxiety at headquarters and in the ranks was at a high level.

The first thing Gage did for protection was a surprise to everyone. On April 20 he ferried all the troops in Charlestown over to Boston. After having built a strong defense at Bunker Hill on the nineteenth, the very next day he ordered it destroyed and every man on the Charlestown peninsula brought back to Boston. The sudden shift demonstrated how nervous he was. He could not afford another wrong move. He had gotten his strategy wrong on the eighteenth and the nineteenth; he had to get it right now. If he did not, he could imagine being forced to surrender, or, more likely, having to retreat to Castle William and the protection of the warships. Retreating to Halifax might be next, if he could manage it. Working with Graves on an undertaking of that magnitude would be a nightmare.

What Graves would do if there was a forced evacuation was anyone's guess. If he ultimately wound up using his warships against the city, a declaration of independence by the Continental Congress was certain, followed by a war that would inevitably draw in the French, and perhaps Spain as well. He had to move fast to get on top of the situation. The militias surrounding the city might not be a functioning army yet, but after what had happened on the nineteenth, he had to take them seriously and prepare for the worst.

While bringing the troops back from Bunker Hill, he was simultaneously strengthening every fortification in the city—on Fort Hill, Beacon Hill, and Boston Neck. Lieutenant Barker observed, "We have now almost finished a battery of ten 24-pounders at the blockhouse; it is fronting Dorchester Hill, where the general is afraid the rebels will erect batteries against us." Not only was Gage's army at risk, the warships in the harbor were as well. If London's hard-liners found it impossible to believe that Gage did not have sufficient troops to enforce the Coercive Acts, they could never imagine that he might not be able to secure Boston, even with the help of the Royal Navy. But that indeed was the case, and no one knew it better than the admiral in charge.

Although Graves had done nothing about it until now, he had been concerned about a small boat attack on his warships ever since he had arrived in Boston. He had written to Lord Sandwich more than once, explaining that whaleboats lay in abundance "in the different creeks round this harbor [and might] in a calm night . . . surprise one of the frigates of the squadron and carry her by suddenly pouring in great numbers of people."

Gage probably never thought about this possibility. There's no evidence that he did. But he was still worried about the numerous small boats lying in the extensive harbor. He could imagine them being employed for an amphibious attack on Boston. Using whaleboats against the great warships may have seemed implausible to him, but he could imagine them being used to ferry a patriot army. In fact, under certain conditions, a large-scale small boat attack on the fleet, combined with an amphibious assault on the city and an uprising within, could succeed.

Graves and Gage were fortunate that the patriots were not thinking in these aggressive terms. No thought was being given at patriot headquarters to preparing an amphibious attack on Gage. Nor did the patriots ever dream that they could capture a British warship of any size, never mind the *Somerset*. But Graves certainly did, and worried about it. When he surveyed the long coastline around Boston and the outlying areas, he saw whaleboats and other small craft that could carry hundreds of armed men to overwhelm any of his warships at night in bad weather. He could even imagine, given the size of the rebel force now surrounding Boston, several ships being attacked the same night.

In spite of the concerns that he and Gage had about the small boats, it was not until seven days after the battle that either of them took action to remove the threat. On April 25 Gage wrote to Graves, informing him that the rebels were moving small boats from Charlestown to Cambridge, presumably to acquire the means of making an amphibious attack on Boston. "I have just received good intelligence that the rebels are carrying all the boats from Charlestown to Cambridge . . . ," he told Graves. "I should therefore wish that the *Somerset*'s boats were immediately employed to seize all boats that can be found, at or near Charlestown, and that they may be secured so that the rebels may not be able to get them. You see what I have often mentioned; that it is of the greatest consequence to seize all the boats you can lay your hands on everywhere."

One can only imagine how irritated Gage must have felt, having to point out to Graves that rebels were moving boats in large numbers right under his nose. If the admiral was unaware of this potentially lethal activity, what was he doing?

Graves was quick to reply that he had been collecting boats all along, which, of course, wasn't the case. In fact, he had been doing nothing. Not only was he not collecting rebel boats, he wasn't even keeping an eye on their activity. Preoccupation with his pocketbook, and his comfort, left him little time to worry about other matters.

Gage's prodding did move the admiral to order Captain John Collins of the sloop *Nautilus* to search Boston's extensive harbor and seize all the small boats he found and destroy them. Collins was told to use fire grapnels (grappling hooks used to tow away enemy fireships) from the *Somerset*, *Boyne*, and *Glasgow* to snare the boats and carry them away. Given the extent of Boston Harbor and the rivers and creeks branching out from it, assigning this monumental task to a single warship amounted to doing very little. Fortunately for Graves, that didn't matter, since the patriots had no plans to utilize small craft.

The growth of the rebel army surrounding the city added significantly to the problem of the small boats. Hundreds of the militiamen came from coastal towns and were familiar with boats and the sea. It would not take many of them on a dark night to swarm aboard a warship, sail it out of the harbor, and hide it. The *Somerset*, for instance, had a nominal crew of 560, not including deserters and the sick. The actual number was smaller. If she was not on full alert, only a small force would be needed to capture her.

Graves finally reacted to this growing menace by doubling the number of guard boats circling every warship at night, having every ship cleared for action during the night, and placing additional armed boats alongside ready to be manned. What he did not do was make any attempt to seize every small boat in the harbor, as Gage wanted him to do, probably judging that it just could not be done with the number of men and ships he had, particularly when he had to be constantly on the alert for an attack.

Gage brought the matter of the boats up again on April 25. Graves sent a quick reply, assuring him that the navy had been working on the small boat problem for four days now, trying to secure all of them in the harbor. Why Graves was just getting around to doing this wasn't explained, but Gage must have thought about it. It's doubtful that he had any confidence in Graves.

———

After Gage moved his troops back from Bunker Hill, the next thing he focused on was getting weapons out of the hands of the people in the city. Boston's rebels were not going to simply give up their guns and bayonets. There would have to be a grand bargain of some sort.

He knew that most families wanted to leave Boston for the safety of the countryside. They did not want to get caught in the middle of a bloody fight. Even getting enough to eat was now a problem. Patriots were also apprehensive about what a desperate general under intolerable pressure might do to them.

For all these reasons, people would be willing to give up their arms in return for simply being allowed to leave. The only reason Gage might want to hold them in the city would be to use them as hostages, and none of them wanted to be put in that position. So a grand bargain was possible—as unlikely as it might have sounded at first—whereby the citizenry gave up their weapons in return for being allowed to depart their beloved town, not knowing if they would ever be able to return, or what condition it would be in when they did.

Gage intended to collect as many weapons as possible. Since so many citizens were anxious to get away, there was every reason to think he would succeed. If he could confiscate a substantial number of muskets, powder, ball, pistols, and bayonets, he would be far more secure. The threat of attack from outside would still be there, but he would have a much better chance against it.

His task was complicated by a senseless refusal to communicate directly with Dr. Warren, who was president of a body (the Provincial Congress) that London considered illegal. Gage felt that he could not talk with him directly, even though speed was essential. Warren had just been voted president, so that he would have authority to make quick decisions. He was now both the political and military leader of the patriots in Massachusetts.

Warren thought it was important that he and Gage deal with each other directly, and even more important that the two of them develop some rapport, perhaps even to the point where they could trust each other. On April 20 he wrote a long letter to Gage, hoping to open communications. He emphasized how important it was for them to work together for the benefit of all concerned. "Be assured, sir," he told him, "as far as my influence goes, everything which can reasonably be required of us to do shall be done, and everything promised shall be religiously performed." Gage ignored Warren's overture and insisted on dealing only with John Scollay, Boston's legally elected first selectman, even though Scollay looked to Warren for leadership, and Warren, in turn, was keeping Sam Adams and John Hancock abreast of events and seeking their guidance. At the moment, Adams and Hancock were in Worcester waiting for the other members of the Massachusetts delegation to the Continental Congress. They remained there until April 24, when they departed for Philadelphia. The Second Continental Congress, as we have seen, was scheduled to meet on May 10.

Warren wanted to get as many people as possible out of Boston to places of safety, where they could find sustenance. The scarcity of food in the city was already a major problem. De Berniere wrote: "In the course of two days from a plentiful town, we were reduced to the disagreeable necessity of living on salt provisions and fairly blocked up in Boston."

With Gage wanting to get the weapons, and Warren wanting to evacuate the people, an improbable bargain was struck. Citizens would relinquish their weapons, and in return Gage would allow any who wanted to leave to do so. Gage continued to refuse to deal directly with Warren, which delayed matters for no reason. Instead, he called a meeting of the Boston selectmen at Province House, which they readily agreed to. He told John Scollay that he wanted him to urge the Boston town meeting to give up all the weapons in the city in return for individual passes to leave town.

James Bowdoin presided over the town meeting. He was visibly ill, still suffering from consumption, the same malady that had prevented him from attending the First Continental Congress. Guided by the selectmen, the town meeting accepted the deal.

Scollay also agreed, after another town meeting, not to attack Gage's troops under any circumstances. He did not want a battle that destroyed the city. When the final agreements between the city and Gage were formally presented to Warren on April 22, he quickly approved.

Having completed this grand bargain, Warren, with the support of the Provincial Congress, agreed to allow Loyalists outside the city to move into Boston, on condition that they surrender their weapons before entering.

The decision for these families was not any easier than it would be for the patriot families leaving the city. Coming to Boston would mean giving up all the Loyalists owned for an uncertain future. They were no doubt confident that His Majesty would prevail in the end and that their estates would be restored, but that might take some time. Living with this uncertainty, however, was preferable to worrying all the time that angry rebels who had suffered at the hands of the redcoats might take their property and put them out in the cold, or even kill them.

On April 24, five days after the great battle, the people of Boston surrendered an impressive array of weapons: almost 1,800 muskets, 600 pistols, nearly 1,000 bayonets, and 40 blunderbusses. They were not in pristine condition. The owners made sure the British couldn't use them. That didn't matter to Gage; getting them out of rebel hands was enough. Lieutenant Barker wrote in his diary, "I fancy this will quiet him [Gage] . . . for he seemed apprehensive that if the lines should be attacked, the townspeople would raise and assist; they would not give up their arms without the general promising that they should have leave to quit the town, as many as pleased."

Although greatly relieved, this was not the end of the matter for

Gage. The exodus from Boston was so extensive that he now had to worry about a city on a tiny island having only Loyalists and redcoats in it. He would be open to an artillery attack. To prevent that, he needed hostages. Once he had the weapons, he had a big incentive to renege on the agreement and retain a large number of rebels in the city.

38

The Siege: Part Two

WHILE Dr. Warren was dealing with Gage, he was also coordinating with the Continental Congress. Sam Adams, John Hancock, and the rest of their delegation now had the responsibility of gathering support for Massachusetts on a scale never imagined before. Congress was forced to assume the role of a new government, as if there had been a revolution. The victory on April 19 had changed everything. The patriots now had an army. Dr. Warren and the Massachusetts Provincial Congress were looking to the Continental Congress for direction and support. It was a daunting and novel responsibility, made even more so by the knowledge that Congress was dealing with a British government that still considered it an illegal body.

A parley at this moment was needed more than ever. It was not too late to stop fighting and start talking. Yet everyone in Philadelphia and Cambridge recognized how difficult it would be to arrange a negotiation at this point. They also had a high appreciation of how necessary it was. On April 27, Warren wrote to Arthur Lee in

London, "The next news from England must be conciliatory, or the connection between us ends, however fatal the consequences may be. Prudence may yet alleviate the misfortunes and calm the convulsions into which the empire is thrown by the madness of the present administration." Unfortunately, prudence was the last thing the Continental Congress could expect from London.

The political battles that Dr. Warren was conducting, as important and time-consuming as they were, did not occupy all, or even most, of his time. He was concentrating on organizing the patriot army. There wasn't one yet. It was a gigantic task, and he had the responsibility of bringing it into being as quickly as possible.

His first concern was retaliation. George III was not likely to take a defeat of this magnitude lying down. Warren rushed to get Massachusetts and New England prepared. On April 20 he wrote a circular letter to all the towns in Massachusetts. "Gentlemen—The barbarous murders committed on our innocent brethren, on Wednesday, the 19th instant, have made it absolutely necessary that we immediately raise an army to defend our wives and our children from the butchering hands of an inhuman soldiery, who, incensed at the obstacles they met with in their bloody progress, and enraged at being repulsed from the field of slaughter, will, without the least doubt, take the first opportunity in their power to ravage this devoted country with fire and sword."

Warren's extravagant language was not an exaggeration, as will be seen. When the king found out what had happened on April 19, he ordered a vicious retaliation, using the only instrument he had at the moment, the Royal Navy. It was fortunate for the patriots that His Majesty had a wildly exaggerated idea of what his tiny fleet in American waters could accomplish.

The people of New England's seacoast towns were understandably worried. Many fled from their homes and went inland to stay with relatives and friends. They were terrified at the thought of the big warships attacking their defenseless towns. Meanwhile, to Warren's great surprise, General Gage was turning out to be a desperate officer without integrity. Like most of the patriots, Warren had assumed that Gage could be trusted to carry out any bargain they made with him.

But that was turning out not to be the case. Following the agreement to exchange arms for exit passes, Warren discovered that Gage was quietly breaking his promise. At first, there had been a steady migration out of the city, but Gage soon found ways to drastically slow it down. Once he had the weapons, he felt that he had more flexibility. He wanted to keep a large number of rebels in the city as hostages.

He soon brought a complete halt to the exodus. Even the Scollays were not permitted to leave. It was a desperate move. Gage was sacrificing any relationship he had with both the selectmen and Dr. Warren, which, given how strong the patriot army was becoming, could turn out to be another major mistake that would come back to haunt him.

On May 14 Warren reported to Sam Adams in Philadelphia, "General Gage, I fear, has trepanned [deceived] the inhabitants of Boston. He has persuaded them to lay down their arms, promising to let them remove with their effects, but he suffers them to come out but very slowly, contriving every day new excuses for delay." Soon, the delay turned into a total prohibition.

One of the people Gage did not prevent from leaving the city was Henry Knox, who rode out of town with his wife, Lucy, in their carriage to Cambridge. Knox would become of signal importance to the patriot army. Washington would give him responsibility for bringing the artillery from Fort Ticonderoga that allowed the patriots to finally drive the British out of Boston the following March, using threats alone, without having to destroy the city.

Benjamin Edes also managed to escape from the city with his printing press. Of course, he did not attempt to get a pass from Gage. One dark night, he simply brought the press down to a secluded cove, placed it in a small boat, and rowed seven miles up the Charles River to Watertown, where he began publishing the *Boston Gazette* again. It was hard to read, however. He had left some of his best type behind. Nonetheless, he was an important figure in Watertown, which had become the de facto capital of Massachusetts, since the Provincial Congress was meeting there.

With the grand exchange of people brought to an end unilaterally, the lines between the two sides were now drawn tightly. The

British were stumbling into a major war. Warren had offered the olive branch, but he was ignored. More than sixteen thousand patriot militiamen were already surrounding Boston. There was no telling how many more were coming. French support for them was a certainty; so was help from the Dutch, and no doubt from Spain as well.

———

Meanwhile, Dr. Warren and his associates were busy building the army. It was obviously going to take some time. They had plenty of it. General Gage was not planning to attack them. By the same token, Warren had no intention of attacking Boston, either. He had his hands full organizing the militiamen into a real army. He had no time to plan an offensive that entailed movement over the water.

Admiral Graves and his superiors had the enormous advantage of the Royal Navy's reputation. The patriots never dreamed that Graves was vulnerable. Warren certainly didn't. He was still thinking entirely about defense, not offense. As improbable as it might sound after all that had happened, he kept hoping that London would at long last come to its senses and begin a dialogue.

Warren's headquarters were in Hastings House, adjacent to Harvard College. The facilities of the college were made available to help with housing and food. He was working closely with General Heath and the new commander in chief of the army, forty-seven-year-old Lieutenant General Artemus Ward, another veteran of the French and Indian War.

Ward had not participated in the fighting on the nineteenth because of a painful bladder stone, but the day after, he mounted his horse in Shrewsbury and rode thirty-six agonizing miles to Hastings House. Along the way, he passed a stream of militia companies marching toward Cambridge. They warmed his heart.

Dr. Warren, General Heath, Major General John Thomas, six colonels, and six lieutenant colonels greeted Ward when he arrived. The job ahead was daunting. The patriot militias that had chased Lord Percy back to Boston were in continual flux. Many of the farmers and artisans who answered the call on April 19 were going home to tend to the things they dropped when they left for the battlefield. A number of them wanted to search the combat areas with loved ones for missing comrades and relatives. The aftermath of all great battles involved this gruesome task.

Military leaders from the other New England colonies were assisting Warren. Their support was critical. Nearly every Connecticut town sent militia. Leading the Connecticut men were Brigadier General Joseph Spencer, who was in overall command, and Brigadier General Israel Putnam, a storied hero of the French and Indian War.

The Rhode Island Assembly sent fifteen hundred men under the command of Brigadier General Nathanael Greene. He brought with him several fieldpieces. New Hampshire's hero, John Stark, brought a large contingent as well. He had responded immediately to the alarm on the nineteenth, organizing a meeting of militias at Medford, New Hampshire, and marching to the battle zone. In Keene, Captain Isaac Wyman also answered the call with his men and was on the road to Concord quickly that day. Both Wyman and Stark were veterans of the French and Indian War. Stark had been second in command of Rogers' Rangers. A New Hampshire frontier fighter, Major Robert Rogers led a special force of backwoodsmen who became partial substitutes for the Indian allies Britain lost early in the war. The rangers performed effectively in the backcountry as scouts and raiders.

Newspapers in Massachusetts were calling the new patriot army "the Grand American Army." It was anything but. Although the militiamen had done spectacularly well on April 19, they had a long way to go before they were an army. To begin with, the companies and regiments came from different colonies and were responsible to their own provinces. Establishing unity of command was an immediate need, which Warren and his colleagues accomplished in the first couple of weeks. At that point, the army was becoming more cohesive, but divisiveness remained.

Most of the militiamen were from Massachusetts. The coming and going continued. Many of the men who had fought on the nineteenth had already gone home, and more had arrived to replace them. The newcomers were mostly from distant counties in Massachusetts, as well as from the Maine District of Massachusetts. Warren and Ward were doing their best to sign the men on for a specific period of time, and they were succeeding, but it was slow going.

While they were organizing the army, they were blocking the roads in and out of Boston, at Roxbury and Charlestown, keeping Gage penned within the city. In a remarkably short time, they were able to create a tight cordon around the city that extended from Dorchester in the west to Chelsea in the east. Nothing could get in or out of town without their approval. General Thomas, another veteran of the French and Indian War and a superb leader, was in command in the Roxbury area.

Since Ward and Warren could now cut off food and other supplies going into Boston by land, Gage became totally dependent on Graves for supplies. Endless bickering ensued, as the admiral, seeking to squeeze the maximum amount of profit out of the situation, made supplies scarce. Gage sent complaints to London, but little happened.

The king was now as unhappy with the admiral as he was with Gage. Not only was Graves not supplying Boston with food, but no seaports, large or small, had been firebombed. His Majesty began to wonder aloud if Graves was aware there was a war going on.

Since the army that Warren and Ward had already put together was far more powerful than the one Gage had, the only recourse the king had at the moment was to firebomb seaport towns and intimidate the rebels that way. Admiral Graves would have had no hesitation carrying out such a reckless plan, but the strategy had limits, which the king failed to recognize.

To begin with, Graves did not have that many warships, and he had more to think about than just Boston. The entire country was lining up solidly behind Massachusetts. In addition, if he attacked a town, it would take more than one warship, and consume a great deal of ammunition that was not easy to replace. More importantly, it would damage the warships. Since they would be firing for hours, just the recoiling of the giant cannon would tear at their insides. They would then have to be taken out of active service for repairs, and the only place to get that done now was at Halifax, which had limited facilities.

Boston, it seems, was turning more and more into a nightmare for Britain. She might have extricated herself from it rather easily, and at no expense, by accepting Dr. Warren's plea for conciliation. The patriots were more than ready for it, but His Majesty was not. War had been declared, and he intended to win.

39

Earth-Shattering News

WHILE coping with his other tasks, Dr. Warren was conscious of the need to get the patriot version of what had happened on April 19 to both London and the rest of the colonies as quickly as possible. Isaac Bissell and a string of post riders had already carried news of the massacre at Lexington to the other colonies. Joseph Palmer, a prominent member of the Committee of Safety, had dispatched Bissell immediately after the bloody encounter on Lexington Green.

Dr. Warren rushed a fuller account later. To make the patriot version of events credible, a hundred eyewitnesses, including British prisoners, were interviewed. Elbridge Gerry led a committee of nine that took the testimony. Local justices of the peace certified it. Once the evidence was collected, Warren sent it to the rest of the colonies. By May 11, a detailed account of the fighting had reached all the way to Savannah, where the weekly *Georgia Gazette* published the full story. By that time, newspapers in Connecticut, New York, Pennsylvania, Maryland, Virginia, and the Carolinas had already printed accounts. The *Virginia Gazette*'s depiction was particularly vivid.

Warren was even more anxious to get the full story to London. Richard Derby, a prominent Salem merchant and member of the Provincial Congress, offered his yacht-like schooner *Quero* to race across the Atlantic with the patriot account. His son John, an experienced sea captain, volunteered to take it. Warren eagerly accepted their offer. It was important to get the patriot version to London ahead of Gage's official report. John Derby looked like the man who could do it.

On April 27, eight days after the battle, Derby set out from Salem Harbor. He was in a race. On the twenty-fourth, Lieutenant Joseph Nunn, Gage's aide, had already left Boston aboard the British packet *Sukey* with the official version. Fortunately for the patriots, neither Lieutenant Nunn nor William Brown, the *Sukey*'s skipper, had any idea that they were in a race. Gage was unaware of Warren's drive to get the patriots' side of the story before the British public first.

William Carleton, the *Quero*'s master, was with Derby when they left Salem in the dead of night. A thin haze covered a half moon. As the schooner fell away from Derby's pier, they quickly had all her sails up. They were going to need them. Patrolling off nearby Marblehead Harbor was the *Lively*, under Captain Thomas Bishop, one of Admiral Graves's best officers. Bishop was not on the lookout for the *Quero*, particularly. Her mission had been kept a tight secret.

Derby had no trouble avoiding the *Lively*. The *Quero* raced into the Atlantic for the 3,000-mile run to the English Channel. Warren had given Derby instructions to follow a roundabout route to London that would have taken him first to Ireland, then over the Irish Sea to Scotland or England, and from there overland to London. Warren was afraid that if Derby took a direct route, a British cruiser might pick him up in the English Channel.

Ignoring his instructions, Derby set a course directly for the channel and the Isle of Wight, close to Britain's largest naval base at Portsmouth. He knew the waters well and saw no reason to follow Warren's instructions, especially when he was in a race with the

Sukey and following Warren's directions might make it impossible to reach the British capital ahead of Lieutenant Nunn.

The *Quero* was off Portsmouth long before the *Sukey* even got to the channel. The Salem vessel was carrying only ballast, while the *Sukey* was loaded with cargo. Early on the morning of May 26, Derby and Carleton landed on the Isle of Wight in a place they knew well. The minute they landed, Derby stepped off the boat with his package, while Carleton put back out into the channel and sailed down to Plymouth, where he planned to rendezvous with Derby after the mission was completed.

Derby lost no time renting a pair-oared wherry, a light rowboat that brought him into bustling Portsmouth. As luck would have it, waiting beside the dock when he arrived was a post chaise that ran overnight to London along one of England's best turnpikes. Derby climbed aboard and was in the capital the next day. The *Sukey* was still far out at sea.

Once in London, Derby went straight to Benjamin Franklin's lodgings on Craven Street, but to his chagrin, Franklin had already left for America on March 21. He would not reach Philadelphia until May 9, after the war he had done so much to avert had already started.

In addition to the other material Derby was carrying, he had a special message for Dr. Franklin from Dr. Joseph Warren. "We most ardently wish," it read, "that the several papers herein enclosed may be immediately printed and dispersed through every town in England, and especially communicated to the Lord Mayor, Aldermen, and Common Council of the city of London. . . . we are confident [that you will communicate our belief] that it is the united efforts of both Englands that must save either. But whatever price our brethren in one may be pleased to put on their constitutional liberties, we are authorized to assure you that the inhabitants of the other, with the greatest unanimity, are inflexibly resolved to sell theirs only at the price of their lives."

Derby went next to the lodgings of Franklin's associate and rival Arthur Lee, a close friend of Dr. Warren's mentor, Sam Adams. Lee moved fast to get Derby's sensational documents to the London press. He took them first to his friend the lord mayor of London,

John Wilkes, a bitter foe of the king and the ministry and a friend of the patriots. Wilkes understood immediately the significance of the documents and brought them directly to the antigovernment *London Evening Post*, which published them the next day. Other newspapers printed special editions, and soon the whole city and a good part of the country had the disturbing account of a major British defeat in Massachusetts.

When Lord Dartmouth saw the story, he was aghast. Arresting Derby was the first thing he thought of, but he decided not to do it. He did order a search of the Isle of Wight for Derby's boat, but nothing turned up. In the meantime, Derby hurried off to Plymouth for a rendezvous with Carleton and the *Quero*. Soon they were far out to sea beyond Dartmouth's reach.

On June 1 an exasperated American secretary wrote to Gage, "An account has been printed here, accompanied with depositions to verify it, of skirmishes between a detachment of the troops under your command, and different bodies of the provincial militia." Dartmouth assured Gage that he did not believe the reports. It seemed to him to be "plainly made up for the purpose of conveying every possible prejudice and misrepresentation of the truth." At the same time, he added that "it is very much to be lamented that we do not have some account from you of this transaction." He then went on to note that he knew Gage's dispatches were aboard the *Sukey*, and he awaited her appearance "with great impatience, but till she arrives I can form no decisive judgment of what happened."

The king was more than a little irritated that he did not have Gage's version of events, but at the same time he refused to believe a story based entirely on documents supplied by the rebels. He told everyone within reach to withhold judgment until the official account from General Gage arrived. But where was it? As the days went by with no word from Boston, His Majesty's impatience turned to anger.

The *Sukey* did not reach London until June 9. Lieutenant Nunn was so out of touch that, instead of rushing his dispatches to Whitehall, he slept on board the *Sukey* until late the following morning. Lord Dartmouth was relieved to finally receive Gage's account, but when he read it, he was shocked. He could not help but be annoyed by its brevity. Even before seeing what Gage had to say, the fact that he said so little would itself suggest a disaster had occurred. Indeed it had. No matter how much Gage diminished and sugar-coated it, Lieutenant Colonel Smith had suffered a major defeat, and would have surrendered his entire column had not Lord Percy come to the rescue. Gage wrote of Smith's being "a good deal pressed," and of Percy's arriving "opportunely," and then having to fight "a continual skirmish for the space of fifteen miles, receiving fire from every hill, fence, house, barn, &c. His Lordship kept the enemy off, and brought the troops to Charlestown, from whence they were ferried over to Boston."

Gage went on to extol Percy's effort. "Too much praise cannot be given Lord Percy," he wrote, "for his remarkable activity and conduct during the whole day." He assured Dartmouth that "Lieutenant Colonel Smith and Major Pitcairn did everything men could do, as did all the officers in general, and the men behaved with their usual intrepidity."

Dartmouth must have wondered why, if the men and their leaders were doing "everything men could do," things had turned out so badly. The answer could only be that Gage had let them down by placing them in an impossible situation.

At the end of his report, Gage presented a list of the killed, wounded, and missing, and, lest Dartmouth and the king think the numbers rather high, he insisted—although obviously he had no way of knowing—that "the loss by those who attacked is said to be great."

Having briefly described the "skirmish," as Gage always referred to the disaster, he pointed out that "[t]he whole country was assembled in arms with surprising expedition." This was bad enough, and accounted for the defeat, but far worse was what followed. "[S]everal thousand are now assembled about this town threatening an attack, and getting up artillery. And we are very busy in making preparations to oppose them."

Suddenly, the army in Boston was at risk, something that astonished Dartmouth, who now had the odious task of reporting all of this to the king. He knew His Majesty would be livid, and he was.

Gage's claim that the rebels had fired first didn't matter. The plain fact was that Gage had suffered a major defeat. Nothing could gainsay that.

His Majesty was naturally upset with his feckless commander, but even more with the rebels. He vowed to make them pay for the insult to British arms. On June 10 he told Dartmouth, "I am not apt to be over sanguine, but I cannot help being of opinion that with firmness and perseverance America will be brought to submission . . . old England . . . will be able to make her rebellious children rue the hour that they cast off obedience: America must be a colony of England or treated as an enemy. Distant possessions standing upon an equality with the superior state is more ruinous than being deprived of such connections."

The thought of pulling back and entering into a negotiation before a full-scale civil war developed never entered his mind. In a fit of rage, similar to the one he had had after being informed of the Tea Party, he ordered Dartmouth to immediately unleash naval attacks on New England's coastal towns. It was a lashing out by a petulant monarch that made no political or military sense. He was declaring all-out war on his own subjects, even though they were still open to negotiations.

Dartmouth must have had great qualms about pursuing such an ill-considered policy, but he carried out the king's instructions, writing to the Admiralty:

It is His Majesty's firm resolution of which I am directed to inform your Lordships, that every measure be pursued for suppressing, by the most vigorous efforts, by sea and land, this unnatural rebellion which menaces the subversion of the present happy constitution. To this end it is His Majesty's pleasure that the admiral commanding upon the Boston station, do carry on such operations upon the sea coasts of the four governments in New England as he shall judge most effectual for suppressing in conjunction with His Majesty's land forces, the rebellion which is now openly avowed and supported in those colonies.

While Dartmouth may have had doubts about the king's response, the rest of the cabinet did not. His Majesty had firm support for a tough policy, and this included Lord North, who was beginning to concede that England was, after all, in a war, and that the conflict had to be treated as such. The argument with Massachusetts and the rest of the colonies had gone beyond words. This was a major revolt that had to be put down.

Expecting the Royal Navy to do it, however, was a desperate strategy that was bound to fail. It would add immeasurably to patriot ranks. Ordering the great warships to attack coastal towns without warning could only bring many moderates, and even a good number of Tories, over to support the patriots. A declaration of independence was a certainty.

Lord Sandwich moved swiftly to carry out the king's instructions. Ordering Admiral Graves to prey on defenseless seaport towns was something the first lord had always supported. The inadequate number of warships that Graves had on the North American station, and the limitations on what they could do, remained serious problems but were ignored.

Graves was now being forced into the same position that Gage had been in, having London demand results without supplying the resources. When the king issued his latest order, the total number of warships of all kinds on the North America station amounted to twenty-four. Seven were in Boston, one at Marblehead, two in the Piscataqua River, off Portsmouth, New Hampshire, two patrolling the entire coast of Maine, one in the Bay of Fundy, and another at Halifax. Three were off Rhode Island, and one at each of the following places: New York, Philadelphia, Chesapeake Bay, North Carolina, and South Carolina. Another was off the coast of Florida, and still another in the Bahamas.

With a fleet of this size scattered along the American coast, even Horatio Nelson would have had a hard time carrying out the king's directive. At least Lord Sandwich recognized the need for more warships. He promised to double the size of the North America fleet, but that was only a promise. It would take months to fulfill.

Conclusion

STUNNING success at the Battle of Lexington and Concord brought the colonies together as never before. Doubts about whether they stood a chance against the British colossus lessened dramatically. All the talk about what fools Americans were to think they could stand up to the world's dominant empire wasn't heard much anymore.

More proof of America's fighting ability was exhibited in the weeks that followed, as patriots won an uninterrupted string of victories on land and sea. On May 10, Vermont's Green Mountain Boys and Benedict Arnold captured Fort Ticonderoga, along with eighty heavy artillery pieces, twenty brass guns, a dozen mortars, small arms, powder, and ball. They also seized nearby Crown Point and its military stores, as well as Fort George.

Arnold then raced north up Lake Champlain to St. Jean on the Richelieu River with seventy armed men in bateaux and captured a 60-foot armed British schooner. He renamed her, appropriately enough, *Enterprise*. She carried two brass 6-pounders, which were enough for him to command the lake.

Admiral Graves was unaware that a major naval event had occurred in his area of responsibility. He had given no thought to securing Lake Champlain. Nor did he understand the strategic significance of Arnold's move. A critical element of the land-sea corridor linking Canada with Manhattan was now in patriot hands.

Of more concern to Graves were the embarrassing patriot victories right under his nose in Boston Harbor. In May he suffered defeats at Chelsea Creek, Peddock's Island, and Deer Island. At the battle of Chelsea Creek, the admiral's nephew, Lieutenant Thomas Graves, lost the armed schooner *Diana* to a large contingent of patriots led by Brigadier General Israel Putnam and New Hampshire's John Stark.

The same patriots who were successful at Chelsea Creek took a large number of sheep and cattle from Peddock and Deer Islands. When Graves sent an armed barge to investigate, they captured it as well and took five prisoners.

Another unexpected naval victory occurred the first week of June off distant Machias, in the Maine District of Massachusetts. Jeremiah O'Brien and Benjamin Foster captured the converted merchant schooner *Margaretta*. Graves had sent her to support Loyalists in the distant town. She was under the command of midshipman James Moore, from the flagship *Preston*. He was a favorite of the admiral's, and was killed in the action. James Fenimore Cooper called this episode "the Lexington of the Sea."

Given the fact that the minuscule *Margaretta* had only four old cannon for armament, Cooper's description was a notable exaggeration. Nonetheless, it was America's first significant naval victory on blue water. There had been an earlier victory in Buzzard Bay during the first week of May. Daniel Egery and thirty patriots from Dartmouth, Massachusetts, challenged the 14-gun sloop of war *Falcon* and stole her tender, which was loaded with supplies. Somehow, this daring episode failed to interest Cooper.

The success of patriot arms created more confidence that in a war with Britain on their own territory they could prevail. On the other hand, in spite of the military success, many patriots were shocked that relations with the mother country had reached this point. The thought of war appalled them. This was particularly true of Quakers in Pennsylvania, but it was not confined to them. Many people wanted to step back and see if there weren't alternatives. While they pondered what these might be, the conflict continued, almost as if it had a life of its own.

———

It was up to Congress to deal with the growing call for making one last attempt at negotiations. Brave and articulate John Dickinson of Pennsylvania led the delegates who were profoundly disturbed at the quickening pace of events. They wanted to try, at least one more time, to plead with His Majesty to rethink where all this was going, and substitute talks for guns.

While Congress was trying to decide whether or not to launch another peace initiative, on June 17 patriot fighters again showed their strength at the Battle of Bunker Hill. This time the redcoats were under the command of Major General William Howe, one of Britain's finest. Lieutenant General Gage was still in Boston, still in command, but Howe took the lead in this action.

All he could manage was a Pyrrhic victory, however. The patriots came very close to beating him. They decimated his ranks, even though at the end of the day they were forced to retreat—but not surrender. The orderly withdrawal itself was evidence of how beaten down the redcoats were. Howe lost half his men, including a large number of officers, among them Major Pitcairn.

Howe's overconfidence and lack of respect for provincials was his undoing. He had been a favorite of General James Wolfe during the last war and had absorbed Wolfe's attitudes toward Massachusetts militiamen. He would never make light of the patriot fighters again, nor employ the same tactics. Like Lord Percy, he came away with a better understanding of rebel strengths, which made him a more formidable opponent.

The reaction of Congress, and of the patriots in general, to the fight at Bunker (actually Breed's) Hill was mixed. The near victory was applauded. The knowledge that only lack of ammunition prevented Howe's outright defeat was frustrating. The high price he was made to pay in casualties was heartening. But the death of Dr. Warren was a crushing blow, and the burning down of Charlestown by Admiral Graves was devastating. The wanton destruction sank deep into the consciousness of the patriots and never would be forgiven. As much as anything else that the British high command had done so far, destroying Charlestown hardened patriot hearts against them.

The Continental Congress was now forced to adopt a two-track strategy of pursuing the war with all the vigor it could muster, and at the same time trying to open a dialogue with His Majesty to get beyond the madness that was gripping the empire. John Dickinson pushed hard to get Congress to send the king an Olive Branch Petition. John Adams led the opposition. As far as he was concerned, the king had long since demonstrated that he had no interest in conciliation. Sending him another plea for talks could only signal weakness and make the job of the men on the front lines that much harder.

In the end Dickinson won. Even Adams voted for the resolution. He did not want to appear overly bellicose, and Massachusetts still needed a unified Congress to be successful. The Olive Branch Petition was sent to London on July 8. The king reacted as Adams had predicted, scorning Dickinson's carefully worded plea, refusing even to read it. The Congress then did not have a choice but to concentrate on defending America.

The lesson His Majesty had taken away from the defeat at Lexington and Concord was that, more than ever, Britain needed to enforce the Coercive Acts and gain complete control of her colonies. Although he made it clear that he was not going to change his policy, he was forced to make one major adjustment. After the humiliating defeat at Lexington and Concord, and those that followed, particularly at Bunker Hill, which he read as a defeat, he could no longer pretend that the rebels could be forced to submit on the cheap. A much larger commitment of resources would be necessary.

On June 15, five days after the official account of Lexington and Concord reached His Majesty, the cabinet met at Lord North's to discuss how large a force would be needed to crush the Americans. At subsequent meetings, on July 21 and 26, the figure of twenty thousand additional troops was agreed to, the same figure that General Gage had argued was necessary back in the fall of 1774 but which London, accusing Gage of being timid, had dismissed as preposterous. Not surprisingly, the noble lords sitting around North's dinner table never discussed whether or not they had made a huge miscalculation.

Nor did any of them consider that they might be making the same mistake again of grossly underestimating what it would take to force America to submit. And, of course, no one at the table was willing to consider the question of whether America was conquerable at all, particularly when France, and to a lesser degree Spain and Holland, were ready to support the rebellion.

Here was another excellent opportunity for Lords North and Dartmouth to lead for a change and save both lives and the empire, but they let their chance pass and fell in with the rest of their irate colleagues, whose hubris was blinding them. Their lordships opted for the lash, never dreaming that the war they were so anxious to continue, instead of being brief, as they still assumed, would be long, and end not in victory but defeat.

While the ministry was gearing up for a larger war, the king insisted on immediate action from his navy. His earlier call for quick naval action against New England's seaport towns had not happened, and this lapse drew more of his ire. Lord Sandwich was quick to inform Graves of the king's displeasure. "If the rebellion continues," he told him, "we must have no further delicacies. Therefore, I repeat to you what I have said in my former letters, that you may be blamed for doing too little, but can never be censured for doing too much."

Graves still wasn't getting the message. The only town he had destroyed was Charlestown, and that did not seem to matter, since the outcome of the larger battle was a blow to British pride. A few more "successes" like it, and the rebels would be independent. The firebombing of Charlestown thus was discounted. Graves continued to be criticized for not destroying more towns. Sandwich wrote again, urging him to bomb indiscriminately. "In the letters that I have lately troubled you with," he said, "I have pointed out to you that the eyes of the whole nation are upon you, that much is expected. . . . I have told you at the same time that you may be found fault with for doing too little, but that there is no danger of blame for a vigorous exertion of your strength."

In the same letter, Sandwich warned Graves that there were many complaints about his inactivity. "They say that you do not seem to consider America as a country you are actually at war with." The first lord ended his reprimand by insisting again that Graves get on with the attacks: "Let me tell you again . . . that we are at war with the rebels of America, and that delicacies and forms are no longer to be attended to."

In less than a month, on September 17, the king's patience was exhausted, and Graves was relieved of command. His Majesty had had enough. General Gage was recalled at the same time, and for the same reason—not being aggressive enough. On September 26, 1775, the king's "mild general" received the long-expected order to return to London.

Lord Dartmouth was replaced as well for not being aggressive enough. George Germain, a longtime ally and friend of the king's going back to his days as Prince of Wales, became the American secretary. Germain would have charge of the land campaigns for the duration. Unlike Dartmouth, he was confident, at all times and through each change of strategy, that he knew exactly how to win the war. And unlike Dartmouth, he was willing to fight for what he believed. Even though he and Sandwich, who also remained in place for the rest of the war, never got along, Germain was always pressing for more firebombing, which was at least one thing that he and the first lord had in common, along with an inexplicable, deep-seated distaste for, indeed hatred of, their American opponents.

———

Given the king's determination to make the rebels "rue the hour they cast off obedience," and the patriots' belief that obedience meant a species of deprivation similar to the one on full display in Ireland, the war begun at Lexington and Concord would continue. Both sides were confident in ultimate victory. Neither thought the fighting would last as long as it did or anticipated the extent of its human and material cost.

George III remained committed to forcing "his" colonies to submit. The fighting would conclude only when Parliament finally asserted itself, overruled him, and agreed to American independence. Through it all, His Majesty remained steadfast. If Parliament had not intervened, the war, however senseless, would have continued, but it could never have been won. As Franklin, Chatham, Burke, Fox, and so many other of the king's critics had been pointing out for years, the Americans were never going to allow themselves to be ruled as Ireland was. Their subservience could not be obtained by any power on earth. If they were going to remain part of the empire, they would have to be treated as equal partners. They were free people; they would never be anything else.

Acknowledgments

I FIRST want to thank my immensely talented agent, Rob McQuilkin, for his indispensable help. In our many years of collaboration, I have always relied on his wise counsel, and at no time more than in moving this book from conception to publication. He was there every step of the way, offering his special brand of professional guidance.

At Norton, Starling Lawrence, a gifted leader, did his usual superb job of editing with skilled assistance from Janet Byrne and Emma Hitchcock.

Retired Vice Admiral George Emery read the entire manuscript, offering insights into the least understood part of this seminal battle: its naval dimension. Admiral Emery has an unsurpassed knowledge of America's early naval history. I owe him a special debt of gratitude for sharing some of it with me.

I also owe a special debt to Kia Campbell of the Library of Congress for her expert assistance. America's great national library has been an essential resource for me over many years, as have other exceptional institutions, the foremost being Harvard's Widener and Houghton Libraries, the American Antiquarian Society, Britain's National Archives at Kew, the Massachusetts Historical Society, and the Boston Public Library.

My wife, Kathleen, who has had an abiding interest in American history since her days as a history major at the University of New Hampshire, provided a supportive environment for my work while being very busy with her own. I will be forever grateful for her help.

Notes

INTRODUCTION

4   **"attacked the king's troops"**: Hugh Percy to General Edward Harvey, April 20, 1775, in Hugh Percy, *Letters of Hugh, Earl Percy, from Boston and New York, 1774–1776* (hereinafter Percy, *Letters*), ed. Charles K. Bolton (Boston: Charles E. Goodspeed, 1902), 53.

4   **"when opposed to regular troops"**: John Pitcairn, R.M. (Royal Marines), to Lord Sandwich (First Lord of the Admiralty), February 14, 1775, in *Naval Documents of the American Revolution* (hereinafter *NDAR*), ed. William Bell Clark et al., 12 vols. (Washington, DC: U.S. Government Printing Office, 1964–), vol. 1, 89.

4   **"ever to presume to do it"**: G. D. Scull, ed., *Memoir and Letters of Captain W. Glanville Evelyn of the Fourth Regiment (King's Own) from North America, 1774–1776* (Oxford: James Parker & Co., 1879), 53–55.

4   **"reluctant revolutionaries"**: Robert A. Gross, *The Minutemen and Their World* (New York: Hill & Wang, 1976), 30–41.

6   **"that a few may be raised above it"**: Franklin to Joshua Babcock, January 13, 1772, in *The Papers of Benjamin Franklin* (hereinafter *Franklin Papers*), ed. William Willcox et. al., 42 vols. (New Haven, CT: Yale University Press, 1959–2017), vol. 19, 6–7.

7   **"pensions are spent out of the country"**: Ibid., 22–23.

7   **They were independent, economically and politically**: J. Hector St. John de Crèvecoeur, *Letters from an American Farmer*, ed. Ernest Rhys (New York: E. P. Dutton, 1940; London, 1792), 39–55.

9   **"lawless riot and confusion"**: Franklin to John Ross, May 1, 1765, in *Franklin Papers*, vol. 4, 78.

11   **"continual necessity in the midst of natural plenty"**: Franklin to Joseph Galloway, February 25, 1775, in *Franklin Papers,* vol. 21, 509.

11   **"without the consent of himself, or representative"**: Revere to Mathias Rivoire, October 6, 1781, in Charles Ferris Gettemy, *The True Story of Paul*

Revere, His Midnight Ride, His Arrest and Court-Martial, His Useful Public Services (Boston: Little, Brown, 1905), 97.

12 **"independence and unconditional submission":** John Brooke, *King George III: A Biography of America's Last Monarch* (New York: McGraw-Hill, 1972), 175.

I. THE FINAL STRAW

13 **Lawlessness reigned supreme:** *The Massachusetts Spy, or Thomas's Boston Journal* and the *Boston Gazette*, December 18, 1773.

15 **North did as the king directed and kept the tax:** J. Steven Watson, *The Reign of George III, 1780–1815* (Oxford: Clarendon Press, 1960), 143–46; George III to Lord North, March 5, 1770, in *The Correspondence of King George the Third from 1760 to December 1783* (hereinafter *Correspondence of King George*), ed. Sir John Fortescue, 6 vols. (London: Macmillan, 1927–28), vol. 3, 136.

15 **authority became an obsession:** Bernard Donoughue, *British Politics and the American Revolution* (London: Macmillan, 1964), 250.

16 **wanted to end it:** Stanley Ayling, *The Elder Pitt, Earl of Chatham* (New York: David McKay, 1976), 290.

16 **as well as North:** Peter D. G. Thomas, *Lord North* (London: Allen Lane, 1976), 18.

16 **"protect their subjects and their property":** John A. Cannon, *Lord North: The Noble Lord in the Blue Ribbon* (London: Historical Association, 1970), 10.

17 **"the public voice?":** Ibid., 9–10.

17 **relating to America:** G. E. Mingay, *English Landed Society in the Eighteenth Century* (London: Routledge and Kegan Paul, 1963), 11.

17 **"join in the worst":** Franklin to William Franklin, March 22, 1775, in *Franklin Papers*, vol. 21, 582.

2. GENERAL THOMAS GAGE AND GEORGE III

19 **including Boston:** Ayling, *The Elder Pitt*, 344–46.

20 **by jury of one's peers:** Edmund S. Morgan and Helen M. Morgan, *The Stamp Act Crisis: Prologue to Revolution* (Chapel Hill, NC: University of North Carolina Press, 1995), 62–69.

20 **the will to use it:** John Richard Alden, *General Gage in America: Being Principally a History of His Role in the American Revolution* (Baton Rouge: Louisiana State University Press, 1948), 196.

21 **in the legislatures:** Ibid.

21 **"dependence on the mother country":** Gage to Hillsborough, September 26, 1768, in *The Correspondence of General Thomas Gage with the Secretar-*

ies of State, and with the War Office and the Treasury, 1763–1775 (hereinafter *Gage Correspondence*), ed. Clarence Edwin Carter, 2 vols. (New Haven, CT: Yale University Press, 1931–33), vol. 1, 197.

21 **"in a perpetual heat"**: Gage to Barrington, September 8, 1770, in *Gage Correspondence*, vol. 2, 556–57.

22 **"owes to its mother country"**: George III to North, February 4, 1774, in *Correspondence of King George,* vol. 3, 59.

23 **"without any military force"**: Alan Valentine, *Lord North,* 2 vols. (Norman: University of Oklahoma Press, 1967), vol. 1, 319.

24 **"his hands would be tied up"**: *Collections of the Massachusetts Historical Society,* 4th Series (Boston, 1858), vol. 4, 371.

24 **fear of being replaced**: For a different view see John Shy, *A People Numerous and Armed: Reflections on the Military Struggle for American Independence* (New York: Oxford University Press, 1976), 94–95.

3. BENJAMIN FRANKLIN EXCORIATED

25 **government wanted to encourage**: Franklin to Thomas Cushing, February 15, 1774, in *Franklin Papers*, vol. 21, 90; Bernard Bailyn, *The Ordeal of Thomas Hutchinson* (Cambridge, MA: Harvard University Press), 285.

26 **political decisions of their betters**: William M. Fowler Jr., *The Baron of Beacon Hill: A Biography of John Hancock* (Boston: Houghton Mifflin, 1979), 150–51.

27 **House of Representatives**: John K. Alexander, *Samuel Adams* (New York: Rowman & Littlefield, 2011), 150–53.

27 **"solemnity to the decision"**: Burke to the committee of correspondence of the General Assembly of New York, February 2, 1774, in *The Correspondence of Edmund Burke* (hereinafter *Burke Correspondence*), ed. Lucy S. Sutherland et. al., 9 vols. (Cambridge: Cambridge University Press, 1960), vol. 2, 522.

27 **congratulating him on his victory**: Gage to Hutchinson, February 2, 1774, in Thomas Hutchinson, *The Diary and Letters of His Excellency Thomas Hutchinson* (hereinafter Hutchinson, *Diary*), ed. Peter Orlando Hutchinson, 2 vols. (Boston: Houghton Mifflin, 1884–86; London: Sampson Low et al., 1883), vol. 1, 99–100; Bailyn, *The Ordeal of Thomas Hutchinson*, 285–86.

28 **"a foreign independent state"**: *Franklin Papers*, vol. 21, 58–59.

28 **America was irresistible**: Ibid., 94.

29 **the death penalty**: Bailyn, *The Ordeal of Thomas Hutchinson*, 298–99; Carl Van Doren, *Benjamin Franklin* (New York: Penguin, 1991), 490–91.

29 **"pursued by a wolf"**: Benjamin Franklin, "An Open Letter to Lord North," *The Public Advertiser*, April 15, 1774, in *Franklin Papers*, vol. 21, 183–86.

4. BRITAIN CLOSES THE PORT OF BOSTON

31 **"stronger than I have ever known it":** *Burke Correspondence*, vol. 2, 521–22.

31 **"meets with no opposition":** Franklin to Thomas Cushing, March 22, 1774, in *Franklin Papers*, vol. 21, 152.

31 **"incited other places to tumults":** William Cobbett, *The Parliamentary History of England from the Earliest Period to the Year 1803* (hereinafter Hansard's Debates), 36 vols. (London: T. C. Hansard, 1814), vol. 17, 1163–65.

32 **in the thinking of Britain's rulers:** Lawrence Gibson, *The Coming of the Revolution, 1763–1775* (New York: Harper & Row, 1954), 19–22.

32 **unclear by design:** Peter Force, ed., *American Archives*, 4th Series, 6 vols. (Washington, DC: M. St. Claire Clarke and Peter Force, 1837–46), vol. 1, 61–66.

33 **"connection and dependence":** *Burke Correspondence*, vol. 2, 527.

34 **the ministers reluctantly approved:** Cabinet minutes, April 7, 1774, in William Walter Legge, 2nd Earl of Dartmouth, *The Manuscripts of the Earl of Dartmouth*, 2 vols. (hereinafter *Dartmouth Papers*), Royal Commission on Historical Manuscripts (London, 1887–96), vol. 2, 883; Alden, *General Gage in America*, 203–4.

35 **"violent against America":** Franklin to Thomas Cushing, April 16, 1774, in *Franklin Papers*, vol. 21, 191.

5. DECLARING WAR ON MASSACHUSETTS

37 **removing the judicial system entirely from popular control:** Force, *American Archives*, 4th Series, vol. 1, 104–12.

38 **putting them beyond the law:** Alden, *General Gage in America*, 210.

38 **on May 20 a triumphant king signed it:** Force, *American Archives*, 4th Series, vol. 1, 129–32.

39 **"no revenue is to be found":** Hansard's Debates, vol. 17, 1216.

40 **"but in the arts also":** William Stanhope Taylor and John Henry Pringle, eds., *Correspondence of William Pitt, Earl of Chatham*, 4 vols. (London: John Murray, 1838–40), vol. 4, 322–26.

41 **"the people of America":** Quoted in Kenneth McNaught, *The Penguin History of Canada* (London: Penguin, 1969), 50.

41 **"right of representation":** Warren to Adams, August 15, 1774, in Richard Frothingham, *Life and Times of Joseph Warren* (Boston: Little, Brown, 1865), 340.

41 **forced to accept it:** McNaught, *The Penguin History of Canada*, 49–52.

6. SUPPORT FOR BOSTON BROADENS

43   **dissolved the House the following morning:** Jared Sparks, ed., *The Writings of George Washington*, 12 vols. (Boston: Russell, Odiorne, and Metcalf, 1834–37), vol. 2, 486.

44   **to support Massachusetts:** Kenneth Coleman, *The American Revolution in Georgia, 1763–1789* (Athens: University of Georgia Press, 1958), 42–43.

45   **every reason to remain aloof:** W. Walker Stephens, ed., *The Life and Writings of Turgot, Comptroller General of France, 1774–76, for English Readers* (New York: Burt Franklin, 1971), 295–96, 321–24.

45   **what every Frenchman wanted—revenge:** Orville T. Murphy, *Charles Gravier, Comte de Vergennes: French Diplomacy in the Age of Revolution, 1719–1787* (Albany: State University of New York Press, 1982), 217.

47   **"your fortitude and discretion":** *Gage Correspondence*, vol. 2, 158–62.

48   **"return to their masters here?":** Hansard's Debates, vol. 17, 1208.

7. DEFIANCE ESCALATES

49   **"measures to extricate it":** Governor Hutchinson to his brother, Elisha, June 1, 1774, in Hutchinson, *Diary*, vol. 1, 150–51.

51   **first governor of the Bay Colony, John Winthrop:** *Boston Gazette*, May 30, 1774.

52   **new Coercive Acts arrived:** Massachusetts Historical Society, *Proceedings of the Massachusetts Historical Society*, 1st Series (1791–1883), vol. 12, 47; John Andrews, "Letters of John Andrews, Esq., of Boston, 1772–1776," ed. Winthrop Sargent, *Proceedings of the Massachusetts Historical Society*, 1st Series, vol. 8, 316–412, reprinted as *Letters of John Andrews, Esq., of Boston, 1772–1776*, ed. Winthrop Sargent (Cambridge: J. Wilson & Son, 1866), 55; Gage to Dartmouth, July 5, 1774, in *Gage Correspondence*, vol. 1, 358–59.

52   **"regiments so near us":** Samuel Adams to Stephen Hopkins, May 30, 1774, in Frothingham, *Life and Times of Joseph Warren*, 312–13.

53   **convening a general Congress:** Fowler, *The Baron of Beacon Hill*, 165.

53   **"thinking on it":** Franklin to Joseph Galloway, February 18, 1774, in *Franklin Papers*, vol. 21, 110–11.

54   **the lack of them:** Esther Forbes, *Paul Revere and the World He Lived In* (Boston: Houghton Mifflin, 1942), 114–22.

55   **"must take place":** Adams to William Checkley, May 14, 1774, in William Vincent Wells, *The Life and Public Services of Samuel Adams*, 3 vols. (Boston: Little, Brown, 1865), vol. 2, 193.

55 **behind the destruction of the tea:** Frothingham, *Life and Times of Joseph Warren*, 218–86.

56 **a similar amount for his son:** John K. Alexander, *Samuel Adams: The Life of an American Revolutionary* (New York: Rowman & Littlefield, 2011), 179.

8. A DEEPENING CRISIS

59 **"going greater lengths":** Montagu to Sandwich, March 3, 1773, in *The Private Papers of John, Earl of Sandwich, First Lord of the Admiralty, 1771–1782*, ed. G. R. Barnes and J. H. Owens (hereinafter *Sandwich Papers*), 4 vols. (London: Naval Records Society, 1932–38), vol. 1, 49–50.

59 **"end in fatal consequences":** Montagu to Sandwich, June 1, 1773, ibid., 50.

59 **"to the king's service":** John Adams, *The Works of John Adams, Second President of the United States: with a Life of the Author, Notes and Illustrations by His Grandson, Charles Francis Adams*, 10 vols. (Boston: Little, Brown, 1850–56), vol. 2, 306–7.

59 **pace with the French:** N. A. M. Rodger, *The Insatiable Earl: A Life of John Montagu, 4th Earl of Sandwich* (New York: W. W. Norton, 1993), 126–71.

60 **"the satire of his opponents":** Horace Walpole, *Journal of the Reign of George III from 1771 to 1783*, ed. John Doran, 2 vols. (London: Bentley, 1859), vol. 1, 170–71.

61 **additional schooners in Marblehead:** Neil R. Stout, *The Perfect Crisis: The Beginning of the Revolutionary War* (New York: New York University Press, 1976), 89.

63 **a roundtrip of twenty-eight miles:** *Boston Gazette*, August 1, 1774.

63 **"every sentiment of humanity":** Bowdoin to Franklin, September 6, 1774, in *Franklin Papers*, vol. 21, 282.

63 **a Continental Congress was illegal:** Alexander, *Samuel Adams*, 177–79.

64 **"to think of opposing us":** Hugh, Earl Percy, to Rev. Thomas Percy, April 17, 1774, in *Letters of Hugh, Earl Percy, from Boston and New York, 1774–1776*, 25.

64 **"come to extremities":** Ibid., 27.

64 **"to be well served":** Lord Percy to the Duke of Northumberland, July 27, 1774, ibid., 28.

65 **"out of their wits":** Ibid., 28–29.

65 **"despise them completely":** Percy to Henry Reveley, August 8, 1774, ibid., 31.

65 **"no affection for his army":** Lt. John Barker, *The British in Boston: Being the Diary of Lieutenant John Barker of the King's Own Regiment from November 15, 1774, to May 31, 1776, with Notes*, ed. Elizabeth Ellery Dana (Cambridge, MA: Harvard University Press, 1924), 47.

9. THE COUNTIES STRIKE BACK

68 **flee to Boston for protection:** Ray Raphael and Marie Raphael, *The Spirit of '74: How the American Revolution Began* (New York: The New Press, 2015), 53–64.

69 **going their own way:** Stephen E. Patterson, *Political Parties in Revolutionary Massachusetts* (Madison: University of Wisconsin Press, 1973), 91–124.

69 **unreliability of British friendship:** Richard Berleth, *Bloody Mohawk: The French and Indian War & American Revolution on New York's Frontier* (Delmar, New York: Black Dome Press, 2009), 15–20.

70 **"All that is valuable in life is at stake," it declared:** Quoted in Ray Raphael, *The First American Revolution: Before Lexington and Concord* (New York: The New Press, 2002), 61.

70 **"subjects in Great Britain":** Ibid., 62.

71 **"they are put upon":** Gage to Dartmouth, October 30, 1774, in *Gage Correspondence*, vol. 1, 381–82.

73 **"the minutest tittle of its charter":** Frothingham, *Life and Times of Joseph Warren*, 349.

75 **"they knew not how to fight":** Charles Lee, "Strictures on a Pamphlet, Entitled a 'Friendly Address to all Reasonable Americans . . . ,'" in *The American Revolution: Writings from the Pamphlet Debate, 1773–1776*, 383–96, ed. Gordon Wood (New York: Penguin Random House, 2015).

10. HIS MAJESTY REFUSES TO BEND

76 **news from Boston:** Hutchinson, *Diary*, vol. 1, 152–53.

77 **"they will soon submit":** George III to Lord North, July 1, 1774, in *Correspondence of King George*, vol. 3, 116; Bailyn, *The Ordeal of Thomas Hutchinson*, 278.

78 **"a flame in every colony":** Gage to Barrington, July 18, 1774, in *Gage Correspondence*, vol. 2, 649.

11. THE POWDER ALARM

83 **"their whole number":** Joseph Warren to Samuel Adams, September 4, 1774, in Frothingham, *Life and Times of Joseph Warren*, 355–56.

83 **for troops as well:** Samuel Cooper to Benjamin Franklin, September 9, 1774, in *Franklin Papers*, vol. 21, 297–302.

84 **"no prospect of putting the [Coercive] acts in force but by first making a conquest of the New England provinces":** Gage to Dartmouth, September 25, 1774, in *Gage Correspondence*, vol. 1, 376–77.

84 **"by forcible means":** Gage to Dartmouth, September 2, 1774, ibid., 369–72.

85 **"mad as they are here"**: Gage to Dartmouth, September 12, 1774, ibid., 373–34.

85 **the colonists to submit**: Bailyn, *The Ordeal of Thomas Hutchinson*, 302–7.

85 **strong and well armed**: Gage to Barrington, August 27, 1774, in *Gage Correspondence*, vol. 2, 651.

86 **"His Majesty's royal predecessors"**: Frothingham, *Life and Times of Joseph Warren*, 364.

12. THE COLONIES UNITE

87 **"civility, compliance, and respect"**: John Adams to Abigail Adams, August 28, 1774, in *The Book of Abigail & John: Selected Letters of the Adams Family, 1762–1784*, ed. L. H. Butterfield, Marc Friedlaender, and Mary-Jo Kline (Cambridge, MA: Harvard University Press, 1975), 68–69.

88 **"as likely as in her liberation"**: John Adams to William Tudor, October 7, 1774, in Frothingham, *Life and Times of Joseph Warren*, 386.

89 **"pursuing vigorous measures"**: John Adams to Abigail Adams, June 17, 1775, in *The Portable John Adams*, ed. John Patrick Diggins (New York: Penguin Classics, 2004), 146.

90 **"changing of measures"**: Franklin to Thomas Cushing, September 15, 1774, in *Franklin Papers*, vol. 21, 306.

90 **extend to Massachusetts**: Alden, *General Gage in America*, 212.

91 **"grave and serious indeed"**: John Adams to Abigail Adams, September 8, 1774, in *The Book of Abigail & John*, 70–71.

13. THE SUFFOLK RESOLVES

93 **"tedious to me"**: John Adams to Abigail Adams, October 9, 1774, in *The Book of Abigail & John*, 78–79.

95 **"any person whatsoever"**: Worthington Chauncey Ford et. al., eds., *Journals of the Continental Congress, 1774–1789*, 34 vols. (Washington, DC: U.S. Government Printing Office, 1904–1937), vol. 1, 32–37.

96 **"pacific Quakers of Pennsylvania"**: John Adams to Abigail Adams, September 18, 1774, in Frothingham, *Life and Times of Joseph Warren*, 366.

97 **prevent them at home**: Jack N. Rakove, *The Beginnings of National Politics: An Interpretive History of the Continental Congress* (Baltimore: Johns Hopkins University Press, 1979), 46–49.

14. CONGRESS COMPLETES ITS WORK

98 **"secret" meetings in Philadelphia**: Hutchinson, *Diary*, November 18, 1774, vol. 1, 296; Donoughue, *British Politics and the American Revolution*, 208.

99   **approval of both:** The text of the Galloway plan is in Jack P. Greene, ed., *Colonies to Nation, 1763–1789: A Documentary History of the American Revolution* (New York: W. W. Norton, 1975), 241–42.

99   **any chance of passing:** David Ammerman, *In the Common Cause* (New York: W. W. Norton, 1975), 59.

100   **"poison us also":** Franklin to Joseph Galloway, February 25, 1775, in *Franklin Papers*, vol. 21, 508–10.

101   **direct threat to "religion, laws, and liberties":** Ford, ed., *Journals of the Continental Congress, 1774–1789*, vol. 1, 63–73.

102   **moving it toward becoming a separate government:** Ibid., 75–80, for the full text of the Association.

102   **forming a revolutionary government:** Useful summaries of the work of the First Congress are given in Ammerman, *In the Common Cause*, 35–101; Merrill Jensen, *The Founding of a Nation* (New York: Oxford University Press, 1968), 483–507; and Rakove, *The Beginnings of National Politics*, 42–62.

103   **"they have sent you":** Gage to Barrington, February 10, 1775, in *Gage Correspondence*, vol. 2, 669.

15. SLAVES

105   **any other overseas operation:** Donald L. Robinson, *Slavery in the Structure of American Politics, 1765–1820* (New York: Harcourt Brace Jovanovich, 1971), 469.

105   **many people in the Bay Colony found slavery reprehensible and wanted to get rid of it:** Ibid.

106   **"a right to freedom as we have":** Abigail Adams to John Adams, September 22, 1774, in *Adams Family Correspondence*, ed. L. H. Butterfield and Marc Friedlaender, 13 vols. (Cambridge, MA: Harvard University Press, 1963–2017), vol. 1, 162.

106   **for the time being:** For a somewhat different view of John Adams and slavery, see David McCullough, *John Adams* (New York: Simon & Schuster, 2001), 130–36.

107   **not in the same way:** Harriet Jacobs, "Incidents in the Life of a Slave Girl," in *The Oxford Book of the American South*, ed. Edward L. Ayers and Bradley C. Mittendorf (New York: Oxford University Press, 1997), 50–64.

108   **the market value of his own:** E. Stanly Godbold Jr. and Robert H. Woody, *Christopher Gadsden and the American Revolution* (Knoxville: University of Tennessee Press, 1982), 65.

108   **more than a quarter of the African slaves imported into the United States came after the Declaration of Independence:** Edward Country-

man, *Americans: A Collision of Histories* (New York: Hill & Wang, 1996), 185–93.

108 **"a gloomy perspective to future times"**: Patrick Henry to Robert Pleasants, January 18, 1773, in Bernhard Knollenberg, *Growth of the American Revolution: 1766–1775* (New York: Simon & Schuster, 1975), 328; Robert D. Meade, *Patrick Henry, Patriot in the Making* (Philadelphia: Lippincott, 1957), 299–300.

109 **Benjamin Franklin thought the same thing**: Van Doren, *Benjamin Franklin*, 216–17.

109 **including African slaves**: Phillis Wheatley, "Letters," *Proceedings of the Massachusetts Historical Society*, 1st Series, vol. 7, 267–78.

16. THE PERVERSE EFFECTS OF THE POWDER ALARM

112 **did not arrive in Boston until December 15**: Gage to Dartmouth, December 15, 1774, in *NDAR*, vol. 1, 23.

112 **Admiral Graves received a similar order on the same day from Philip Stephens**: Graves to Philip Stephens, December 15, 1774, ibid.

113 **for larger armies**: Hutchinson, *Diary*, October 10, 1774, vol. 1, 259–60.

113 **troops Gage was calling for weren't needed**: Sylvia R. Frey, *The British Soldier in America* (Austin: University of Texas Press, 1981), 9.

114 **"they will come to submit"**: *Correspondence of King George*, vol. 3, 1508.

114 **London would support him**: George III to Dartmouth, October 10, 1774, in Donoughue, *British Politics and the American Revolution*, 206.

17. THE MARCH TO WAR

116 **in each village**: Allen French, *The Day of Concord and Lexington: The Nineteenth of April, 1775* (Boston: Little, Brown, 1925), 21.

117 **doubtless exaggerated**: Gordon S. Wood, *The Radicalism of the American Revolution*, 51; Bernard Knollenberg, *Growth of the American Revolution, 1776–1775* (Indianapolis: Liberty Fund, 2003), 261.

117 **militias of Middlesex County**: Gross, *The Minutemen and Their World*, 70.

118 **"at this juncture"**: Gage to Barrington, November 2, 1774, in *Gage Correspondence*, vol. 2, 658–59.

119 **warships of various types**: Gage to Barrington, October 3, 1774, ibid., 656.

120 **dismissed it out of hand**: Barrington to Dartmouth, December 24, 1774, in *Dartmouth Papers*, vol. 2, 887.

120 **"in a state of open rebellion"**: Hutchinson, *Diary*, November 1, 1774, vol. 1, 272–74.

120 **as a basis for negotiations**: November 12, 1774, ibid., 292–93.

18. CHATHAM'S OPPOSITION

122 **a thriving empire again:** Pitt became the 1st Earl of Chatham and moved to the House of Lords on August 4, 1766.

123 **answering members' questions:** Van Doren, *Benjamin Franklin*, 336–52.

124 **"the splendor of lightning":** A phrase describing Pitt that Franklin liked, *Franklin Papers*, vol. 21, 542.

125 **"as the South Sea":** "Journal of Negotiations in London," ibid., 548.

125 **"Reduced to a Small One":** *Franklin Papers*, vol. 23, 87–94.

125 *Acquisition of Canada:* *Franklin Papers*, vol. 9, 590–95.

125 **"might be restored":** *Franklin Papers*, vol. 21, 543.

126 **parliamentary majorities:** Ayling, *The Elder Pitt*, 203–9.

127 **"proceedings of the Congress":** Franklin to Thomas Cushing, September 15, 1774, in *Franklin Papers*, vol. 21, 306–7.

128 **Franklin's true position was:** Van Doren, *Benjamin Franklin*, 494.

129 **"maturity of your errors":** William Pitt, *Correspondence of William Pitt, Earl of Chatham*, ed. W. S. Taylor and W. H. Pringle, 4 vols. (London, 1838–40), vol. 4, 377–84; Ayling, *The Elder Pitt*, 414.

130 **"the person who drew it up":** Memoir written on board ship, March 22, 1775, *Franklin Papers*, vol. 21, 581–82.

130 **spineless American secretary:** Ibid.

130 **by a vote of 61 to 32:** Hansard's Debates, vol. 18, 198–215.

130 **"to common respect":** Franklin to Charles Thomson, February 5, 1775, in *Franklin Papers*, vol. 21, 475–79.

131 **"bribe their representatives":** *Franklin Papers*, vol. 21, 583.

19. LORDS NORTH AND DARTMOUTH SECRETLY SEARCH FOR PEACE

132 **and it had been since December:** Peter D. G. Thomas, *Lord North* (London: Allen Lane, 1976), 82.

132 **opposite of what he wanted:** King to North, December 15, 1774, in *Correspondence of King George*, vol. 3, 156.

134 **the Jacobites in the 1740s:** *Franklin Papers*, vol. 21, 551.

134 **going to sway him:** For Franklin's list of recommendations for a reconciliation, see *Franklin Papers*, vol. 21, 553–62.

135 **if they had succeeded:** R. Hingston Fox, *Dr. John Fothergill and His Friends* (London: Macmillan, 1919), 332–33.

136 **had broad support:** Hansard's Debates, vol. 18, 33–34, 38–40, 45–46; see also *Franklin Papers*, vol. 21, 503.

136 **"intolerable wrongs":** Ayling, *The Elder Pitt*, 416.

137 **ingratiate himself with the ministry:** Franklin to Joseph Galloway, February 25, 1775, in *Franklin Papers*, vol. 21, 508.

137 **submission in Massachusetts:** Bernard Donoughue, *British Politics and the American Revolution*, 231.

20. THE DECISION FOR WAR

140 **prepare for possible conflict in the spring of 1775:** Graves to Stephens, December 16, 1774, in *NDAR*, vol. 1, 28.

140 **Rochford was the senior secretary of state:** Hutchinson, *Diary,* January 27–30, 1775, vol. 1, 363–64; Nick Bunker, *An Empire on Edge* (New York: Random House, 2015), 349–54.

143 **could not recruit a single person:** "Captain John Cochran to Governor John Wentworth, December 14, 1774, in *NDAR*, vol. 1, 18–19; Governor John Wentworth to Vice Admiral Samuel Graves, December 14, 1774, in *NDAR*, vol. 1, 19.

143 **as large as twenty-four pounders:** James Rivington's *New York Gazetteer,* December 2, 1774; in *NDAR*, vol. 1, 20–21.

143 **orders for Gage to go on the offensive:** Hutchinson, *Diary,* January 30, 1775, vol. 1, 364–65.

144 **they were of no interest:** Sir George Otto Trevelyan, *The American Revolution: Part I. 1766–1776* (London: Longmans, Green, and Co., 1899), 280–81.

21. PARLIAMENT VOTES FOR WAR

145 **by the lopsided vote of 296–106:** Hutchinson, *Diary,* January 30 to February 4, 1775, vol. 1, 364–69.

145 **Parliament's decision:** George III to Lord North, February 8, 1775, in *Correspondence of King George,* vol. 3, 1588–89.

146 **"the language of a highwayman":** Franklin to Joseph Galloway, February 25, 1775, in *Franklin Papers,* vol. 21, 510.

149 **"the troops must march into the country":** Gage to Barrington, February 10, 1775, in *Gage Correspondence,* vol. 2, 669.

22. THE COUNTRY PEOPLE

151 **"by battalions, officers and all":** Wolfe to Lord George Sackville, August 7, 1758, William Beckles, ed., *The Life and Letters of James Wolfe* (London: W. Heinemann, 1909), 392; John Shy, *Toward Lexington: The Role of the British Army in the Coming of the American Revolution* (Princeton: Princeton University Press, 1965), 415–18.

151 **could not have agreed more:** Lt. Alexander Johnson to Lord Loudoun, December 20, 1756, in Douglas Edward Leach, *Roots of Conflict: British*

Armed Forces and Colonial Americans, 1677–1763 (Chapel Hill: University of North Carolina Press, 1986), 130–31.

152 **including higher education:** David Hackett Fischer, *Albion's Seed: Four British Folkways in America* (New York: Oxford University Press, 1989), 130–34.

152 **and of their officers:** See, for instance, Seth Metcalf, *Diary and Journal of Seth Metcalf,* ed., William S. Piper (Boston, 1939); Edna V. Moffet, ed., "The Diary of a Private on the First Expedition to Crown Point," *New England Quarterly* 5 (1932): 602–18.

153 **happily in their place:** Sylvia R. Frey, *The British Soldier in America: A Social History of Military Life in the Revolutionary Period* (Austin: University of Texas Press, 1981), 3–21; Mark Urban, *Fusiliers: Eight Years with the Redcoats in America* (London: Faber & Faber, 2007), 1–18.

154 **"slaves to their officers":** Fred Anderson, *Crucible of War: The Seven Year's War and the Fate of Empire in British North America* (New York: Vintage Books, 2001), 286–88.

154 **their courage inspired:** Fred Anderson, *A People's Army: Massachusetts Soldiers and Society in the Seven Years' War* (Chapel Hill: University of North Carolina Press, 1984), 155–61.

155 **around forty thousand:** Anderson, *Crucible of War,* 317–20.

23. THE COUNTRY PEOPLE FIND MANY SUPPORTERS

158 **with few troops if he had a mind to:** B. D. Bargar, *Lord Dartmouth and the American Revolution* (Columbia: University of South Carolina Press, 1965), 161.

158 **Britain was threatening:** Trevelyan, *The American Revolution: Part I. 1766–1776,* 28–99.

159 **from the port every year:** Richard Frothingham, *History of the Siege of Boston, and of the Battles of Lexington, Concord, and Bunker Hill* (Boston: Little, Brown, 1873), 20.

159 **in ships built there:** Lawrence Henry Gipson, *The Coming of the Revolution 1763–1775* (New York: Harper & Brothers, 1954), 23–25.

161 **"for the new empire":** *Correspondence of King George,* vol. 4, 351.

24. TENSIONS MOUNT

164 **"both blood and treasure":** Gage to Dartmouth, October 30, 1774, in *Gage Correspondence,* vol. 1, 383.

164 **"a few months ago":** Gage to Dartmouth, January 18, 1775, ibid., 390.

165 **a colonial world that didn't exist:** Dartmouth to Gage, April 15, 1775, ibid., 190–96.

166 **kept them under strict control:** Frederick Mackenzie, *Diary of Frederick Mackenzie*, 2 vols., ed. Allen French (Cambridge, MA: Harvard University Press, 1926, 1930), vol. 1, 30–31.

166 **"without some convulsion":** Gage to Dartmouth, March 28, 1775, in *Gage Correspondence*, vol. 1, 394–95.

25. STILL WAITING

169 **"very bad people":** Pitcairn to Sandwich, March 4, 1775, in *Sandwich Papers*, vol. 1, 59–62.

170 **"the Yankees will":** Ibid.

173 **"to act solely on the defensive so long as it can be justified on the principles of reason and self-preservation":** Allen French, *General Gage's Informers* (New York: Greenwood Press, 1968; Ann Arbor: University of Michigan Press, 1932), 17–19; John H. Scheide, "The Lexington Alarm," *Proceedings of the American Antiquarian Society*, vol. 50, part 1 (1940), 49–79.

173 **"subjugate this people":** *The Massachusetts Spy, or Thomas's Boston Journal*, March 30, 1775.

173 **"taking other routes":** David Hackett Fischer, *Paul Revere's Ride* (New York: Oxford University Press, 1994), 81–82.

174 **exactly the opposite:** Barker, *British in Boston*, 18.

175 **no orders had arrived from London:** Lord Percy to Rev. Thomas Percy, April 8, 1775, in Percy, *Letters*, 48.

176 **"endeavor to starve us":** Ibid.

176 **turn away ships in distress:** M. Garnier to Vergennes, April 7 and 11, 1775, in *NDAR*, vol. 1, 450–53.

176 **"application to you for their assistance":** Alden, *General Gage in America*, 227–28.

177 **retribution from the rebels:** Graves to Philip Stephens, April 11, 1775, in *NDAR*, vol. 1, 177.

177 **"bring them into the field":** Gage to Josiah Martin, Governor of North Carolina, April 12, 1775, in *NDAR*, vol. 1, 180.

26. FATEFUL ORDERS

179 **"grown to maturity":** Gage to Barrington, March 28, 1775, in *Gage Correspondence*, vol. 2, 671–72.

179 **"in support of law and government":** Dartmouth to Gage, January 27, 1775, ibid., 179–83.

180 **"presumed will prove successful":** Gage to Dartmouth, September 2, 1774, in *Gage Correspondence*, vol. 1, 371–72.

180 **"shelter in Boston"**: Gage to William Barrington, September 25, 1774, in *Gage Correspondence*, vol. 2, 654–55.

180 **thoroughly intimidated**: Gage to Dartmouth, December 15, 1774, *Gage Correspondence*, vol. 1, 387.

183 **"with firmness and decision"**: Dartmouth to Gage, January 27, 1775, in *Gage Correspondence*, vol. 2, 179–83.

183 **a little over five thousand**: Dartmouth to Gage, April 14, 1775, ibid., 190–96; Donoughue, *British Politics and the American Revolution*, 266–67.

27. GAGE'S DECISION

185 **"attract support for the king"**: John R. Galvin, *The Minute Men: The First Fight: Myths and Realities of the American Revolution* (Dulles, VA: Potomac Books, The History of War Edition, 2006), 101–2.

188 **"the bottom of the Common"**: "Letter from Paul Revere to Jeremy Belknap, January 1, 1798," *Proceedings of the Massachusetts Historical Society* 16 (1878): 371–76; Forbes, *Paul Revere and the World He Lived In*, 235.

188 **"ordered to be in readiness"**: Mackenzie, *Diary*, vol. 1, 18; *NDAR*, vol. 1, 192.

28. CROSSING THE RUBICON

190 **lead her to destroy him**: For another view of Mrs. Gage, see Fischer, *Paul Revere's Ride*, 96–97.

192 **"judgment and discretion"**: Galvin, *The Minute Men*, 99–102.

29. PAUL REVERE

196 **of the Fifth Regiment**: French, *General Gage's Informers*, 32.

201 **no way the Somerset could miss them**: Paul Revere, "Letter from Paul Revere to Jeremy Belknap, circa 1798."

201 **"going up the road"**: Ibid.

202 **an affirmation of slavery in Massachusetts**: Forbes, *Paul Revere and the World He Lived In*, 37–38.

202 **Lexington at midnight**: Ibid.

202 **whatever the cost**: Arthur B. Tourtellot, *Lexington and Concord: The Beginning of the War of the American Revolution* (New York: W. W. Norton, 1959), 34–45.

203 **the rest of the militia**: Harlow Giles Unger, *John Hancock: Merchant King and American Patriot* (Hoboken, NJ: Wiley, 2000), 192–93.

205 **Militiamen hurried to village greens in preparation for a march to the battle zone**: Galvin, *The Minute Men*, 110–11.

30. THE BRITISH MARCH TO CONCORD BOGS DOWN

207 **if challenged:** Mackenzie, *Diary*, vol. 1, 18.

208 **the Royal Welch Fusiliers:** A fusil was a light flintlock musket.

208 **only twenty were there:** Ibid.

210 **to stop all of them:** "The Journal of Captain Edward Le Cras, R.N.," in *NDAR*, vol. 1, 192.

211 **"up to their middies":** Barker, *British in Boston*, 31–32.

213 **defeat and surrender:** French, *The Day of Concord and Lexington*, 226–27.

31. A MASSACRE AT LEXINGTON

216 **"disperse, and not to fire":** John Parker, (Affidavit) No. 4, Lexington, April 25, 1775, Library of Congress, "Depositions Concerning Lexington and Concord, April 1775."

216 **"on the basis of reason":** William Heath, *Memoirs of Major-General William Heath*, ed. William Abbatt (New York: William Abbatt, 1901), 6; French, *The Day of Concord and Lexington*, 96.

217 **real enough, they said:** Galvin, *The Minute Men*, 116; Thomas B. Allen, *Tories: Fighting for the King in America's first Civil War* (New York: Harper-Collins, 2010), 55–56.

219 **"and then platoons":** "Letter from Paul Revere to Jeremy Belknap, circa 1798"; Elbridge Henry Goss, *The Life of Colonel Paul Revere*, 2 vols. (Boston: Joseph George Cupples, 1891), vol. 1, 213–25.

220 **and James Brown:** Frothingham, *History of the Siege of Boston, and of the Battles of Lexington, Concord, and Bunker Hill*, 367.

222 **beyond any doubt:** George III to Lord Sandwich, July 1, 1775, in *Sandwich Papers*, vol. 1, 63.

223 **had obviously colluded:** Pitcairn's full report is in French, *General Gage's Informers*, 52–54.

225 **"draw once more the British fire?":** Harold Murdock, *The Nineteenth of April, 1775* (Boston: Houghton Mifflin, 1923), 23–25.

226 **"glorious day for America":** Frothingham, *Life and Times of Joseph Warren*, 459.

226 **received such a command:** French, *The Day of Concord and Lexington*, 96–97.

32. THE ROAD TO CONCORD

228 **cakewalk in Lexington:** Mackenzie, *Diary*, vol. 2, 145–46.

230 **Tuesday the eighteenth:** Ruth R. Wheeler, *Concord: Climate for Freedom* (Concord: Concord Antiquarian Society, 1967), 105–12.

235 **largely on their own:** Galvin, *The Minute Men*, 206.

33. THE CONCORD FIGHT

239 **just off the bridge:** See General Galvin's description of how Laurie deployed his men, *The Minute Men*, 147–55.

239 **that warm blood:** John Harris, *America Rebels* (Boston: Boston Globe Co., 1976), 145.

240 **an experienced commander:** Lemuel Shattuck, *A History of the Town of Concord* (Concord, MA: Russell, Odiorne, 1835), 97.

241 **the redcoats grim:** Ibid., 125.

34. THE BLOODY ROAD BACK TO LEXINGTON

243 **"behind hedges and walls":** Jeremy Lister, *Narrative* (Cambridge: Harvard University Press, 1931), 29.

243 **general action commenced:** For a different interpretation, see Galvin, *The Minute Men*, 166.

246 **had the opportunity:** Charles H. Bradford, *The Battle Road: Expedition to Lexington and Concord* (Boston: The Rotary Club of Boston, 1975), 58–63.

246 **"near expended":** Barker, *British in Boston*, 32–33.

246 **"incessant" patriot fire:** J. D. Tyler, ed., "Account of Lexington," *William and Mary Quarterly*, 3rd Series, X (January 1953), 99–107.

247 **"increased rather than lessened":** Henry De Berniere, "Narrative of Occurrences, 1775," *Collections of the Massachusetts Historical Society*, 2nd Series, vol. 4 (Boston, 1816), 167.

247 **"Upon this they began to form under a very heavy fire":** Ibid.

35. LORD PERCY TO THE RESCUE

249 **"we afterwards found these houses were full of men, and only forsaken by the women and children":** Mackenzie, *Diary*, vol. 1, 53–54.

249 **"the morning at Lexington":** Ibid.

250 **"they shouted repeatedly, and the firing ceased for a short time":** Ibid., 54.

250 **"they retired":** Barker, *British in Boston*, 34.

251 **"which was extremely necessary for our men who were almost exhausted with fatigue":** Ibid., 35.

251 **"their pleasure":** Ibid. 360–67.

251 **before marrying someone else:** R. Wheeler, *Concord: Climate for Freedom* (Concord, MA: Concord Antiquarian Society, 1967), 113.

36. A MASTERFUL RETREAT

255 **his men on alert:** Mackenzie, *Diary*, vol. 1, 23.

256 **"brisk on both sides":** Heath, *Memoirs*, 8.

256 **"left him solely to their care"**: Ensign Lister, *Narrative*, 43.

257 **"the hair of his earlock"**: Frothingham, *Life and Times of Joseph Warren*, 460–61.

257 **eleven militiamen dead**: Harris, *America Rebels*, 159–60.

257 **until he was ninety-five**: Ellen Chase, *The Beginnings of the American Revolution*, 3 vols. (New York: Baker and Taylor, 1910), vol. 3, 146–48.

258 **"killing great numbers of the rebels"**: De Berniere, "Narrative of Occurrences, 1775," 84.

259 **"as it is perhaps imagined at home"**: Percy to General Harvey, April 20, 1775, in Percy, *Letters*, 52–53.

259 **a carpenter at Harvard College**: Harris, *America Rebels*, 162.

260 **"the road shorter"**: Percy to Gage, April 20, 1775, in Percy, *Letters*, 51.

261 **He wanted a negotiation, having no idea how impossible that was at this point**: For a different view of Pickering's tardiness see Douglas P. Sabin, *April 19, 1775: A Historiographical Study* (West Linn, OR: Sinclair Street Publishing, 2011), 194.

261 **supplies in clandestinely**: Benjamin W. Labaree, *Patriots and Partisans: The Merchants of Newburyport, 1764–1815* (New York: W. W. Norton, 1975), 40.

261 **decision was a wise one**: Heath, *Memoirs*, 8–9.

262 **on the eighteenth and nineteenth of April**: Le Cras's Log, in *NDAR*, vol. 1, 199.

263 **"burning and laying waste the whole country"**: "Narrative of Vice Admiral Samuel Graves," *Graves's Conduct*, I, 73, 74, Massachusetts Historical Society transcript; *NDAR*, vol. 1, 193.

264 **"come to their assistance"**: Barker, *British in Boston*, 31–37; *NDAR*, vol. 1, 200.

37. THE SIEGE OF BOSTON: PART ONE

266 **"batteries against us"**: Barker *Diary* entry for May 4, 1775.

267 **"pouring in great numbers of people"**: Graves to Philip Stephens, July 24, 1775, in *NDAR*, vol. 1, 200–201.

267 **worried about it**: George C. Daughan, *If By Sea: The Forging of the American Navy from the Revolution to the War of 1812* (New York: Basic Books, 2008), 40.

267 **"hands on everywhere"**: Gage to Graves, April 25, 1775, in *NDAR*, vol. 1, 221.

268 **carry them away**: Graves's secretary, George Gefferina, to Captain John Collins, April 26, 1775, in *NDAR*, vol. 1, 226–27.

268 **ready to be manned**: "Narrative of Vice Admiral Samuel Graves," *Graves's Conduct*, I, 74–75.

270 **"shall be religiously performed"**: Warren to Gage, April 20, 1775, in Frothingham, *Life and Times of Joseph Warren*, 467.

270 **"blocked up in Boston"**: De Berniere, "Narrative of Occurrences, 1775," 98.

271 **"as many as pleased"**: Barker, *British in Boston*, 124.

38. THE SIEGE: PART TWO

274 **"the present administration"**: Warren to Arthur Lee, April 20, 1775, in Frothingham, *Life and Times of Joseph Warren*, 471.

274 **"with fire and sword"**: Warren's circular letter, April 20, 1775, ibid., 466.

275 **"new excuses for delay"**: Warren to Sam Adams, May 14, 1775, ibid., 483.

275 **without having to destroy the city**: North Callahan, *Henry Knox, General Washington's General* (New York: Rinehart & Co., 1958), 30.

275 **was meeting there**: Forbes, *Paul Revere and the World He Lived In*, 275.

278 **but it was slow going**: Frothingham, *History of the Siege of Boston, and of the Battles of Lexington, Concord, and Bunker Hill*, 100–101.

39. EARTH-SHATTERING NEWS

281 **particularly vivid**: Arthur B. Tourtellot, *Lexington and Concord* (New York: W. W. Norton, 1959), 233.

282 **"at the price of their lives"**: Warren to Franklin, April 26, 1775, in *NDAR*, vol. 1, 226.

283 **"no decisive judgment of what happened"**: Dartmouth to Gage, June 1, 1775, in *Gage Correspondence*, vol. 2, 198–99.

284 **"with their usual intrepidity"**: Gage to Dartmouth, April 22, 1775, in *Gage Correspondence*, vol. 1, 396–97.

284 **"said to be great"**: Ibid.

284 **"preparations to oppose them"**: Ibid.

285 **"deprived of such connections"**: George III to Dartmouth, June 10, 1775, in Donoughue, *British Politics and the American Revolution*, 275.

285 **"supported in those colonies"**: Dartmouth to Lords Commissioners of the Admiralty, July 1, 1775, in *NDAR*, vol. 1, 1307–9.

286 **another in the Bahamas**: Disposition of the squadron under Vice Admiral Samuel Graves, in *NDAR*, vol. 1, 47.

CONCLUSION

288 **victory on blue water**: James Fenimore Cooper, *The History of the Navy of the United States* (Annapolis: Naval Institute Press, 2000), 39.

288 **failed to interest Cooper:** Daughan, *If By Sea*, 17–27.

290 **Dickinson joined the fight:** John Ferling, *A Life of John Adams* (New York: Henry Holt; Knoxville: University of Tennessee Press, 1992), 121–23.

291 **"doing too much":** Sandwich to Graves, July 30, 1775, in *Sandwich Papers*, vol. 1, 66–67.

292 **"no longer to be attended to":** Sandwich to Graves, ibid., 68–72.

292 **His Majesty had had enough:** Sandwich to Graves, September 17, 1775, ibid., 73–74.

292 **return to London:** Alden, *General Gage in America*, 272–86.

Select Bibliography

PRIMARY SOURCES

Adams, John. *The Works of John Adams, Second President of the United States: with a Life of the Author, Notes and Illustrations by His Grandson, Charles Francis Adams.* 10 vols. Boston: Little, Brown, 1850–56.

Adams, John, and Abigail Adams. *The Book of Abigail & John: Selected Letters of the Adams Family, 1762–1784.* Edited by L. H. Butterfield, Marc Friedlaender, and Mary-Jo Kline. Cambridge, MA: Harvard University Press, 1975.

Adams, Samuel. *The Writings of Samuel Adams.* Edited by Harry Alonzo Cushing. 4 vols. New York: Putnam, 1904–08.

Andrews, John. "Letters of John Andrews, Esq., of Boston, 1772–1776." *Proceedings of the Massachusetts Historical Society*, 1st Series, vol. 8, 316–412. Reprinted as *Letters of John Andrews, Esq., of Boston, 1772–1776.* Edited by Winthrop Sargent. Cambridge, MA: John Wilson and Sons, 1866.

Barker, John, Lt. *The British in Boston: Being the Diary of Lieutenant John Barker of the King's Own Regiment from November 15, 1774, to May 31, 1776, with Notes.* Edited by Elizabeth Ellery Dana. Cambridge, MA: Harvard University Press, 1924.

Barnes, G. R., and J. H. Owen, eds. *The Private Papers of John, Earl of Sandwich, First Lord of the Admiralty, 1771–1782.* 4 vols. London: Navy Records Society, 1932–36.

Barrett, Captain Amos. "An Account of the Battle of Concord." Edited by Henry True. In *Journals and Letters of Rev. Henry True.* Marion, OH: Printed for Henry True, 1906.

Bartlett, Russell John, ed. *Records of the Colony of Rhode Island and Providence Plantations in New England, 1770–1776.* Vols. 7 and 8. Providence, RI: A. C. Greene, 1856–65.

Beloff, Max., ed. *The Debate on the American Revolution, 1761–1783,* Dobbs Ferry, NY: Sheridan House, 1989.

Bradford, Alden, ed. *Speeches of the Governors of Massachusetts from 1765 to 1775:*

And the Answers of the House of Representatives to the Same; with Their Resolutions and Addresses for That Period and Other Public Papers Relating to the Dispute between This Country and Great Britain Which Led to the Independence of the United States. Boston: Richardson and Lord, 1822.

Burke, Edmund. *The Correspondence of Edmund Burke.* Edited by Lucy S. Sutherland et. al. 9 vols. Cambridge: UK: Cambridge University Press, 1960.

Burnett, Edmund Cody. *Letters of Members of the Continental Congress.* 8 vols. Washington, DC: The Carnegie Institution, 1921–26.

Butterfield, L. H., and Marc Friedlaender, eds. *Adams Family Correspondence*, 13 vols. Cambridge, MA: Harvard University Press, 1963–2017.

Clarke, Jonas, *Opening of the War of the Revolution, 19th of April, 1775.* Lexington, MA: Lexington Historical Society, 1901.

Cobbett, William, ed. *The Parliamentary History of England from the Earliest Period to the Year 1803.* 36 vols. London: T. C. Hansard, 1814. Vols. 16–18.

Commager, Henry Steele, and Richard B. Morris, eds. *The Spirit of Seventy-Six: The Story of the American Revolution as Told by Its Participants.* Indianapolis: Bobbs-Merrill, 1958.

Curtis, Edward H. *The Organization of the British Army in the American Revolution.* New Haven, CT: Yale University Press, 1926.

Dartmouth, William Walter Legge, 2nd Earl of. *The Manuscripts of the Earl of Dartmouth.* 3 vols. London: Royal Commission on Historical Manuscripts, 1887–96.

De Berniere, Henry. "Narrative of Occurrences, 1775." *Proceedings of the Massachusetts Historical Society.* 2nd Series, vol. 4. 1816.

Donne, W. Bodham, ed. *Correspondence of George III with Lord North, 1768–83.* 2 vols. London: Murray, 1867.

Emerson, William. "Diary." In Ralph Waldo Emerson, *Miscellanies.* Boston: Houghton Mifflin, 1863.

Force, Peter, ed. *American Archives: Fourth Series, Containing a Documentary History of the English colonies in North America from the King's Message to Parliament of March 7, 1774, to the Declaration of Independence by the United States.* 6 vols. Washington, DC: M. St. Clair Clarke and Peter Force, 1837–46.

Ford, Worthington Chauncey, et al., eds. *Journals of the Continental Congress, 1774–1789.* 34 vols. Washington, DC: U.S. Government Printing Office, 1904–37.

Fortescue, Sir John, ed. *The Correspondence of King George the Third from 1760 to December 1783.* 6 vols. London: Macmillan, 1927–28.

Franklin, Benjamin. *The Papers of Benjamin Franklin.* Vols. 19–22. Edited by William B. Willcox. New Haven, CT: Yale University Press, 1976–82.

———. *Benjamin Franklin's Letters to the Press, 1758 to 1775.* Edited by Vernon W. Crane. Chapel Hill: University of North Carolina Press, 1954.

Gage, Thomas. *The Correspondence of General Thomas Gage, 1763–1775.* Edited by Clarence Edwin Carter. 2 vols. New Haven, CT: Yale University Press, 1931–33.

"General Gage's Order Book from December 10, 1774, to June 6, 1775." Manuscript Collection, Boston Public Library, File MS R, 1.4.

Heath, William. *Memoirs of Major General William Heath.* Edited by William Abbatt. New York: William Abbatt, 1901.

Hudson, Charles. *History of the Town of Lexington, Middlesex County, Massachusetts, from Its First Settlement to 1868.* Boston: Houghton Mifflin, 1913.

Hughes, Edward. "Lord North's Correspondence, 1766–83." *English Historical Review* 62 (April 1947): 218–38.

Hutchinson, Thomas. *Diary and Letters of His Excellency Thomas Hutchinson.* Edited by Peter Orlando Hutchinson. 2 vols. Boston: Houghton Mifflin, 1884–86; London: Sampson Low et al., 1883.

Labaree, Leonard W., ed. *Royal Instructions to British Colonial Governors, 1670–1776.* 2 vols. New York: D. Appleton-Century, 1935.

Lincoln, William, ed. *The Journals of Each Provincial Congress of Massachusetts in 1774 and 1775, and of the Committee of Safety.* Boston: Dutton and Wentworth, 1838.

Livermore, George. *An Historical Research Respecting the Opinions of the Founders of the Republic, on Negroes as Slaves, as Citizens, as Soldiers.* Boston: A. Williams, 1862.

Mackenzie, Frederick. *Diary of Lieutenant Frederick Mackenzie.* Edited by Allen French. 2 vols. Cambridge, MA: Harvard University Press, 1926, 1930.

Percy, Hugh, Earl. *Letters of Hugh, Earl Percy, from Boston and New York, 1774–1776.* Edited by Charles K. Bolton. Boston: Charles E. Goodspeed, 1902.

Pitt, William. *Correspondence of William Pitt, Earl of Chatham.* Edited by W. S. Taylor and J. H. Pringle. 4 vols. London, 1838–40.

Putnam, Rufus. *The Memoirs of Rufus Putnam.* Edited by Rowena Buell. Boston: Houghton Mifflin, 1903.

Revere, Paul. "Letter from Paul Revere to Jeremy Belknap, circa 1798." Edited by Charles Deane. *Proceedings of the Massachusetts Historical Society* 16 (1879): 370–76.

Rowe, John. *The Diary of John Rowe, a Boston Merchant, 1764–1779.* Edited by Edward L. Pierce. Cambridge: J. Wilson & Son, 1895.

Scull, G. D., ed. *Memoir and Letters of Captain W. Glanville Evelyn, of the Fourth Regiment (King's Own) from North America, 1774–1776.* Oxford: James Parker and Co., 1879.

Simmons, R. C., and P. D. G. Thomas, eds. *Proceedings and Debates of the British Parliament Respecting North America, 1774–1783.* 6 vols. Millwood, NY: Kraus International, 1982–87.

Smith, Paul, et al., eds. *Letters of Delegates to Congress, 1774–1789.* 26 vols. Washington, DC: Library of Congress, 1976–2000.

Sparks, Jared, ed. *The Writings of George Washington.* 12 vols. Boston: Russell, Odiorne, and Metcalf, 1834–37.

Stephens, W. Walker, ed. *The Life and Writings of Turgot, Comptroller General of France, 1774–76, for English Readers.* New York: Burt Franklin, 1971.

Walpole, Horace. *Journal of the Reign of George III from 1771 to 1783.* Edited by John Doran. 2 vols. London: R. Bentley, 1859.

———. *The Letters of Horace Walpole, Earl of Oxford.* Edited by John Wright. London: R. Bentley, 1840.

———. *The Letters of Horace Walpole.* Edited by Mrs. Paget Toynbee. Oxford: Clarendon Press, 1903–05.

Warren-Adams Letters: Being Chiefly a Correspondence among John Adams, Samuel Adams, and James Warren. 2 vols. *Collections of the Massachusetts Historical Society* 72 (Boston, 1917) and 73 (Boston, 1925).

Wells, William Vincent. *The Life and Public Services of Samuel Adams.* 3 vols. Boston: Little, Brown, 1865.

Willard, Margaret Wheeler, ed. *Letters on the American Revolution.* Boston: Houghton Mifflin, 1925.

Willson, Beckles. *The Life and Letters of James Wolfe.* London: William Heinemann, 1909.

Wood, Gordon, ed. *The American Revolution: Writings from the Pamphlet Debate, 1773–1776.* New York: Penguin Random House, 2015.

Wroth, Kinvin L., ed. *Province in Rebellion: A Documentary History of the Founding of the Commonwealth of Massachusetts.* Cambridge, MA: Harvard University Press, 1975.

SECONDARY SOURCES

Adams, James T. *Revolutionary New England, 1691–1776.* Boston: Atlantic Monthly Press, 1923.

Akers, Charles W. *The Divine Politician: Samuel Cooper and the American Revolution in Boston.* Boston: Northeastern University Press, 1982.

Alden, John R. "Why the March to Concord?" *American Historical Review* 49 (April 1944): 446–54.

———. *General Gage in America: Being Principally a History of His Role in the American Revolution.* Baton Rouge: Louisiana State University Press, 1948.

———. *General Charles Lee: Traitor or Patriot?* Baton Rouge: Louisiana State University Press, 1951.

Alexander, John K. *Samuel Adams: The Life of an American Revolutionary.* New York: Rowman & Littlefield, 2011.

Allen, Thomas B. *Tories: Fighting for the King in America's First Civil War.* New York: HarperCollins, 2010.

Anderson, Fred. *Crucible of War: The Seven Years' War and the Fate of Empire in British North America, 1754–1766.* New York: Random House, 2000.

———. *A People's Army: Massachusetts Soldiers and Society in the Seven Years' War.* Chapel Hill: University of North Carolina Press, 1984.

Anderson, Terry L. "Economic Growth in Colonial New England." *Journal of Economic History* 39 (March 1979): 243–57.

Andrews, Charles M. *The Colonial Background of the American Revolution.* New Haven, CT: Yale University Press, 1931.

Ayers, Edward L., and Bradley C. Mittendorf, eds. *The Oxford Book of the American South.* New York: Oxford University Press, 1997.

Ayling, Stanley. *The Elder Pitt, Earl of Chatham.* New York: David McKay, 1976.

Baldwin, Alice M. *New England Clergy and the American Revolution.* Durham, NC: Duke University Press, 1928.

Bancroft, George. *History of the United States.* 10 vols. Boston: Little, Brown, 1846.

Bargar, B. D. *Lord Dartmouth and the American Revolution.* Columbia: University of South Carolina Press, 1965.

Beck, Derek W. *Igniting the American Revolution, 1773–1775.* Naperville, IL: Source Books, 2015.

Bell, J. L. *The Road to Concord: How Four Stolen Cannon Ignited the Revolutionary War.* Yardley, PA: Westholme Publishing, 2016.

Berleth, Richard. *Bloody Mohawk: The French and Indian War and American Revolution on New York's Frontier.* Delmar, NY: Black Dome Press, 2009.

Berlin, Ira. *The Long Emancipation: The Demise of Slavery in the United States.* Cambridge, MA: Harvard University Press, 2015.

———. *Many Thousands Gone: The First Two Centuries of Slavery in North America.* Cambridge, MA: Harvard University Press, 2000.

Bidwell, Percy Wells, and John I. Falconer. *History of Agriculture in the Northern United States, 1620–1860.* Washington, DC: Carnegie Institute, 1925.

Borneman, Walter R. *American Spring: Lexington, Concord, and the Road to Revolution.* Boston: Little, Brown, 2014.

Brindenbaugh, Carl. *Cities in Revolt: Urban Life in America, 1743–1776.* New York: Oxford University Press, 1971.

Bridenbaugh, Carl, and Jessica Bridenbaugh. *Rebels and Gentlemen: Philadelphia in the Age of Franklin.* New York: Oxford University Press, 1965.

Brooks, Paul. *Trial by Fire: Lincoln Massachusetts and the War of Independence.* Lincoln, MA: Lincoln Bicentennial Commission, 1975.

Brown, Robert D. *Revolutionary Politics in Massachusetts: The Boston Committee of Correspondence and the Towns, 1772–1774.* Cambridge, MA: Harvard University Press, 1970.

Burnett, Edmund Cody. *The Continental Congress.* New York: Macmillan, 1941.

Bushman, Richard L. *King and People in Provincial Massachusetts.* Chapel Hill: University of North Carolina Press, 1992.

Cannon, John A. *Lord North: The Noble Lord in the Blue Ribbon.* London: Historical Association, 1970.

Carretta, Vincent. *Phillis Wheatley: Biography of a Genius in Bondage.* Athens: University of Georgia Press, 2011.

Chase, Ellen. *The Beginnings of the American Revolution.* 3 vols. New York: Baker and Taylor, 1910.

Coburn, Frank. *Battle of April 19, 1775, in Lexington, Concord, Lincoln, Arlington, Cambridge, Somerville, and Charlestown, Massachusetts.* Lexington, MA: Published by the Author, 1912. Rev. ed., 1922.

———. *Truth and Fiction About the Battle on Lexington Common.* Lexington, MA: Published by the Author, 1918.

Coleman, Kenneth. *The American Revolution in Georgia, 1763–1789.* Athens: University of Georgia Press, 1958.

Cook, Don. *The Long Fuse: How England Lost the American Colonies, 1760–1785.* New York: Atlantic Monthly Press, 1995.

Countryman, Edward. *Americans: A Collision of Histories.* New York: Hill & Wang, 1996.

Crèvecoeur, Hector St. John de. *Letters from an American Farmer.* Edited by Ernest Rhys. New York: E. P. Dutton, 1940.

Dandridge, Danske. *American Prisoners of the Revolution.* Charlottesville, VA: The Micnie Co., 1911.

Deane, Phyllis, and W. A. Cole. *British Economic Growth, 1688–1959: Trends and Structure.* Brookfield, VT: Ashgate Publishing Co., 1993.

Drake, Samuel Adams. *History of Middlesex County.* Boston: Estes and Lauriat, 1897.

Duval, Kathleen. *Independence Lost: Lives on the Edge of the American Revolution.* New York: Random House, 2015.

Egnal, Marc. "The Economic Development of the Thirteen Original Continental Colonies, 1720–1775. *William and Mary Quarterly,* 3rd Series, vol. 32. 1975.

Ferling, John. *A Life of John Adams.* New York: Henry Holt, 1996.

Fischer, David Hackett, *Albion's Seed: Four British Folkways in America.* New York: Oxford University Press, 1989.

———. *Paul Revere's Ride.* New York: Oxford University Press, 1994.

Flavell, Julie. "British Perceptions of New England and the Decision for a Coercive Policy, 1774–1775." In *When Britain and America Go to War: The Impact of War and Warfare in Anglo-America,* 95–115, edited by Julie Flavell and Stephen Conway. Gainesville, FL: University Press of Florida, 2004.

Fleming, Thomas. *The First Stroke: Lexington, Concord, and the Beginning of the American Revolution.* Honolulu, HI: University Press of the Pacific, 1978.

Forman, Samuel. *Dr. Joseph Warren: The Boston Tea Party, Bunker Hill, and the Birth of American Liberty.* New Orleans: Pelican, 2011.

Forbes, Esther. *Paul Revere and the World He Lived In.* Boston: Houghton Mifflin, 1942.

Fowler, William M. *The Baron of Beacon Hill: A Biography of John Hancock.* Boston: Houghton Mifflin, 1980.

———. *Samuel Adams: Radical Puritan.* New York: Longman, 1997.

Fox, R. Hingston. *Dr. John Fothergill and His Friends.* London: Macmillan, 1919.

French, Allen. *The Day of Concord and Lexington: The Nineteenth of April, 1775.* Boston: Little, Brown, 1925.

———. *General Gage's Informers.* Ann Arbor: University of Michigan Press, 1932.

———. *The First Year of the American Revolution.* Boston: Houghton Mifflin, 1934.

———. "General Haldimand in Boston, 1774–75." *Proceedings of the Massachusetts Historical Society* 66 (1942): 80–95.

Frey, Sylvia R. *The British Soldier in America: A Social History of Military Life in the Revolutionary Period.* Austin: University of Texas Press, 1981.

———. *Water from the Rock: Black Resistance in a Revolutionary Age.* Princeton, NJ: Princeton University Press, 1991.

Frothingham, Richard Jr. *History of the Siege of Boston, and of the Battles of Lexington, Concord, and Bunker Hill.* Boston: Little, Brown, 1873.

———. *Life and Times of Joseph Warren.* Boston: Little, Brown, 1865.

Galvin, John R. *The Minute Men: The First Fight: Myths and Realities of the American Revolution.* Dulles, VA: Potomac Books, The History of War Edition, 1989.

George, M. Dorothy. *London Life in the Eighteenth Century.* London: Penguin, 1965.

Gettemy, Charles Ferris. *The True Story of Paul Revere, His Midnight Ride, His Arrest and Court-Martial, His Useful Public Services.* Boston: Little, Brown, 1905.

Gipson, Lawrence Henry. *The British Empire Before the American Revolution.* 9 vols. Caldwell, ID: Claxton Printers, 1936–70.

———. *The Coming of the Revolution, 1763–75.* New York: Harper & Brothers, 1954.

Godbold, E. Stanly Jr., and Robert H. Woody. *Christopher Gadsden and the American Revolution.* Knoxville: University of Tennessee Press, 1982.

Goss, Elbridge H. *The Life of Colonel Paul Revere.* 2 vols. Boston: Joseph George Cupples, 1891.

Graymont, Barbara. *The Iroquois in the American Revolution.* Syracuse: Syracuse University Press, 1972.

Greene, Jack P. Jr., and J. R. Pole, eds. *The Blackwell Encyclopedia of the American Revolution.* Oxford: Basil Blackwell, 1994.

Greene, Lorenzo J. *The Negro in Colonial America.* New York: Atheneum, 1974.

Haffenden, Philip S. *New England in the English Nation, 1689–1713.* Oxford: Clarendon Press, 1974.

Hambrick-Stowe, C. E., and Donna D. Smerlas. *Massachusetts Militia Companies and Officers in the Lexington Alarm.* Boston: New England Historic Genealogical Society, 1976.

Harper, L. A. "The Effect of the Navigation Acts on the Thirteen Colonies."

In *The Era of the American Revolution*, edited by Richard B. Morris, 3–39. New York: Columbia University Press, 1939.

Jacobs, Harriet. "Incidents in the Life of a Slave Girl." In *The Oxford Book of the American South: Testimony, Memory, and Fiction*, edited by Edward L. Ayers and Bradley C. Mittendorf, 50–63. New York: Oxford University Press, 1997.

Jones, Edward Alfred. *The Loyalists of Massachusetts: Their Memorials, Petitions, and Claims*. London: St. Catherine Press, 1930.

Knollenberg, Bernard. *Growth of the American Revolution: 1766–1775*. New York: The Free Press, 1975.

Labaree, Leonard W., *Royal Government in America: A Study of the British Colonial System Before 1783*. New York: Frederick Ungar, 1958.

———. *Patriots and Partisans: The Merchants of Newburyport, 1764–1815*. New York: W. W. Norton, 1975; Cambridge, MA: Harvard University Press, 1962.

Leach, Douglas Edward. *Roots of Conflict: British Armed Forces and Colonial Americans, 1677–1763*. Chapel Hill: University of North Carolina Press, 1986.

Lemire, Elise. *Black Walden: Slavery and Its Aftermath in Concord, Massachusetts*. Philadelphia: University of Pennsylvania Press, 2009.

Lockridge, Kenneth A. *Literacy in Colonial New England: An Enquiry into the Social Context of Literacy* in the Early Modern West. New York: W. W. Norton, 1974.

Macaulay, Thomas Babington, Lord. *Critical and Historical Essays, Contributed to the Edinburgh Review*. 3 vols. London: Brown, Green, and Longmans, 1848.

MacEacheren, Elaine. "Emancipation of Slavery in Massachusetts: A Reexamination, 1770–1790." *Journal of Negro History* 55 (October 1970): 289–306.

Maier, Pauline. "Coming to Terms with Samuel Adams." *American Historical Review* 81 (February 1976): 12–37.

Main, Jackson T. *The Social Structure of Revolutionary America*. Princeton, NJ: Princeton University Press, 1965.

Marston, Jerrilyn Greene. *King and Congress: The Transfer of Political Legitimacy, 1774–1776*. Princeton, NJ: Princeton University Press, 1987.

Martyn, Charles. *The Life of Artemas Ward: The First Commander-in-Chief of the American Revolution*. New York: Artemas Ward, 1921.

Mason, Bernard. *The Road to Independence: The Revolutionary Movement in New York, 1773–1777*. Lexington: University of Kentucky Press, 1966.

McCullough, David. *John Adams*. New York: Simon & Schuster, 2001.

McCusker, John J., and Russell R. Menard. *The Economy of British America, 1607–1789*. Chapel Hill: University of North Carolina Press, 1985.

McManis, Douglas R., *Colonial New England: A Historical Geography*. New York: Oxford University Press, 1975.

McNaught, Kenneth. *The Penguin History of Canada*. London: Penguin, 1969.

Meade Robert D. *Patrick Henry, Patriot in the Making*. Philadelphia: Lippincott, 1957.

Miller, Kerby A. *Emigrants and Exiles: Ireland and the Irish Exodus to North America*. New York: Oxford University Press, 1988.

Mingay, G. E. *English Landed Society in the Eighteenth Century*. London: Routledge and Kegan Paul, 1963.

Moore, George A. *Notes on the History of Slavery in Massachusetts*. New York: D. Appleton, 1866.

Morgan, Edmund S. *American Slavery American Freedom: The Ordeal of Colonial Virginia*. New York: W. W. Norton, 1975.

Morgan, Edmund S., and Helen M. Morgan. *The Stamp Act Crisis: Prologue to Revolution*. Chapel Hill: University of North Carolina Press, 1953.

Morris, Richard B. "The Effect of the Navigation Acts on the Era of the American Revolution." In *The Era of the American Revolution*, edited by Richard B. Morris. New York: Columbia University Press, 1939, 3–39.

Murdock, Harold. *The Nineteenth of April, 1775*. Boston: Houghton Mifflin, 1923.

———. *Late News of the Excursions and Ravages of the King's Troops on the Nineteenth of April, 1775*. Cambridge, MA: Harvard University Press, 1927.

Murphy, Orville T. *Charles Gravier, Comte de Vergennes: French Diplomacy in the Age of Revolution, 1719–1787*. Albany: State University of New York Press, 1982.

Namier, Lewis B. *England in the Age of the American Revolution*. London: Macmillan, 1930.

Nelson, James L. *With Fire and Sword: The Battle of Bunker Hill and the Beginning of the American Revolution*. New York: St. Martin's Press, 2011.

O'Brien, Maire, and Conor Cruise O'Brien. *Ireland: A Concise History*. London: Thames and Hudson, 1995.

Palfrey, John Gorham. *History of New England*. Boston: Little, Brown, 1890.

Patterson, Stephen E. *Political Parties in Revolutionary Massachusetts*. Madison: University of Wisconsin Press, 1973.

Philbrick, Nathaniel. *Bunker Hill: A City, a Siege, a Revolution*. New York: Viking, 2013.

Phillips, Kevin. *1775: A Good Year for Revolution*. New York: Penguin, 2012.

Rakove, Jack N. *The Beginnings of National Politics: An Interpretive History of the Continental Congress*. Baltimore: Johns Hopkins University Press, 1979.

Raphael, Ray. *The First American Revolution*. New York: The New Press, 2002.

Raphael, Ray, and Marie Raphael. *The Spirit of '74: How the American Revolution Began*. New York: The New Press, 2015.

Ripley, Ezra. *A History of the Fight at Concord*. Concord, MA: Allen and Atwell, 1827.

Risjord, Norman K. *Jefferson's America, 1760–1815*. Madison WI: Madison House Publishers, 1991.

Ritcheson, Charles R. *British Politics and the American Revolution*. Norman: University of Oklahoma Press, 1954.

Rodger, N. A. M. *The Insatiable Earl: A Life of John Montagu, 4th Earl of Sandwich*. New York: W. W. Norton, 1993.

Ryan, D. Michael. *Concord and the Dawn of Revolution*. Charleston, SC: History Press, 2007.

Robinson, Donald L. *Slavery in the Structure of American Politics, 1765–1820*. New York: Harcourt Brace Jovanovich, 1971.

Robinson, William H. *Phillis Wheatley and Her Writings*. New York: Garland Publishing, 1984.

Sabin, Douglas P. *April 19, 1775: A Historiographical Study*. West Linn, OR: Sinclair Street Publishing, 2011.

Sabine, Lorenzo. *The American Loyalists: Or, Biographical Sketches of Adherents to the British Crown in the War of the Revolution*. Boston: Charles C. Little and James Brown, 1847.

Scheide, John H. "The Lexington Alarm." *Proceedings of the American Antiquarian Society*, vol. 50, part 1 (1940), 49–79.

Schlesinger, Arthur M. *The Colonial Merchants and the American Revolution, 1763–1776*. New York: Atheneum, 1968; New York: Columbia University Press, 1918.

Shattuck, Lemuel. *A History of the Town of Concord*. Concord, MA: Russell, Odiorne, 1835.

Shepherd, James F., and Gary M. Walton. *Shipping, Maritime Trade, and the Economic Development of Colonial North America*. Cambridge: Cambridge University Press, 1972.

Sherrard, O. A. *Lord Chatham*. 3 vols. London: Bodley Head, 1952–58.

Shy, John. *Toward Lexington: The Role of the British Army in the Coming of the American Revolution*. Princeton, NJ: Princeton University Press, 1965.

———. *A People Numerous and Armed: Reflections on the Military Struggle for American Independence*. New York: Oxford University Press, 1976.

Smith, E. A. Joseph, and Thomas Cushing. *History of Berkshire County, Massachusetts, with Biographical Sketches of Its Prominent Men*. New York: J. B. Beers, 1885.

Stark, James Henry. *Loyalists of Massachusetts and the Other Side of the American Revolution*. Boston: W. B. Clarke, 1910.

Stout, Neil R. *The Perfect Crisis: The Beginnings of the Revolutionary War*. New York: New York University Press. 1976.

Thomas, P. D. G. *The House of Commons in the Eighteenth Century*. Oxford: Clarendon Press, 1971.

———. *Lord North*. London: Allen Lane, 1976.

Thomas, Peter. *Tea Party to Independence: The Third Phase of the American Revolution*. New York: Oxford University Press, 1991.

Tolman, George. *Events of April Nineteenth*. Concord MA: Concord Antiquarian Society, 1902.

Tourtellot, Arthur B. *Lexington and Concord: The Beginning of the War of the American Revolution*. New York: Doubleday, 1959.

Trevelyan, Sir George Otto. *The American Revolution: Part I. 1766–1776*. London: Longmans, Green, and Co., 1899.

Triber, Jayne E. *A True Republican: The Life of Paul Revere*. Boston: University of Massachusetts Press, 1998.

Tyler, J. E., ed. "Account of Lexington." *William and Mary Quarterly*, 3rd Series, 10 (January 1953): 99–107.

Unger, Harlow Giles. *John Hancock: Merchant King and American Patriot*. Hoboken, NJ: Wiley, 2000.

Valentine, Alan. *Lord North*. 2 vols. Norman: University of Oklahoma Press, 1967.

Van Doren, Carl. *Benjamin Franklin*. New York: Penguin, 1991 (one vol.); New York: Viking, 1938 (originally 3 vols.).

Warden, G. B. *Boston, 1689–1776*. Boston: Little, Brown, 1970.

Watson, J. Steven. *The Reign of George III, 1760–1815*. Oxford: Clarendon Press, 1960.

Weeden, William B. *Economic and Social History of New England, 1620–1789*. Boston: Houghton Mifflin, 1891.

Wheeler, Ruth R. *Concord: Climate for Freedom*. Concord, MA: Concord Antiquarian Society, 1967.

Williams, Basil. *William Pitt, Earl of Chatham*. 2 vols. London: Longmans, Green, and Co., 1913.

Wood, Gordon S. *The Radicalism of the American Revolution: How a Revolution Transformed a Monarchical Society into a Democratic One Unlike Any That Had Ever Existed*. New York: Knopf, 1992.

Wood, Gordon S., ed. *The American Revolution: Writings from the Pamphlet Debate, 1773–1776*. New York: Penguin Random House, 2015.

Zilversmit, Arthur. *The First Emancipation: The Abolition of Slavery in the North*. Chicago: University of Chicago Press, 1967.

WEBSITES

Bell, J. L.: Boston1775.blogspot.com
oxforddnb.com
anb.org

Index

Page numbers in *italics* refer to illustrations.